ABOLITION LABOR

ABOLITION LABOR

The Fight to End Prison Slavery

Andrew Ross
Tommaso Bardelli
Aiyuba Thomas

OR Books
New York · London

First printing 2024

Cataloging-in-Publication data is available from the Library of Congress. A catalog record for this book is available from the British Library.

Typeset by Lapiz Digital Services.

paperback ISBN 978-1-68219-398-3 • ebook ISBN 978-1-68219-455-3

Contents

Authors' Note

This book was researched and written under the auspices of the NYU Prison Research Lab, an arm of the NYU Prison Education Program (PEP). The Research Lab consists of a small group of faculty members and a rotating group of formerly incarcerated students who are trained in social science methods, and work on joint faculty-student projects together.

The inspiration for *Abolition Labor*, and much of its content, is drawn from interviews conducted with formerly incarcerated men and women in the states of New York, Alabama, Georgia and Texas by the authors. Quotations in the text are drawn from these interviews. Many of the names of the interviewees have been altered.

We incurred our own debts while producing this book—first and foremost among them, to past and present PEP students and faculty: Zach Gillespie, Mychal Pagan, Aunray Stanford, Hashani Forrester, Lynne Haney, Julie Livingston, Thuy Linh Tu, Shabnam Javdani, David Knight, Debanjan Roychoudhury, and Nikhil Singh. Michelle Daniel provided invaluable help in Alabama. Thanks are also due to the PEP team; Kaitlin Noss, Dylan Brown, Zoe Vongtau and Rich Villar for support and assistance. Early results from this research were presented at the Columbia/NYU Workshop on Carcerality, Law and Punishment.

We are grateful to Kassandra Manriquez and Paolina Lu for work on transcribing interviews, and Kassandra, again, for providing expert fact-checking. Myha Hill and her Stuyvesant crew also helped with transcriptions. Our gratitude goes to the OR Books team—Colin Robinson, Emma Ingrisani, and Olivia Heffernan—for making the production of this book a smooth, even enjoyable, experience. Finally and most importantly, we thank the interviewees who generously shared their time and knowledge with us.

Introduction

In February 2016, President Obama signed a bill that banned goods made by certain prisoners and other workers who toil under conditions of forced labor. Oregon senator Ron Wyden, who helped push the bill through Congress, triumphantly declared that "this law slams shut an unconscionable and archaic loophole that forced America to accept products made by children or slave labor."[1] To what immoral loophole was he referring? Not the most well-known one—the notorious Punishment Clause in the 13th Amendment that abolished slavery and involuntary servitude in the U.S. "except as a punishment for crime." That constitutional loophole is the legal basis for imposing forced labor in America's prisons, which hold more than 20 percent of the world's incarcerated population. These facilities annually produce goods and services worth tens of billions of dollars from the labor of largely unpaid prisoners.[2]

The bill signed by Obama turned a blind eye to this domestic injustice and the trade it upholds. Instead, it was aimed solely at shutting down the import of prison-made products *from other countries*. And the loophole in question was a legacy from an earlier embargo, the 1930 protectionist Smoot-Hawley Tariff Act, which banned most but permitted some goods if there was high domestic demand for them.[3] In closing this loophole by banning *all* imports, the U.S. government was able to dust off its standing as a humanitarian champion of the fight against global slavery. Yet this step forward only exposed a widening moral gap between the zero tolerance shown toward prison labor overseas and the longstanding acceptance of the same conditions at home, where the majority of the 1.2 million Americans incarcerated in state and federal prisons work under duress, for nothing or for penny wages.[4] It is repugnant that goods made by foreign prisoners are forbidden while those produced by our own are freely purchased by government agencies. In many states, these goods are available on the open market, not to mention overseas, since there is no corresponding ban on exports from the U.S.

Later that year on September 9, as if in response, the biggest prison strike ever broke out, in large part as a protest against domestic "prison slavery."[5] Masterminded by the Free Alabama Movement, it was observed in twenty-four states—including Texas, Mississippi, Oregon, Illinois, Virginia, California, Georgia, Washington, South Carolina, Michigan, and Florida, in addition to Alabama—and an estimated 57,000 prisoners participated in as many as 46 facilities.[6] The strike was not an isolated action; it was preceded and followed by several others. And it resonated far beyond the prison walls as initiatives got underway, all across the country, to eliminate the 13th Amendment's prison slavery exception from state constitutions and to pave the way for fair pay for incarcerated workers. A nationwide network, the Abolish Slavery National Network, sprang up to coordinate these efforts. By the fall of 2023, majorities in seven states had voted on amendments to end prison slavery (joining Rhode Island, that had done so in 1843), and many other bills were being prepared for consideration, including on Capitol Hill itself.

These efforts, on the inside and the outside, occupy a significant place in the new abolition movement. They are closely chronicled in this book, and we, the authors, support and participate in them. The campaign to end penal servitude speaks directly and explicitly to the unfinished business of Emancipation. By all norms of international law, constitutional slavery is a crime against humanity, and should be annulled. No one should be compelled to work or be punished for refusing to do so. Unpaid, or penny-wage, labor is a stark violation of human and labor rights. No less oppressive are the unregulated and often demeaning conditions under which incarcerated people work in the U.S. The legacy of hard labor, imposed as part of a "debt to society," is no more acceptable than capital punishment or a life sentence without parole.

Despite the moral clarity of these tenets, at this point in time, the outcome of efforts to "end the exception" is by no means straightforward. In some states where constitutional amendments have passed, daily life behind the walls is unaltered; forced labor continues as before, and wages have not budged.⁷ Men and women still face punishment, including beatings, lock-downs, sexual assault, loss of family visitation rights, elimination of good time credit, and solitary confinement for refusing to work. Removing the threat of coercion from a work assignment will take much more than a change in the letter of the law, and establishing the right to fair pay and labor protections is an even harder road. In Colorado (the first state to pass an anti-slavery amendment in 2018) the effort to implement the changes has involved closely fought litigation in the courts. In New York, the 13ᵗʰ Forward coalition (in which we are active members) is exploring a range of legislative approaches. In addition to pushing an amendment to end slavery, the coalition is attempting to pass a statutory bill on fair pay, standard labor protections, and the right to organize. It remains to be seen whether litigation or legislation will be more effective, or whether the impact of such new laws and rights can penetrate the thick culture of custodial rules and rituals through which guards and officials have run facilities with impunity for generations. Penal history shows us that prison reformers have come and gone, but the customary, violent praxis of the jailhouse "screw" has proven as deeply resistant to change as that of the rank-and-file in police departments.

The amendments and acts may fall short unless these correctional officers face immediate consequences for violating the new laws, or unless prisoners have a pathway to pursue legal action against them.

Some abolitionists have questioned the focus on ending the exception and winning worker rights. The energy is misdirected, they say, if it simply results in the recapture of wages by the state to pay for room and board in addition to restitution, court fines, family support, and other facility costs.[8] States already deduct up to 80 percent of the paltry wages on offer, and any pay hike might further feed, or subsidize, the system. So, too, it has been argued that the legal status of prisoners as akin to "slaves of the state" cannot be redeemed by adopting the identity of "workers" with its associated rights. The American carceral system is too tethered to the violent legacy of slavery and white supremacy for the dignity and value of work to be fulfilled under conditions of captivity.[9]

We respect these arguments, based, as they are, on sound speculation. In response, we believe that the anti-slavery logic deployed by the movement to end the exception is a *necessary*, though not *sufficient*, approach to eliminating forced work. It also speaks to the very real afterlives of slavery that permeate many aspects of the criminal justice system and which are unduly felt by African Americans held captive within it.[10] Based on our interviews and our own experience, we also believe that, for those on the inside, the provision of meaningful jobs on a voluntary basis and the establishment of fair wages would have a transformative impact. For one thing, these measures, if properly implemented and protected against garnishing by the state, would alter the balance of power significantly within carceral facilities. Taking away the discretionary power of staff to discipline and punish around work assignments is no small thing in a system governed, at all times, by the threat of institutional violence. Such advances are also likely to open the door to other prisoner rights that are not directly tied to labor: the right to vote, to litigate, or to access skill-building educational programs in systems that proclaim their commitment to rehabilitation.

So, too, many of the formerly incarcerated people we interviewed for this book spoke frankly about the difference it would have made in their lives to earn surplus income that is not swallowed up by the purchase of marked-up items from the commissary store: of being able to relieve their debt-burdened families from having to support them; of saving enough money to reenter society on a stable footing; of contributing toward earning future benefits such as Medicare, Social Security or unemployment insurance; and of freeing themselves from the need to participate in the risky—and predatory—trade in contraband goods that is a direct by-product of ultra-low pay that has been stagnant for decades, while the price of goods has risen considerably.[11]

As for the long-term abolitionist goal of decarceration, we believe that criminal justice officials would almost certainly be pressured to shrink their prison populations if faced with considerably higher wage bills. The greatly increased cost of keeping open facilities in which imprisoned men and women do all the work of maintenance—cooking, cleaning, repairing, and laundry, among other housekeeping tasks—would make it difficult—politically and economically—to sustain mass incarceration's vast archipelago. Of course, paying fair wages is not the only route to decarceration. There are many other ways for abolitionists to do that work. Like Angela Davis, we believe, ultimately, in "creating the kind of society where prisons are no longer necessary." But prison slavery abolition is a *necessary* step on the pathway to justice, even though the road beyond still needs to be built.

Living Off the Land

Scholars in the field of prison studies increasingly reject the view that prisons are "total institutions" (as Erving Goffman defined them), quarantined off from the free world. Prisons are now seen as porous and heavily entangled with society beyond the walls: they shape this society and are shaped by it. Journalists and analysts have exposed the profiteering character of the prison-building boom of the late twentieth and early twenty-first century, and they have charted the many ways in which private firms continue to extract revenue from the $80 billion price-gouging prison industry.[12] As Ruth Wilson Gilmore has argued, the U.S. prison boom was never really about crime control: the rise of the carceral archipelago was shaped by economic crises of the 1970s and 1980s, creating streams of profit from the "idle time" of those placed behind bars. As she puts it, "prisons enable money to move because of the enforced inactivity of people locked in them. It means people extracted from communities—and people returned to these communities but not entitled to be of them—enable the circulation of money on rapid cycles. What's extracted from the extracted is the resource of life: time."[13]

Others have focused on the direct impact of mass incarceration on the outside economy. Bruce Western and Katherine Beckett have demonstrated that official unemployment figures were artificially depressed (by as much as 2 percent) as a result of mass incarceration, and are further affected by the barriers to employment that most prisoners face on release.[14] Scholars like Noah Zatz and Erin Hatton have described how penitentiary punishment and carceral labor extend far beyond the prison walls; not only in the requirements set by parole, probation, work-release, workfare, immigrant confinement, and pre-trial detention, but also in a variety of low wage or precarious work sectors.[15] Tasseli McKay has estimated the colossal costs, to black women in particular, of maintaining communications with and economic care for incarcerated spouses or children.[16] Our own research has shown how the cost to family members of supporting their loved ones behind bars takes a huge toll on their household budgets and their ability to earn a livelihood.[17]

Proponents of the influential "warehousing" thesis, like Loïc Wacquant, argue that mass incarceration offered a way to absorb and store away large fractions of the working class who were displaced by deindustrialization and social-welfare retrenchment.[18] In this book, we present another view. The interviews we conducted with incarcerated persons suggest that the prison economy closely conforms to the "lousy wage and a hustle on the side" formula that holds sway in the free-world neoliberal economy. Far from a human depository, the prison exists in more of a continuum with the outside, just as its techniques of discipline have become quite common far beyond the walls—in carcerality at large. Unlike most studies of prison labor, which tend to focus exclusively on formal work assignments or jobs in the "correctional industries," we have tried to document the labor that goes into the informal economy's many industrious schemes for generating additional income.[19] These hustles, infinite in variety, are often what keep prisoners alive. In some states, like Alabama where correctional oversight is threadbare, they keep the prisons afloat, intersecting with and supplementing the role of maintenance labor. In most cases, they are extractive exchanges, because they drain resources from one prisoner to benefit another, and they are routinely shadowed by force or the threat of violence. Rarely are they disconnected from the outside world.

Paying fair wages would go a long way toward diminishing these forms of extraction, ranging from formal wage theft to the unpaid labor of self-care, the high cost of addiction, and the exploitation of families and friends who support loved ones inside. Yet little has been written about the potential economic impact of fair pay for incarcerated workers. At the height of mass incarceration, more than two million people had effectively been pulled out of the labor market and incapacitated, while most of them were doing work that would generate a great deal of income if performed by free-world workers.[20] In any other context, this would be classified as wage theft on a grand scale. According to one national estimate, the disparity between the local minimum wage and the penny-wages paid in prison amounts to $14 billion annually.[21] So, too, the abiding experience of being paid a pittance or nothing at all habituates imprisoned people to accept sub-standard, underpaid employment on release, while the threat of carceral poverty is an effective form of discipline for those on the outside who might otherwise chafe at such precarious conditions. In many ways, the incarcerated population is close to an ideal capitalist workforce behind bars, while also serving as what Marx called the "reserve army of labor" on reentry.[22]

Exiting prison with little more than a bus ticket and $40 or less in "gate money" leaves many people with few alternatives. They go right back to the "street," with harmful consequences for their own safety and for the general public. As one of the women we interviewed for this book reported, "I know so many women who get to the Port Authority [New York City's central bus station], and never even make it out of there. They end up right back in jail, because 'how am I even going to survive?'" While lawmakers may balk at the cost of paying fair wages for prison labor, a full accounting of the savings is arguably greater, beginning with—but not limited to—the reduction in social services for housing, healthcare, and unemployment, as well as a decrease in public safety and correctional expenditures. In 2023, Worth Rises commissioned an economist consultancy to estimate the impacts of paying a minimum, or prevailing, wage for formal job assignments in prison. The fiscal costs would range from $8.5 billion to $14.5 billion per year, but they would be far outweighed by the tangible benefits to incarcerated workers, to their families and children, to crime victims, and to society at large. The report estimated that they are between $26.8 billion and $34.7 billion per year, or a net benefit of $18.3 billion and $20.3 billion per year.[23]

The arguments we put forth in these pages are not the result of armchair speculation. One of us is formerly incarcerated, and the other two teach regularly in a prison education program. As members of the NYU Prison Research Lab, we conducted interviews with men and women who have served time. For this book, we did almost a hundred in-depth interviews—primarily in New York, Alabama, Texas, and Georgia—with system-impacted people and with advocates who are active in the movement. In addition to testimony about formal work assignments, we gathered a wealth of detail about the informal economy in which most people are forced to find a hustle to stay alive in prison. Due to the dismal state of institutional food, undernourishment is guaranteed and the threat of starvation is real. We also investigated the continuity of prison work-life with pre-carceral and post-carceral experiences. The low-road jobs that are available outside of prison do not pay enough to support a working-class household, and so almost everyone has a hustle, on the side, to make ends meet. If a breadwinner becomes incarcerated, the illegal activities that may have led to their arrest and detention continue on the inside. The art of living off the proceeds of the "street" carries over, often quite seamlessly, inside prison, where it is referred to as "living off the land." And given the stigma or "mark" that prevents so many ex-felons from finding sustainable employment on release, it is no surprise to find people picking up the hustle where they left off, rendering them permanent outsiders in the labor market.[24] Up to 70 million Americans have some kind of criminal record that hampers their formal employment prospects.[25] Under these circumstances, many have to eke out an off-the-books livelihood, putting them at some considerable risk of being reincarcerated.

What we drew from our research was a holistic picture of the roles occupied by prison labor in the daily lives of those who perform it. We were able to document a wide range of experiences, from state to state and from prison to prison. How a job is inter-preted can even vary from cell block to cell block, depending on the character or whims of the guard in charge. *Captive Labor*, the ACLU's comprehensive national survey (2022) records the vast diversity of jobs performed by men and women behind the wall:

> They work as cooks, dishwashers, janitors, groundskeep-ers, barbers, painters, or plumbers; in laundries, kitch-ens, factories, and hospitals. They provide vital public services such as repairing roads, fighting wildfires, or clearing debris after hurricanes. They washed hospital laundry and worked in mortuary services at the height of the pandemic. They manufacture products like office furniture, mattresses, license plates, dentures, glasses, traffic signs, garbage cans, athletic equipment, and uni-forms. They cultivate and harvest crops, work as welders and carpenters, and work in meat and poultry processing plants.[26]

"In most instances," the authors note, "the jobs these people in prison have look similar to those of millions of people working on the outside." Yet those who perform them are toiling at min-imal cost (from 13 cents to 52 cents an hour on average). They are under the complete, captive control of their "employers," and with no protections against exploitation or abuse.[27] No one would hesitate to denounce these conditions if they existed on the out-side. Nor would most people tolerate these abuses if more was known about them. In our minds, racial and class prejudice are the primary reasons why there is not more public curiosity about what people who are "civilly dead" are forced to do behind the walls.

During the COVID pandemic, prisoners' labor received a spurt of uncommon attention because, in almost every state, they were forced to manufacture hand sanitizers, face masks, and personal protective equipment while being denied the use of these products for themselves. They dug mass graves and built coffins, and they performed laundry and mortuary services for hospitals at grave risk to their own safety.[28] In other words, they became "essential workers" in the public eye, even though none were accorded the status of "heroes" bestowed upon frontline employees and delivery workers at that time. For more than a century, prisoners have labored on public works programs, maintaining roads, parks, cemeteries, landfills, and forests. But this socially accepted profile of providing a public benefit was troubled by the exposure of the morbid and unsafe nature of their labor during the pandemic. Awareness of their involuntary servitude was further heightened by the media generated by the passage of anti-slavery amendments. The next battle, over wages and worker rights, will bring even more attention.

Michel Foucault once described prison life as an "economy of suspended rights," sequestered off from the outside world.[29] These include the rights accorded to free-world workers. It would be naïve to imagine that we can end this state of segregation any time soon. But the movement to do so is not simply a matter of basic human rights. It is also a necessary part of the fight against poverty, which is the number one factor driving incarceration.[30] Putting poor people in cages and taking away their rights has provided a more dirt-cheap labor opportunity for the state and for corporations than would be available on the outside.

Field and Factory

Much of the testimony we gathered included accounts of extreme cruelty and barbarism. Texas is one of seven states—along with Arkansas, Alabama, Florida, Georgia, Mississippi, and South Carolina—where zero compensation is offered for the vast majority of prison labor.[31] It is also one of the Southern prison systems which maintains large agricultural operations on land previously occupied by slave plantations. Donna Fairchild, a native Texan who worked as a manager in a manufacturing plant before she was incarcerated, described to us what it meant to be assigned to work in the fields:

> I went in when I was 30 years old, and they said, "you look young and healthy enough, we're gonna put you on the hoe squad." They call you out at 6:00 am, and it's very much like an old prison movie scene where you might have seen armed guards on horseback watching us. We were doing identical work to the plantation. We might have a big hoe or even a sledgehammer because we also broke rocks. It was like a chain gang but we weren't chained together. We worked year round, during the coldest and the hottest. There was one time we were harvesting cabbage in February and some rows were even flooded and it was 31 degrees. Texas policy is that inmates don't work outside if it's below freezing, and they aren't provided with things to keep them warm . . . Everyone was miserable, shivering, trying to get it done fast, because the lieutenant told us if we got all the cabbage picked, we would go back in. I don't know if you've ever picked cabbage; you have to like, twist it, so it breaks off, and it has a bottom plant. If you pull up the whole plant, you're gonna get a disciplinary ticket, because they can't grow another head of cabbage. So you have to hold down the bottom of the plant with your knees and twist. Everyone was wet from the knees down, and I remember thinking that they don't really care what happens to me. I felt like I could have died and they would not have cared.

Texas summer temperatures can be brutal. There is no air-conditioning in most of the prisons, and a dozen or more

fatalities were attributed to the heatwaves of 2023 which saw prolonged periods of triple-digit temperatures.[32] Outside in the fields
under direct sunlight, the conditions can be much worse:

> We were out there in 104 degrees weather. We weren't
> issued sunscreen, and medical said only white people
> needed it, so any person of color was not getting free
> sunscreen from the prison. We were made to pull weeds
> down a row, and the ground would be hard and dry from
> the sun. And we would have to stand up and bend over
> at the waist to pick weeds, because you weren't allowed to
> squat. If we were picking corn, and you've missed an ear
> of corn, or stand up for too long, that's a disciplinary case
> too—it's a refusal to work. You get an incomplete work
> assignment, and you go to disciplinary court inside of
> prison. Punishments for one infraction can range from
> no phone calls home for 30 days or no outside rec. For
> three refusals to work, I lost my contact visits for four
> months, 45 days of no commissary purchases or rec.

Donna went on to describe the dreaded "strip shack" where
everyone had to be searched for contraband each time they came
in and out for lunch and at the end of their shift:

> If we're on our menstrual cycle, we have to remove our
> tampon or a pad and strip down. Everybody's hot and
> sweaty, so some of the officers would comment on how
> bad we stunk. And if we had blood on us, they would
> tell us that we were disgusting. You don't have an oppor-
> tunity to use the bathroom very easily out in the field.
> They have a tractor driver that brings around a trailer
> with some porta potties on it, but only once in the morn-
> ing and once in the afternoon. If I was on my cycle

I would hold up my tampon and wave it like, please choose me. But they're only going to choose four or five people to go—everybody doesn't get the opportunity to go. So I've changed my tampon in the field, and that's why it was such an issue when we get to the strip shack. It was so common for people to have made a mess, because we weren't able to take care of our hygiene that way at work.

Federal regulations governing workplace safety and health standards do not apply to prison labor, and so we heard many different versions of Donna's misery—and lack of dignity on the job—from others.[33] But what about the backbreaking demands with respect to her productivity in the fields? Outside of agriculture, this kind of pressure would be most familiar to prisoners across the country who work in the factory facilities that are part of industrial programs. The vast majority of these are state or federal industry enterprises, located in public prisons: private prisons control less than 8 percent of the beds nationally, and are mostly concentrated in a handful of Southern prisons. Local, state, or federal governments, in other words, are the primary beneficiaries of these "correctional industries." Despite the public misperception that corporations are exploiting prison labor en masse, only 1 percent of incarcerated people are employed in facilities on private contracts with firms, where they are required to be paid a local minimum wage that is subject to deductions of up to 80 percent (for room and board, and other costs, such as restitution fines, family support payments, court fees, and discharge money).[34]

In states where prisoners are actually paid as a rule, the industry jobs command the highest wage rates, and sometimes include bonuses for meeting productivity quotas. In New York, for example, where hourly pay ranges from 10 cents to 65 cents, workers for Corcraft—the state-owned enterprise—earn double pay if they hit the quota. The topmost compensation is for work that requires a higher level of skill. This includes making office furniture, license plates, street signs, garbage cans, eyeglasses, and other products for purchase by state entities. Emilio Delgado, a Brooklynite who worked in Corcraft shops in several facilities, explained what the difference in pay meant: "It's more like you being a middle-class prisoner than being a lower-class one because with that little money you are able to buy more commissary. The most you can get paid per hour was 65 cents and so you could get a 100 percent bonus and get paid 65 cents more. That would be 1.30 an hour." Even so, he added, "the lowest a person would get paid on the outside for this was probably maybe $25 an hour."

For many of Delgado's peers, the sharp disparity between $1.30 and $25 an hour marked these jobs out as especially exploitative. Since working in industry was mostly optional, they refused to pursue what they labelled as "plantation" or "slave jobs." Maintenance jobs in cleaning or laundry or cooking, which make up the vast majority of prison jobs, were less labor intensive and were not producing for the market. In effect they were "housework," normally gendered as "women's" labor. Yet these jobs also offered a variety of perks in the form of opportunities to make money in the informal economy. Porters, for example, received the lowest pay, but their ability to move around the prison and facilitate the black market trade could bring substantial rewards. But there were some, like Delgado, who sought out the industry positions because they could not rely on outside support or lacked the inclination to hustle, and so the higher wage, even though it was still paltry, went a long way.

In the absence of any workplace protections, the extra pay usually came at the cost of a compromise in safety. Delgado confessed: "Thank God I don't have any long lasting effects. But I've seen guys lose fingers rolling out sheet metal. I've seen them lose fingers trying to go ahead and stop the press and putting their hand in between there because they put in a wrong piece of metal and the license plate was going to be upside down and they were going to be yelled at." In another shop, where he made chairs, he recalled that the "adhesive was dangerous, and for the first five years, we had no masks, we had no glue room. We only had a handkerchief that we would put around our face when the glue got too strong. I didn't know what that was going to do to me long term."

In rare cases, the skills learned in those industry workplaces translated to jobs on the outside, if employment in the trade could be found, but the majority of our interviewees saw no correlation between their prison work experience and what they were able to secure on reentry. To add insult to injury, they found that listing prison jobs on a resume—even skilled ones—invited disqualification from consideration. By contrast, prison educational programs—from GED to college-level—produced all kinds of benefits in skills and self-development. James Tyler, who grew up in a Hudson River Valley city, and earned his B.A. in a college prison program, reported that "one of the biggest benefits is it gave me the ability to write and speak about my world. It gave me the tools to talk about my experience, and subsequently, to reshape my experience, because if you know the things that you're suffering from, if you know the problems that are in your life, you can find solutions. Education gives you those tools, right? So now I know the mechanism of oppression. And now I know how not to succumb to those mechanisms."

Tyler was one of the many interviewees who offered opinions on the widespread experience of idleness, long regarded by administrators as "the devil's workshop." Referencing the long-standing belief that idle time promotes trouble, he observed that "the structure itself is fearful of it, but the officers would rather have you doing nothing, because it makes their job easier. According to a capitalistic idea of life, you want to keep people busy by making them work, but every officer I've ever encountered, they rather have people sitting down and watching TV because they're easier to watch over." Ultimately, Tyler thought "the biggest fear" of administrators "is not idle time, but time spent in a shared space with multiple people. Anything that allows people to come together, in their mind, they think they're gonna get Attica because of that." We heard other, more opportunistic interpretations of the use that officers made of idleness. "They want violence to occur," observed Marshall DuBose, a Bronx native who had done twenty years in a variety of facilities, "because now they can scream 'we need more officers, yo, we need more protection.'" In many cases, the officers themselves "create the violent atmosphere and then say, we need help." "When I was in Green Haven," he recalled, "a group of COs used to just go around and beat people up for no reason. Like you could be on the phone, they'd just beat you up, and it gets written up an assault against an officer. Now the records and the statistics show more cases of assaults on officers have been occurring, and so therefore, we need more guards." As we learned from others, officers could also claim Worker's Comp time off on account of the emotional distress sustained from the beating they themselves had administered.

Whatever the uses to be made of it, there was no shortage of idle time in the prisons we surveyed. Even in prisons that are under capacity, there are not enough jobs to go around—up to 35 percent prisoners nationally are not assigned a job. Of those who are assigned, more than 80 percent, according to the Bureau of Justice Statistics, are given maintenance jobs—janitorial or cleaning duties, food preparation, laundry, grounds and building maintenance.[35] Yet many of these jobs typically require only an hour or two of work per shift, while many other assigned tasks are simply "make work." This is in sharp contrast with earlier periods of penal history when productive labor was placed at the center of prison life. The days when officials insisted on rebuilding prisoners' character by instilling a Protestant work ethic are long over. Marking time has been the main experience of the era of prison warehousing, especially in systems where educational and vocational training programs, redolent of the reform era, have been stripped to the bone.[36] That said, idle time is not the opposite of labor time, nor is it free or down time. On the contrary, we found it can be a very busy field of activity, bustling with many forms of off-the-books work.

Hustle and Refuse

As a result of movies that depict prison breaks, most of us are familiar with the ingenuity that goes into schemes to escape from high-security facilities. Yet this same creativity applies to almost every aspect of the underground prison economy, where participants—through force of circumstance—have to barter all manner of goods and services and hustle to make money on the side. Moments that could be utilized for business opportunities or for self-care (work on the body and mind) are seldom wasted in prison, and so unoccupied time is few and far between. These entrepreneurial activities range from small-scale, local transactions to large operations coordinated with street organizations on the outside. Some of them, involving drug sales for example, might require work skills acquired before incarceration. Others are angles learned on the inside and are a by-product of the peculiar institutional market where many things have an elevated value that they would not command on the outside. Almost everything has a price.

In any event, it is difficult to draw a line between inside and outside because of the constant flow of money and resources in and out of a prison. For example, we heard of people running outside businesses from their cells, including day-trading and ambitious gambling enterprises. Credit enters the prison in numerous ways, for example, through transferring the value on Green Dot reloadable prepaid cards.[37] Activities that are more restricted as far as their impact on the inside tend to be less profitable. Most others are channeled or filtered through a keenly observed prison hierarchy that reflects some wealth or social affiliations on the outside. Without access to one or the other, and short of resorting to extortion or theft, it is not easy to attain the status of "jail-rich." This underground economy is glorified by the business press as a "hothouse of entrepreneurial finesse," but much of it is highly predatory turf, governed by threats of violence that echo the official protocols of penal servitude.[38]

Trading in drugs and other high-priced contraband is by far the most lucrative hustle, and often depends on a "dirty" CO who is profiting royally from bringing in the goods. In Alabama's chronically understaffed and overcrowded prisons, we were told that many guards would not have signed up for such an unsafe job unless they had the opportunity to earn lucre from smuggling contraband at huge markups—cell phones, weapons, and drugs for up to twenty times the retail price. Some of these COs were gang-affiliated and operated as key links in the organization's supply chain. But the mark-ups can also apply to goods that only circulate inside. The personal stores that many prisoners run, according to the "juggle" system, operate on a high-interest credit system. They are stocked with commissary goods that are given out to someone who must pay back with two of the items. Foodstuff pilfered from the mess hall can be profitably sold or traded, and this food is routinely used as currency, especially pouches of fish or ramen packs. The same principles applied to a whole array of custom services, such as sex, cell-cleaning, meal preparation, sewing, gambling, personal laundry, hairstyling, and letter-writing, etc.

These transactional activities demand resourceful work, as distinct from the more mundane "hard labor" of the formal work assignments. Arguably, the most creative involve home-grown skills in arts and hobby crafts, such as making clothing and jewelry, cakes, sketches, birthday cards, hooch, tattoos, soap sculptures, hair dye and the like from everyday items found or procured in the prison (a practice called "mushfake"). Curtis James, a Bronx native who seemed to have tried his hand at almost every hustle, told us about one of these:

> I used to make porn magazines out of different pictures and sell them. Once I started making them, people asked for requests, like, 'I want only this person in my book.' So I had to go through many books and just cut that person out, and then put them all in one. Some people like girl-on-girl, you know. Some people just want that person by themselves. So it was a variation of things. I was making non-pornographic magazines as well, like model magazines. So I would see a picture in *Cosmopolitan*, I might take that out, and make it a cover for one of my books. For a custom-made book, I'd charge five packs of cigarettes, and for a non-custom, two or three. In a week, I would make ten packs easy. And with ten packs of cigarettes in a prison, you the man.

For someone who gave the impression he had seen everything, James said the most ingenious of all was "the person who cooked on his bed frame. He sprayed the paint off, cleaned it, set a fire underneath the bed, and used it like a surface to fry stuff, like pancakes. That was amazing to me." At another prison, his next-door neighbor upped the ante, by "cooking in the toilet bowl." "He actually used the bowl as a fire," James explained, "because it's porcelain. He would layer it with like tissues and then use some type of oil, or Vaseline, to separate the fire and the water and reduce any smoke. And then he would cook over this stove on metal trays and stuff." "Prisoners," he reminded us, "are real crafty."

No less creative is the devotion to self-care and personal development that occupies a lot of the idle time not spent in pursuit of financial gain. This includes body-building, reading, writing poetry and fiction, making art, religious devotion, and working on your legal case—or the legal cases of others—in the law library. This kind of labor is essential for the mental and physical health of people inside. It is not an understatement to say that such efforts at building dignity and well-being are vital to anyone's survival behind bars. Of all the forms of work we have mentioned, these are arguably among the most important, and also the most challenging, especially in men's prisons. This level of care is more accessible in women's prisons where most people belong to "pseudo-families," with mothers and aunts to look over them. As Mavis Billings, a Long Islander who had served more than twenty years, explained: "I'm not with my own children, and so I get some children. I never really had a relationship with my own. And some women who never have mother figures or anybody who cared, when they leave prison, they're leaving the only family they ever had. And they will absolutely do something to come back." Those who lack this "fictive kin" network and who are unable to take care of themselves (the grievous lack of mental health services in most facilities places this burden on individuals themselves) easily spiral into addiction, ill-health, nihilism, and worse. In the most degraded and dangerous facilities, like those we have reported on in Alabama, the end result, for many, is a premature death.

In some respects, this outcome is the logical upshot of a social order that only offers intolerable options to poor people, and to racialized minorities in particular. All that a neoliberal economy has to offer are demeaning dead-end jobs, predatory loans, meager services, and overpolicing. To refuse these wretched choices is a justified response, as philosopher Tommie Shelby has argued.

> The ghetto poor have not received many of the benefits they have been "promised"—e.g., equality of opportunity and the equal protection of the law. We can, therefore, view their refusal to work in an unjust social scheme as the moral equivalent of a rent strike against a slumlord: they refuse to pay their civic debt until the government makes good on its promise to treat all citizens fairly. There has not been a breach of civic contract but a governmental failure to perform so fundamental that the aggrieved citizens, the ghetto poor, can rightfully refuse to comply with their "agreement" to work.[39]

In prison, where the options are much worse, the moral grounds of this refusal to perform unjust labor are even stronger.

It is fitting then that the crux of the movement to end the 13th Amendment exception lies in the freedom to *refuse* unsafe and ill-paid work imposed by the state on citizens it has failed to protect. The right to refuse is the key element, and it also empowers people to reject other aspects of their incarceration. But the obverse of this freedom from coercion is the right to have access to meaningful jobs, with adequate compensation, transferrable skills, and a career ladder to begin climbing. This should be an attainable goal, on both sides of the wall, but especially in prison systems that pay lip service to rehabilitation.

Burying the Confederacy

Our base for research and advocacy is in New York, where progressive penal reform was born in the 1870s, and where it ran its course for almost a century. It is also the state that sowed the seeds of mass incarceration in the 1970s through the mandatory sentencing provisions of the Rockefeller Drug Laws. New York incubated the "punitive turn" through its high-level backlash to the 1971 Attica uprising at the same time as it allowed custodial union power to thrive as a powerful political force pushing for expansion of the correctional workforce.[40] But the litmus test for abolition, as always, lies in the South. That is why we devoted a good part of our research for this book to Alabama, and, to a lesser extent, to Georgia and Texas. It is apt that Alabama, the final battleground of the civil rights movement in the 1960s, emerged as the crucible of a new prisoner rights movement in the 2010s. With prisons that host some of the most barbarous conditions in the nation, the strikes that began there and spread across the country emerged from a historical backdrop of racial repression that included the longest, and most highly concentrated, period of convict leasing of any state. That history also includes a thirteen-year period, from the mid-1970s, when the federal government took control of the state's prison system in order to remedy conditions of "cruel and unusual punishment" under the Eighth Amendment. By the time the strike wave got underway in 2014-2016, Department of Justice agents were once again paying regular visits to Alabama, and it is highly likely that the system will once again fall under federal oversight in the immediate future.

The Free Alabama Movement (FAM) favored work stoppages over hunger strikes and other forms of protest because of the direct harm inflicted on the prison economy. The reality of the system's dependence on prison labor was exposed when guards and administrators had to step in to prepare and serve food and to perform basic maintenance work. But the refusal to show up for work "on the plantation" (a spirit captured in the title of a FAM manifesto, "Let the Crops Rot in the Fields")[41] was driven by an urgent need to exit a system that was highly dangerous to be in and very difficult to get out of. Decarceration, in other words, was a key objective of the organizers. In state after state, the strikes offered a platform for more specific demands. In addition to the abolition of involuntary servitude, these included the payment of prevailing wages, full voting rights, caps on the overall incarcerated population, secure access to education, rehabilitation and re-entry preparedness programs, restoration of the right to litigate, and a ban on incarcerating mentally ill persons.

Measures like these, if implemented, would help to move prisons away from functioning as vehicles of profit and punishment, would reinstate constitutional rights that are currently denied, and would plant the seeds of restorative justice. But the underlying harms and injustices are not exclusive to prison life. Tens of millions of those who leave prison have great difficulty accessing education, healthcare, sustainable employment, and their full democratic rights. Nor are these social goods guaranteed to the general population in our neoliberal order, and least of all to households struggling to stay afloat. That is why the movement to abolish prison slavery and its effects touches all of us. The first lesson of living in a carceral state is that what starts in prison does not end there.

CHAPTER 1

Ending the Exception

"[Slavery] has been called by a great many names, and it will call itself by yet another name; and you and I and all of us had better wait and see what new form this old monster will assume, in what new skin this old snake will come forth next."
—Frederick Douglass (May 9, 1865)

When Ava DuVernay's influential documentary, *13th*, was released in October 2016, the attention that it drew helped to blow the lid off a chronic abuse of human rights that had been hiding in plain sight in the U.S. Constitution. The film offered a variety of insights into the racialized design of mass incarceration and played up the continuity between the confinements of the modern prison and the captivity of chattel slavery. But, in many quarters, it was most hailed for elevating public awareness about the "loophole" in the 13th Amendment that abolishes slavery and involuntary servitude, "except as a punishment for crime." As a result of this Exception Clause, it has been considered lawful to force incarcerated men and women to work.

Not surprisingly, the buzz generated by the film was most closely tracked by incarcerated people, who made requests to make it available in prisons across the country. Several months after its release, youth educator and advocate Dennis Febo showed the film in a class he taught in New Jersey's Hudson County Correctional Facility. After the screening, Febo reported that his students were in a "somber and depressed mood," but, once they realized that the language of the Thirteenth may be a serious "violation of human rights," they began to talk about what they could do to remedy the injustice. "If we were to remove these fourteen little words in the exception," Febo pointed out, "it could create a cascading effect." At the urging of his students, he decided to jumpstart an initiative for a constitutional amendment to end the penal exception in New Jersey.

New Jersey is one of twenty-six states that has no language in its constitution about slavery or involuntary servitude, and therefore defers to the 13th Amendment itself. Once known as the "slave state of the North," holding almost two-thirds of the enslaved population above the Mason-Dixon Line, it was the last of the Northern states to abolish slavery—as late as January 1866. It even took until 2003 to fully ratify the 14th Amendment.

Today, it has one of the highest rates of Black incarceration in the country.[1] It would surely have been appropriate, then, if New Jersey were the first state to abolish slavery without any exceptions since Rhode Island, which did so in 1843.

Febo had little sense of what was required to amend the constitution, but he drafted a petition, signed by his incarcerated students (as disenfranchised citizens), and sent it to members of the state's Black Legislative Caucus. One of them expressed shock: "Do you mean to tell me that slavery is still legal in New Jersey?" As the idea got traction among the lawmakers, they initially drafted a bill "urging" Congress to take up the issue but they were persuaded to go further with a bill aimed at introducing abolitionist language in the state constitution. The bill got past two committees, but encountered hurdles along the way, and never made it to the Assembly floor in 2022. According to Febo, "the governor didn't want it on the ballot, because the outcome was not predictable, and the state's Department of Justice did not want any admission of forced labor in the language of the bill, even though penal codes in New Jersey explicitly impose criminal charges for not performing labor." The bill, with the language unaltered, was re-introduced in 2023, and again, in a modified version, in 2024.

As he was learning about the process for initiating the amendment, Febo heard that activists in Colorado were working on a similar effort. He flew out to Denver to compare notes with Kamau Allen, a recent Howard University graduate who was running the campaign through the multi-faith organization Together Colorado. Allen then spoke at a New Jersey rally at Febo's request. "Let's dream big," they vowed after the event, "and make this national." They soon found people in other parts of the country who were independently working towards the same goals, and so they all got on a call to share tactics about how to end the exception in each state. Colorado got there first. After winning unanimous support in the legislature, an amendment to the state constitution was approved by voters in November 2018.

The loose group of far-flung organizers eventually coalesced into the Abolish Slavery National Network (ASNN), formed in August 2020.[2] Three months later, voters in Utah and Nebraska joined Colorado by approving abolition amendments with large majorities. In 2022, activists launched legislative initiatives in six states, and—as a result of the November election—Vermont, Oregon, Tennessee, and Alabama also crossed the finish line. By the opening of legislative sessions in 2024, there were as many as eighteen amendment campaigns under way, in Georgia, Kentucky, Arkansas, Michigan, New York, Louisiana, California, Nevada, Virginia, Missouri, Texas, North Carolina, New Jersey, New Hampshire, Wisconsin, Iowa, Ohio, and Washington, D.C.

Though facing unlikely odds (the exception had stood for more than 150 years after all), the ASNN state campaigns have recorded significant wins. Organizers reported that, like that New Jersey senator, many lawmakers were surprised to find that slavery of any kind was still legal or was actually authorized by language in their own state constitutions. According to one nationwide 2021 poll, as many as 88 percent of those surveyed were unaware of the loophole in the U.S. Constitution.[3] The revelation about the continued legality of slavery helped move the measure in some states, even in heavily Republican ones, where a lingering appeal to the "party of Lincoln," the Great Emancipator, still counted for something. By 2023, ASNN had secured eight of the thirty-eight states that would be needed for an amendment "to abolish slavery without exception" to become part of the U.S. Constitution as the 28th Amendment. The coalition had succeeded in winning sponsors of a Congressional bill to promote the initiative at the federal level. The measure was first introduced in 2020 and has been introduced every year thereafter. Compared to the titanic struggle for Emancipation, the fight to abolish prison slavery has made a rapid advance in a short space of time, though not without encountering some significant headwinds from government agencies—like Corrections, Justice, and Finance—all of whom have a vested interest in the punishment industry.

By the time DuVernay's film was released, the arguments and ideals of the "new abolitionism" had begun to work their way beyond liberal and left circles. Angela Davis, Michelle Alexander, and others had popularized the notion that mass incarceration lay in the line of descent, direct or otherwise, from the chattel slavery system, and also that a new abolition movement was needed to dismantling it. Even tough-on-crime Republicans were having second thoughts about the demented American experiment of locking up more than two million of its poorest and most marginalized citizens, though they were primarily concerned about the runaway costs of incarceration. New Jersey, for example, spends $600,000 annually to lock up a juvenile, and New York City spends $550k for each person behind bars at Rikers Island jail.[4] Guided by the spirit of fiscal conservatism (and under the aegis of carefully marketed labels like Right on Crime, or Safe Streets, or Second Chances), right-wing philanthropists like Charles Koch were encouraged to push back against over-criminalization by funding programs aimed at shrinking the population behind bars.[5] On the left, Black Lives Matter and the George Floyd movement expanded the potential field of action by demanding an abolitionist approach to policing and other institutions that fell within the ever-widening orbit of the carceral state. The turn to abolition also ran parallel, or overlapped, with the push for decolonization that coursed through college campuses, museums, and other cultural institutions. Decolonize and Abolish emerged from the COVID pandemic as two high-level directives, exerting pressure and influence over all efforts at radical institutional change.

Abolitionists are careful about how they talk among themselves about their ideals and aspirations, but the use of the term "abolition" in more public discussions about the fate of mass incarceration generates its share of confusion. As with the slogan "Defund the Police," it often invites responses that evoke lawlessness: "Are you suggesting that we close all prisons and let serial killers run free?" Davis has responded to this willful misinterpretation with a more aspirational definition: "Abolition is about creating the kind of society where prisons are unnecessary." In this, her guiding star was W. E. B. Du Bois, who drew lessons about the failure of Reconstruction to build institutions capable of truly liberating formerly enslaved people from the political, economic, and social fetters that still kept them down.[6] Du Bois saw that the abolition of chattel slavery had not been nearly enough. There had been no sustained effort to create a positive vision of "abolition democracy" that more fully implemented the new rights of the 14th and 15th Amendments. The restoration of white supremacy in the South saw the establishment of a new slave-like society that closely resembled the old one in all but name.[7] In particular, criminalization and convict leasing, set in motion through the Black Codes and vagrancy acts of the ex-Confederacy, seamlessly replaced the plantation's property laws as a way to secure and bind the free labor of Black people.

Forced prison labor is only one of the many afterlives of slavery. We can also see its imprint today through disparities in education, homeownership, health rates, political power, and household wealth and debt. But because of the wording of the 13th (the only mention of slavery in the Constitution), the prison is the place where we most *directly* encounter the unfinished business of Emancipation itself. Most scholars have come to agree with Du Bois's judgement that formal declarations of rights (like the three post-bellum Amendments, or the Civil Rights Acts of 1866 and 1964) do not automatically yield social equality: they merely set people down a freedom road that is still largely unbuilt. Ending the exception, at the very least, would be that first step on that road, potentially opening a pathway for further challenges to the carceral state. It might not lead, ultimately, to the dismantling of the prison-industrial complex, not even if it resulted in a safe prison workplace that resembled its free world counterpart, with mandated minimum wages, unions, and other labor protections. But no one can deny that it would be an act of abolition.

How difficult will it be to move beyond the formal repeal of the Exception Clause (sometimes called the Punishment Cause) to more fully ensure the ending of forced prison labor? The widespread reliance on unpaid labor or penny wages to run prisons cheaply and to generate revenue from goods produced for the state or private firms is too central to the carceral economy to cede without a bitter, rearguard fight on the part of its public and private beneficiaries. Nor can we overestimate its importance to the preservation of discipline and punishment behind the prison walls, or how this coercive labor system extends far beyond, with respect to probation, parole, supervised release, addiction programs, and a host of other nonvoluntary employment settings under legal supervision. Even underemployment has its punitive uses, in the withdrawal of work privileges for infractions, typically resulting in lockdowns or solitary confinement. Though most incarcerated people want to be actively and gainfully employed, deprivation of work opportunities has at times even been litigated as a "cruel and unusual punishment" under the Eighth Amendment; and, in one instance, California prisoners staged a strike to demand *more* industry jobs.[8]

Given the time-honored association of punishment with hard labor, how would prisons be transformed if they had to host a fair labor environment where prisoners could choose to work with dignity while earning a savings surplus to relieve household debts and help them get back on their feet on release? Would it significantly alter the distribution of power behind the walls and move us more directly toward the horizon of abolition on the outside? Would the increased cost lead to a drawdown of the incarcerated population? And what impact would the attainment of these labor rights have on the free-world economy?

Badges and Incidents

It took centuries of resistance by enslaved people, a lifetime of Abolitionist campaigning, and a bloody civil war to enshrine Emancipation in the U.S. Constitution. After such Herculean efforts, the content and significance of the 13th Amendment should have been crystal clear. Yet, as prominent legal scholar James Gray Pope has put it, "more than a century and a half since the ratification of the Thirteenth Amendment, its meaning remains a mystery."[9] In Pope's view, both sections of the amendment are sources of uncertainty; not just the first one which bans slavery—albeit with exceptions—but also Section 2, which empowers Congress "to enforce" the ban by passing "appropriate legislation." Almost as soon as the ink was dry, lawmakers on either side of the aisle promoted different interpretations of how far Congress could go in these enforcement efforts. After all, the subjugation and harms that flow from slavery come in many forms, not just the holding and binding of human property. For their part, the Republican framers pushed hard to prohibit all the practices that came to be known as the "badges and incidents of slavery," including the denial of the rights first specified in the Civil Rights Act of 1866 (making contracts, owning property etc.).[10] On the other side of the aisle, Democrats wanted to restrict the scope of Congressional power to the minimum, covering only the core badges and incidents like chattelization and physically coerced labor. Although the degree of latitude under Section 2 remains an "open" question to this day, Pope points out that courts have traditionally honored the narrow reading initially proposed by the Democrat upholders of slave power.

A similar face-off occurred over the interpretation of the Exception Clause in Section 1. In Pope's reading, the text of the Amendment "excepts not persons convicted of crime" *in general*, but only specific "instances of slavery or involuntary servitude that exist 'as a punishment for crime whereof the party shall have been duly convicted.'" According to this view:

> [C]onvicted offenders retain protection against slavery or involuntary servitude unless it has been imposed as a punishment for the specific crime whereof they have been duly convicted. Under this reading, any particular instance of prison slavery or servitude could be challenged if, on the facts, it fell outside the exception. Prisoners might allege, for example, that they had been forced to work not as a punishment for crime but as a means for achieving any number of other possible ends, for example raising revenue for the state, generating private profit, or socializing inmates to accept an inferior status as civilly dead outcasts from society. They might challenge the widespread practice of imposing servitude without a sentence of hard labor; after all, the sentencing authority is—by definition—charged with specifying the punishment, while prison administrators inflict servitude for reasons having nothing to do with the inmate's criminal culpability, for example prison discipline and preparation for labor market re-entry.[11]

Given the uncertainty built into the wording, and the subsequent history of misinterpretation, Pope asks us to consider the (patchy) historical record of the debate over the amendment. In his rendering, Southern Democrats, who initially tried to block the Amendment altogether, were inclined to view the penal exception as a way of authorizing the practice of convict leasing, thereby providing a new supply of unpaid Black labor for planters and industrialists. For their part, the Republican majority vigorously opposed any use of the exception to cover this form of private servitude (including debt peonage, which would enjoy a prolonged life in rural pockets of the South). In addition, some senators insisted that the clause did not except all of those convicted of a crime, but applied strictly to instances where offenders were sentenced to hard labor as a specific punishment.

In the political and paramilitary power play that followed, which ultimately resulted in the failure of Reconstruction and the reassertion of white supremacy in the South, the strength of the Republican framers' argument faded. The Democratic view prevailed, and, over time, courts accepted that any conviction in and of itself strips the offender of protection against slavery or involuntary servitude. As with the "open question" of Congress's power to eradicate the badges and incidents of slavery, the judiciary appears to have deferred to the Democratic interpretation on the grounds that it must be constitutionally valid because it has prevailed for so long. Yet, in Pope's view, there is "nothing in the text, original meaning, or Supreme Court jurisprudence of the Punishment Clause" to prevent them from ruling otherwise.[12]

Leaving aside this "constitutional void," one certainty is that the 13th was written in order to end slavery and not to extend it. The Exception Clause was not *intended* to be a "loophole" to justify slavery and involuntary servitude among prisoners, as some "Thirteenthers" have supposed, though it has long been utilized for that purpose.[13] Why was this potential misuse of the clause not foreseen at the time? One reason is that the language of exception was closely modeled on the 1787 Northwest Ordinance that prohibited slavery in a vast territory now occupied by the Midwestern states west of the Ohio River: "[t]here shall be neither slavery nor involuntary servitude in the said territory, otherwise than in punishment of crimes, whereof the party shall have been duly convicted."[14] The Northwest Ordinance was a monumental win for abolitionists, but it was issued at time when sentencing to hard labor in workhouse or houses of correction was common, and when the memory and practice of indentured servitude was still fresh, especially in regions of the country which had been used by colonists as a de facto penal colony. Indeed, roughly one-quarter of British settlers in the 1700s were convicts transported by private companies and sold by auction to plantation owners.[15] Consequently, the inclusion of an exception for convict labor in a statute that forbade slavery was deemed uncontroversial.

Indenture largely disappeared after the American Revolution, but the association of crime with punishment by hard labor got a new lease of life with the rise of the penitentiary movement toward the end of the century. In the new Northern prisons, labor was central to penitence, and, over time, to the factory model of production that flourished during the nineteenth century. By the time of the 13th Amendment, the language of the Northwest Ordinance had been incorporated, almost as boilerplate, into the constitutions of the slave-free states carved out of the Northwest Territory.[16] Its inclusion in the 13th was more a matter of legal precedent, and a recognition of existing state police powers, than an intentional loophole.[17] In the wake of ratification, the language of the amendment's first section was then adopted, in some version, into other state constitutions. Twenty-three states had exceptions until Colorado's revised amendment in 2018.

In recent years, it has become more common to assert that the Exception Clause was included *in order* to open the door to convict leasing and the criminalization of blackness in the South. According to this view, the exception was a concession to ensure Southern buy-in. In other words, it was yet another sordid racial compromise that began with wrangling between the North and South over the Constitution, such as the arguments that resulted in the Fugitive Slave Clause and the Three-Fifths Clause.[18] Yet many historians believe that the Black Codes, introduced and passed into law with utter transparency, would have done the job anyway, with or without the Exception Clause.[19] Slave holders and their political enablers were intent on restoring their control over Black labor by any means necessary.

Just as important, but typically overlooked, is the political reality that Northern sensibilities also had to be accommodated. If the framers of the 13th had sought to ban *all* forms of forced labor—without exception—they would not have gotten enough Northern support to pass the amendment. After all, the use of convict labor for profit in Northern prisons, where the vast majority of prisoners were white (predominantly Irish and German) immigrants, was widespread and had been a well-established and profitable practice since the establishment of New York's Auburn prison in 1816. Indeed, it was such an inspirational model for the post-bellum convict leasing of Black Southerners that it was known as the "Yankee invention" by those who introduced the lease in the former Confederacy. If anything, the inclusion of the Exception Clause spoke more to the private contract labor system that prevailed in prisons north of the Mason-Dixon line than to the Southern lease that lay in wait. As Rebecca McLennan has pointed out: "Penal servitude was so deeply entrenched and widespread that, without the exemption clause, the Thirteenth Amendment's universal prohibition on slavery and involuntary servitude would have rendered most state prisons unconstitutional."[20]

Even though it was an extremely coercive, profit-driven enterprise, Northern Republicans considered their penal labor system to be a settled instrument of punishment and not an incident of slavery. As Pope puts it, "they read the Exception Clause narrowly to cover only those features of slavery or involuntary servitude that fell within what they conceived as the 'ordinary' or 'usual' operation of a penal system."[21] Chattel slavery, obviously, did not do so, nor did convict leasing because it involved "the extension of servitude outside prison walls, the infliction of servitude for crimes not serious enough to warrant such a severe penalty, the condemnation of prisoners to servitude by anyone other than the sentencing authority, and the selective imposition of servitude on blacks but not on whites guilty of the same crimes."[22] Consequently, if there was an intention behind retaining the exception, it was to uphold a distinction between the politically acceptable enterprise of Northern penal labor, however horrifying in reality, and the heavily villainized institution of Southern chattel slavery.

At least one senator, Charles Sumner—the radical Republican from Massachusetts—foresaw that the language of the exception might encourage the restoration of Southern slavery in a new form, and he proposed an alternative draft of the amendment that left it out: *"All persons are equal before the law, so that no person can hold another as a slave; and the Congress shall have the power to make all laws necessary and proper to carry this declaration into effect everywhere in the U.S."*[23] His version was rejected on the grounds that the wording might have allowed women to claim equal citizenship status. Another Republican, John Kasson, a Congressman from Iowa, tried to pass legislation in 1867 clarifying that the framers permitted forced labor under the Exception Clause only when it was a specific part of a sentence: "except in direct execution of a sentence imposing a definite penalty according to law." His bill passed in the House but went no further.

If either Sumner or Kasson had prevailed, the modern penitentiary system might have looked quite different, especially in light of how the exception has been utilized in the age of mass incarceration. But would either measure have made an immediate difference to the introduction of a new penal labor system in the South or the perpetuation of the existing Northern one? That is more difficult to say. Southern convict leasing was never challenged in the courts on constitutional grounds, nor did it need to be defended on the basis of the Exception Clause. As for the North, the prevailing private contract system did encounter increasingly fierce challenges—not from lawmakers but from advocates of organized labor who had been utilizing the rhetoric of "slave labor" (from as early as the 1830s) to inveigh against the threat posed to "free labor" and open market competition by the contract system. The system was eventually abolished in the 1890s, and the reformists' energy carried over to the South, helping to seal the demise of convict leasing. But notably, the upholders of convict labor did not see any need to cite the exception to defend the Northern system after the ratification of the 13th.

From the 1890s onwards, penal labor—both in the North and South—switched from private contract to a state-use system, where prisoners produced goods for government agencies or else worked on roads and other public infrastructure. Forced labor for state use was defended because of its public benefit, as part of paying the debt to society, and also because the virtues of the work ethic were promoted by prison reformers as an integral component of the prisoner's rehabilitation. By then, it was less common for a sentencing judge to specify hard labor as a distinct penalty—which was the only clear grounds for interpreting the exception, as Kasson's resolution intended. Yet even when it was no longer an explicit part of a sentence, hard labor continued to be imposed, either as a form of discipline, as a means of producing public goods, or as a way of "reforming" a wayward individual. So when hard labor sentencing was prohibited in federal district courts in 1948, wardens and correctional officers continued to impose work assignments regardless, as one of a range of measures that fell under the legal treatment of prisoners.[24]

Why did the persistence of forced penal labor go unchallenged for so long? According to legal scholar, Raja Raghunath, one reason has to do with the legal tradition of prison deference.[25] According to a time-honored "hands-off" doctrine, the judiciary saw prisons as quarantined from the legal protections of the free world, and therefore falling under the sole governance of wardens and state officials. At the ground level, the customs and culture of the guards who meted out punishments and privileges from day to day could be uncompromising, and over time their daily policing habits proved resistant to outside interference, especially from reformers. The notion that prisoners relinquished their rights on conviction was presupposed. In the infamous, and much disputed, judgement of the 1871 Virginia ruling (*Ruffin v. Commonwealth*), a prisoner is "the slave of the state," and therefore "he is civiliter mortuus [civilly dead]; and his estate, if he has any, is treated like that of a dead man."[26] Out of respect for the hands-off doctrine, state and federal courts generally declined to intervene in litigation involving prisons until the 1960s, when the prisoners' rights movement gathered steam. Thereafter, a long season of litigation, fomented by uprisings at facilities all across the country, established that constitutional protections are not suspended behind the prison walls. In 1974, the Supreme Court forcefully proclaimed that there was no "iron curtain" between prisoners and their constitutional rights.[27] By then, labor rights were also part of the picture—the right to fair pay, to form unions, and to enjoy protections.

The engine that drove this movement was a combination of jailhouse lawyering, civil rights politicking, and Black Nationalist ideology. The 1964 success of Black Muslims in winning their constitutional right to worship (in *Cooper v. Pate*) was the legal win, in the words of James Jacobs, that "brought the federal courts into the prisons," while "the abominable conditions in American prisons kept them there."[28] The strong ties that were forged between 1960s figureheads on the inside—such as Eldridge Cleaver, George Jackson, Martin Sostre and Angela Davis—and legal advocates on the outside attracted younger champions in law schools and relatively widespread sympathy among mainstream liberals. An avalanche of prisoner rights petitions were filed in the 1970s.[29] Prisoners, even the lumpen, were politicized. Appalling penal conditions were exposed to the public, and state administrators were put on notice that their personal conduct could fall afoul of judicial review in federal courts. The more radical Black Nationalist wing of the movement held that incarceration, especially for African Americans, was a form of collective servitude, consistent with the kidnapping and shackling of the Middle Passage, and redolent of slavery practices that had never been overturned. For revolutionaries like George Jackson, the barbaric confinement, civil death, and forced penal labor of the modern penitentiary were little more than badges and incidents of slavery. In this view, the carceral system was itself an instrument of state repression, and all Black and Brown prisoners were political prisoners.[30]

By the end of the 1970s, "law-and order" rhetoric had worked its way to the forefront of national politics, and the tradition of judicial deference reasserted its sway over courts. In 1977, the Supreme Court ruled against prisoners' labor unions in *Jones v. North Carolina Prisoners' Union*, and, two years later, rolled back the advances that had been made in winning constitutional protections, in *Bell v. Wolfish* (1979).[31] In the decades to follow, prisoner rights took a back seat as tough-on-crime politics and the decimation of the social safety net transformed incarceration into what Ruth Wilson Gilmore and James Kilgore called "catch-all solutions to social problems."[32] Prisons were reconceived as vehicles for public and private profiteering. Prisoners were no longer seen as culture heroes, asserting their rights alongside their withering critiques of the carceral state. Instead, they were re-criminalized, and vilified as "superpredators."[33]

When the prisoner rights movement revived in the 2010s, it was as much under the aegis of human rights as civil rights. America's bloated prison–industrial complex was such an outlier among nations that the treatment of its prisoners had become a matter of international condemnation. The conditions of forced labor in American prisons were in violation of any number of international conventions to which the U.S. was a signatory: the UN's Declaration of Human Rights and the International Covenant on Social and Political Rights, along with several International Labour Organization conventions (29 and 105). Evidence of racial profiling at every level of the criminal justice system was well-documented and indisputable—from "stop-and-frisk" street harassment and traffic stops to arrest, sentencing, and detention rates, both in prisons and in probation programs.[34] Michelle Alexander's book, *The New Jim Crow* (2010) became a bestseller by showing how mass incarceration had reconstituted the earlier systems of racial control under chattel slavery and Jim Crow segregation. After the Ferguson uprisings in 2014—and after the deaths of Trayvon Martin, Michael Brown, Sandra Bland, Kalief Browder, George Floyd, and so many others—the Black Lives Matter movement forced public attention to focus on the systematic racism, brutality, and extortion that underpinned policing and public surveillance in the neoliberal era. The movement helped to confirm that the punishment ethos of the prison extended far into civil society. The U.S. had indeed become a carceral state.

Against this backdrop, it was no surprise, then, that anti-slavery rhetoric would play a significant role in the new abolitionism. What was arguably more unexpected was the target of this belated attention—the 13th Amendment. It had taken a long time for activists to realize that the Exception Clause might be vulnerable. How consequential would efforts to repeal it turn out to be?

Taking On the State Houses

The movement to end the penal exception has aimed high—at changing the laws of the land. But in most states, the ideas behind it were not hatched by seasoned organizers drawing on extensive legal or scholarly knowledge, nor did these ideas well up from mass grassroots protests. Many of the early movers were justice-impacted or had family members who were serving time. In Colorado, for example, Jumoke Emery, a young community organizer with the faith-based group Together Colorado, was wrongfully arrested and detained at gunpoint in 2014. Finding himself shackled hand and foot in the police van, he thought to himself, "this is what slavery feels like." He spent the weekend in jail, pondering the servitude that he, as a Black man, would endure if convicted. On release, with all charges dismissed, he scanned the Exception Clause for the first time, and consulted with Nathan Woodliff-Stanley, the executive director of Colorado's ACLU. They vowed to overturn the 1876 decision made by Colorado (a non-slaveholding state) to enshrine penal slavery in its constitution a full twelve years after the passage of the 13th. Together Colorado helped to draft an Abolish Slavery bill that won unanimous support in the legislature. Despite a public education effort by a coalition that included the ACLU, NAACP, and interfaith groups, the 2016 amendment vote failed by 1 percent, largely due to confusing, triple-negative language on the ballot.[35]

When the campaign was revived, Kamau Allen, fresh out of college, came on board as co-director. For him, the issue was also deeply personal: "I know that my ancestors were held in bondage as somebody else's property," he explained to us. "My family survived the horrors of chattel slavery in Louisiana, Mississippi, and Georgia. Then, more recently, I've had so many family members who have been locked up. We got a pretty good picture of what life is like for people who've been incarcerated from their own words. And my uncle, Joe Bell Jr., wrongly incarcerated for more than twenty years, was not shy to say that this was an act of slavery." For the second campaign, in 2018, the amendment proposition was more carefully framed and worded, and it was carried with 65 percent of the vote. Along the way, however, Allen reported that the organizers encountered many of the obstacles that have beset campaigns in other states. They were met with their share of racist backlash both online and in real life, when a stack of campaign flyers was ignited on the porch of Emery's house on the eve of the election.[36]

Lawmakers had many probing questions for Allen and other advocates about the real impact of the amendment: "Would this require the Department of Corrections to change their policies? Would this require the legislature to change their prison labor statutes? Would the measure be responsible for people who chose to file actions against the Department of Corrections?" There was also the matter of whether a "fiscal note" would have to be attached to the proposed law. Many legislatures require an estimate of the financial impact of a bill before it can move forward. "Fortunately," Allen reported, "we were able to get away with not having a fiscal note attached because the argument that we made, which is a correct argument, is that this would have no immediate impact on prison labor."

To some supporters, the prospect of no substantive change in prison conditions was a disappointment, but it was clear too that the passage of the amendment was much more than a symbolic act. Lawmakers themselves were aware that the bill might turn out to be very costly and were not slow to voice their concerns. Emery said that he bristled at such questions. "When someone asked this, all I heard is 'Who is going to pick our cotton and cut our sugar cane if we don't have slaves'?" He wanted to ask back, "What is the cost in human lives, and in the brutality behind these prison doors, what is the cost of our mental health as a society, when we throw people away, again and again?" Fiscal accounting aside, Allen pointed out that in Colorado politics at least, "nobody wants to be the legislator that voted against abolishing slavery, because it is a racist stain from our history," and so this helped smooth passage of the bill that authored the amendment ballot vote. Even so, the bill's sponsors and their allies saw the amendment, from the outset, "as an open door" that would lead to further action. Not long after it was passed, the wheels of litigation began to turn, as incarcerated plaintiffs were encouraged to step forward to sue the state for their forced labor conditions.

In the meantime, on the back of the publicity from the win, Allen and Emery received inquiries from all across the country about how to run similar initiatives in other states. In addition to Dennis Febo's efforts in New Jersey, they learned that organizers in Tennessee had slowly been germinating an abolition measure for several years. An amendment in Tennessee has to survive readings and votes in two successive sessions (of two years each) to get to the ballot.[37] In Utah and Nebraska, amendment initiatives were underway, and they won a place on the ballot in 2020, passing with large majorities.[38] The national group of organizers had their first meeting on May 26th of that year. It was the day after George Floyd's murder, and the months of street protest that followed added momentum to the idea of a permanent coalition. The Abolish Slavery National Network (ASNN) was launched on August 28th, the summit day of the month routinely commemorated now as Black August, with representatives present from Colorado, Utah, Nebraska, South Carolina, California, and New Jersey.

Allen volunteered as lead organizer. Max Parthas, a spoken-word artist and tireless champion of the cause, took on the role of Director of State Operations. Parthas, who is associated with the Paul Cuffee Abolitionist Center in South Carolina, had been active on the issue since 2010's national March Forth for Freedom, which he called "the first campaign against legalized slavery since the antebellum period." Like other organizers, his family is justice-impacted: two of his sons spent a combined 34 years behind bars, and he has 21 grandchildren whom he also wants to keep out of prison. He is also the presenter of an online radio show, *Abolition Today* (co-hosted with Yusuf Hassan), and his weekly programs have served as an up-to-date platform for information and debate, promoting the ideas behind the movement.[39]

For Parthas, the Exception Clause is a crystal-clear violation of international anti-slavery treaties and covenants. "Article Four of the UN Declaration of Human Rights doesn't have an Exception Clause for America," he points out. "It just says slavery is abolished in all its forms. It doesn't say, 'Except for America, who can do it to inmates, as long as they've been duly convicted.'" He conceded that the act of ending the exception could ultimately have a major bearing on civil rights, prisoner rights, and even labor rights, but explained that the ASNN leadership decided their best chance of winning was to run campaigns on a primarily moral message, and to laser-focus on closing the loophole to the exclusion of all other goals.

In this regard, Parthas distinguishes ASNN's standpoint from that of other carceral activists: "You have your prison abolitionists, prison slavery abolitionists, slavery abolitionists, and criminal justice reformists, and they're not all on the same page. They're not all fighting for the same thing. They don't all have the same tactics, or the same final agenda." As slavery abolitionists, he and other lead ASNN organizers don't see their cause as reformist ("you can't reform a crime against humanity") and they have to push back against the misconstrued charge that they want to abolish prisons. Even so, Parthas allows that the chosen strategy of ASNN has short-term, mid-term, and long-term goals. The immediate target is constitutional change. Once that is achieved, the badges and incidents of slavery—punishment for refusing to work, warehousing bodies for profit, and the provision of penny wages—can then be challenged without the protection of the exception. The long-term goal is to release millions from the grip of the carceral system, especially those who are "there for drug-related, poverty-related, addiction-related, and mental health-related crimes" and those who are "being used as revenue generators."

Focusing first on the amendments has meant that most ASNN state campaigns steer clear of any mention of prison wages or labor conditions in their campaigning and drafting of bills. Any such talk, it was assumed, would muddy the waters, and could provide an opening to opponents or skeptics looking to sabotage a legislative effort by citing the hefty cost of paying prisoners a fair wage. Yet that is exactly what happened in California, even though the bill being considered by the legislature made no mention of wages and was presented as costless. The California Abolition Act passed every committee and was scheduled for a vote close to the end of the 2021 legislative session. At the last minute, the state's Department of Finance wheeled out an estimate (compiled by a former Department of Corrections and Rehabilitation employee) of the cost of paying a $15 minimum wage: a projected $1.5 billion a year. Though the state was running a $100 billion surplus at the time, this fiscal projection swayed enough Democrats to sink the bill's prospects of passing before the session ended in June.[40] What started out as a strong and clear argument about slavery was effectively hijacked: the narrative of the bill was now about the economics of the prison system.

While the bill said nothing about costs, the economic underpinnings of the state's prison system were no small matter. In Ruth Wilson Gilmore's *Golden Gulag*—her book about the factors that drove California's carceral boom in the 1990s—she showed how building prisons presented a convenient solution for a number of acute needs facing the state and allied capitalist interests.[41] ASNN advocates, for their part, tend to focus specifically on the exploitation of California's prison laborers. CALPIA, the state's prison industry program, is an economy of scale, generating $60 million in gross profits from more than 1400 goods and services produced by 7000 prisoners in 45 adult facilities.[42] In the words of Samual Nathaniel Brown, who authored the first draft of the bill while serving a sentence in California State Prison in Los Angeles County, "people need to know that California for so long has been the largest plantation state in the nation. Mass incarceration looms large here. This is not the Deep South. Forced labor is big business here."[43] Most notoriously, the incarcerated workforce provides hundreds of front-line wildfire fighters who work for the state under the most hazardous conditions. They earn $1 an hour, plus time off their sentences, saving the state $100 million annually in discounted wages. Given the rapid escalation of California's climate-driven distress, they are among the most essential public workers, pressed into service in jobs which they then have great difficulty in securing on release from prison. CAL FIRE, the fire-fighting agency, is now facing a staffing crisis because pandemic-era policies like early releases and reduced sentences have diminished the prison labor supply.[44]

Exposure to hazards on the job is what prompted Brown himself to become active. Serving a life sentence at the time of the first COVID breakout, he was issued inadequate PPE and ordered to clean and sterilize areas of the facility where the state's first infected prisoners were located. His wife Jamilia Land (who serves on ASNN's administrative team) explained that "when he stopped showing up for work, they threatened him with what we call the modern-day whip, the 115—a rules violation report." Getting issued a 115 ticket for refusal to perform the task would have cost him his parole.

Released after 24 years in 2022, he and Land founded the Anti-Violence, Safety, and Accountability Project to promote a new version of the amendment legislation. Land, who also has an incarcerated son, resides close to the state capitol in Sacramento and is such a frequent lobbying presence there that she told us that she is known as the "Tiny Terror," on account of her diminutive size. Along with their broad coalition, the pair worked hard to get the bill reintroduced, this time as the End Slavery in California Act in February 2023. In the interim, California's newly established Reparations Task Force had issued its 500-page preliminary report, aimed at restitution for the harms generated by the badges and incidents of slavery for Black Californians. The report provided a comprehensive description of these harms, in the areas of housing segregation, political disenfranchisement, racial terror, separate and unequal education, environmental racism, and stolen labor. But the Task Force members decided that their first order of business should be to end legal slavery in California. They placed a series of measures at the top of their list of recommendations that reached far beyond the constitutional amendment—measures that would eliminate all of the impacts of involuntary servitude in prisons.[45]

As with the 2021 constitutional amendment bill, the projected dollar costs of the Task Force's proposed reparations were the subject of much fearmongering in the public media. Headlines focused on the initial proposal for $220,000 payments to each Black citizen of the state who could establish lineage to enslaved ancestors. By March 2023, the individual payment had been re-evaluated at $360,000, for an overall cost to the state of $640 billion. By May, the overall cost had climbed to $800 billion, with a sliding scale of individual payments, capped at $1.2 million for those who had spent their entire life in the state. But the proposed measures in the final draft—which contained 115 law and policy recommendations and ran for 1100 pages—were a mix of retroactive cash payments (for items like housing wealth lost due to redlining or the devaluing of residential property in minority neighborhoods) and proactive policies, such as the provision of zero-interest housing loans and subsidized housing.[46]

The task force's approach to mass incarceration and over-policing reflected a similar mix of proactive and retroactive justice. Economists were asked to calculate the potential income lost by incarcerated Black Californians from 1971—when Richard Nixon launched the War on Drugs—until the present day. These consultants concluded that qualified Black people, who were incarcerated far beyond their numbers in the general population, were each owed $115,260 (or $2,352 for each year of California residency) for unpaid prison labor and years of lost earnings.[47] But the recommendations for "ending legal slavery" in prisons were more forward-looking. They included deleting the exception from the constitution, repealing the state's penal code that requires prisoners to work, prioritizing education, mental health treatment, rehabilitative programs, paying a market wage for voluntary labor, prohibiting for-profit companies from contracting prison labor, equalizing the costs of goods and services with outside prices, and re-enfranchising the incarcerated.

These latter recommendations, delivered in the final report on June 29, 2023, were nothing if not ambitious. They went far beyond ASNN's single-minded focus on abolishing involuntary servitude. Yet, initially at least, the report played no role in legislators' consideration of the End Slavery in California Act (AC8). In September 2023, the bill passed in the Assembly with 62 Democrats and 6 Republicans in support and was taken up by the Senate in January 2024. According to Land, there wasn't much discussion of the fiscal costs of the bill, though she anticipated that the issue would return in the course of deliberations in the Senate. More ominously, looking ahead to a possible ballot vote in November 2024, she reported that it would cost an estimated $40 to $60 million to get an amendment over the line in California.

ASNN's anti-slavery initiatives in many states have hardly been plain sailing. More have failed than have passed, though the reasons for these failures have varied. In some states which have no relevant language in their constitutions, the process of inserting an antislavery amendment without exceptions is onerous. It often involves sustained campaigning and politicking over the course of several years to propel a bill through two consecutive legislative sessions. In others like Texas, where prison industries are run with ruthless efficiency, ASNN organizer Vanessa Eldridge told us it that it was all but impossible, initially, to get the attention of legislators. "Our bill was referred to the state affairs committee, and then the chair stopped answering my phone calls," she recalled, "he literally would not have any conversation at all." Texas officials take pride in the toughness of their prisons, and after the 2020 election, the anti-woke backlash that has driven the polarization of politics has backfooted all advocates of racial progress.

In Louisiana, there was strong pushback from the Department of Public Safety and Corrections and from the Department of Justice. The reaction from white supremacists was also virulent. When the bill was first introduced in May 2021, Alan Seabaugh—a Republican representative from Shreveport—called it "one of the most dangerous bills we've seen this session." Seabaugh said he was "afraid this might open the door to a legal challenge for every felony conviction in the state of Louisiana, and that's just not a can of worms I'm willing to open."[48] He and others wanted to retain the legal capacity to sentence people to hard labor. Louisiana is the only state, other than Arkansas, that still applies this form of penal sentence. The bill died in committee in 2021. When it was reintroduced in 2022, Republicans succeeded in amending the original resolution so that the language on the final ballot created some doubt about whether forced labor would still be allowed to continue as part of a criminal sentence. The amendment, as it was now worded, would abolish slavery and involuntary servitude "except as it applies to the otherwise lawful administration of criminal justice." A measure designed to end the exception now seemed to include one. After the legislative sponsor withdrew his support and urged voters to reject it, the amendment failed at the ballot. Journalists had a field day denigrating Louisiana as a pro-slavery throwback.[49]

Curtis Davis, the ASNN activist who promoted the amendment through his action group Decarcerate Louisiana, saw this as a "missed opportunity." He considered the attempt to confuse voters to be "a form of voter suppression... so people didn't know what they were voting on."[50] While incarcerated (or, as he put it, "transported at least two hundred years back in time") in the notorious Angola prison, Davis picked cotton and okra on the former plantation for 25 years. When he broke his foot to avoid the grueling work—a time-honored practice of resistance—he was told that he "was destroying state property."[51] Undaunted by the 2022 ballot debacle, Decarcerate Louisiana pushed successfully for the reintroduction of the amendment bill in May 2023. It passed unanimously in the House but ran into trouble in the Senate when there was more horse-trading around the language regarding involuntary servitude. So, too, the California tactic of a fiscal note (for more than $80 million) was shoehorned into the discussion.[52] The measure failed by the five votes necessary to reach the two-third majority in the Senate required for a constitutional amendment.[53] In response to the bill's defeat and other reactionary measures passed by the legislature, the NAACP issued a travel advisory: "We urge individuals, particularly African Americans, people of color, and members of the LGBTQIA2S+ community, to exercise extreme caution when traveling to or within the State of Louisiana."[54]

In some red states—like Utah, Nebraska and Tennessee—the amendment process has flown beneath the radar. The most low-flying was Alabama, where the abolition initiative was bundled into an omnibus amendment to strip racist language from the state constitution in 2022.[55] The outcome would surely have been more complicated by far if a separate bill had been required to pass through the hard-right legislature. As it was, 75 percent of those who voted on the ballot elected to remove the taint of slavery from the state's constitution. In general, when a clearly worded anti-slavery resolution manages to make it to the popular vote, the outcome has been positive. But most legislators are increasingly aware not only of the fiscal consequences but also of how courts can and will try to implement the measure in ways that can challenge their oversight of the prison system and lead to lawsuits against the state.

After Colorado's 2018 anti-slavery constitutional amendment was adopted, it had little impact on conditions inside prisons, and it did not alter anything in the penal codes of correctional law.[56] The state's department of corrections took the view that the amendment was merely a symbolic modernization of the constitution —that there was no forced labor before the amendment and none subsequently. Clearly, litigation would be required to ensure that the changes were recognized in correctional law. A series of lawsuits filed by prisoners subsequently charged state officials with violating the amendment by maintaining the status quo.

The first such lawsuit in July 2020 alleged that the plaintiffs were forced to provide "slave labor" at 10 cents an hour. They demanded a minimum wage plus benefits enjoyed by other state workers. This suit was dismissed and they did not appeal.[57] In February 2022, two prisoners filed a more serious class action suit challenging the state's power to compel them to work. The plaintiffs had been punished with losing "earned time" credits and being placed in restricted housing units for refusing to work due to health complications from contracting COVID. The suit pointed out that there are still several provisions in the state's penal code compelling prisoners to work, which are in direct violation of the new amendment.[58] Another case, self-litigated by Mark Lamar from prison, was turned down at Colorado's Court of Appeals. This ruling declared that "the voters did not intend to abolish the DOC inmate work program by virtue of passing Amendment A," and that the withdrawal of privileges for refusing to work did not amount to the levels of "physical or legal coercion" that define involuntary servitude.[59] But the judge's narrow definition of involuntary servitude would be challenged through a renewal of the February class action lawsuit that Towards Justice, a progressive legal organization, filed later that year, alleging that the state uses coercive and cruel tactics to compel incarcerated people to work.[60]

When we spoke to Valerie Collins, who was leading the case from Towards Justice, she reported that the process of discovery revealed more than 3,000 incident reports of prisoners being punished for "failure to work" of one kind or another in the disciplinary record for six months in 2022.[61] These records supported her goal of extracting injunctive relief, since she believed that the courts would condemn these practices as unlawful and instruct the Department of Corrections to do something about it. Collins was excited to be working on a case at the forefront of legal history. "Colorado is furthest along," she noted, "and so other states are looking to us." To better plan such lawsuits, Jamilia Land pulled together a "post-election" committee of attorneys from California, Alabama, Nevada, and Colorado. The goal was to build an effective legal strategy for implementing the amendments and challenging state penal codes that still required "able-bodied prisoners" to work. The ultimate goal, of course, would be to change the supreme law of the land.

Law of the Land

Land recalled that the fledgling ASNN group "was focused on building out the states, and didn't have any intentions of running a national campaign for a federal piece of legislation." But then toward the end of 2020 they received a phone call from Oregon senator Jeff Merkley's office to report that he had co-authored a bill for a federal amendment (along with Missouri Democrat representative William Lacy Clay).[62] Merkley and Clay's "Abolition Amendment" has been reintroduced with each session of Congress, and—in the 2022-23 session—it attracted 180 Democratic and 11 Republican co-sponsors in the House, and 14 Democrats in the Senate. On Juneteenth of 2023, New Jersey Senator Cory Booker and Georgia Representative Nikema Williams joined Merkley to introduce it again.

After Merkley's first bill, Kamau Allen and the ASNN group asked Worth Rises—an NGO that challenges profiteering in the prison industry—to run the federal campaign (now called End the Exception) for the national network.[63] Energetically led by its founder, the former attorney and financial analyst Bianca Tylek, the organization has established an impressive track record in taking on the private monopolies of outsourced prison services which generate $80 billion of profit annually for as many as 4000 corporations.[64]

Faced with an extensive array of corporate targets, Tylek and her team decided to prioritize firms that charge an arm and a leg to make a phone call from inside a prison for their initial campaign. They put together an effective playbook for building coalitions in each state and began to rack up wins. Her long-term goal is "dismantling the prison industry" entirely, but going after telecom would open a "door," as she put it, to lead the public "to the industry's other predatory practices." Extortionate phones fees provided obvious "villains" in the form of private equity firms. Abolishing them made for what she calls a "captivating story." Successful campaigns to make phone calls free of charge in several cities (New York and San Francisco) and states (Connecticut, California, and Colorado) bolstered the reputation of Worth Rises as a fighter and winner. But delivering a constitutional amendment for ASNN was a much heavier lift. The U.S. Constitution is notoriously difficult to amend, especially because it requires a high degree of bipartisan support to do so. To amend the Constitution requires a two-thirds vote in both the House and Senate, then ratification by three-quarters of the states. In recent decades, an average of 75 proposed amendments have been introduced by members of Congress in each two-year term. Some have been under consideration for decades, such as the Equal Rights Amendment which was first introduced in Congress in 1923.

However, in the arena of public opinion, an amendment to remove the Exception Clause could muster a good deal of bipartisan support. Even the American Correctional Association, a champion of correctional effectiveness since 1870, voted to support its repeal in 2016.[65] According to polls conducted in 2021 by Worth Rises, 92 percent of those surveyed believe that slavery doesn't belong in the Constitution. However, only 12 percent knew about the existence of the exception, which makes it a challenge to build public pressure on elected representatives.[66] Nonetheless, Dan Rosen, the organization's Washington campaign manager, said he was upbeat about the prospects, noting that the 2022 abolition amendments in several states generated thousands of "irresistible" media headlines about "slavery on the ballot." He was hoping to match the resulting uptick in public awareness with the strong possibility that, despite intense polarization between Democrats and Republicans, "the leadership in both houses is looking for something to agree on, and this is a moral, not a partisan political issue." Once twelve or thirteen state-level amendments have been passed, he believed that "the federal campaign will have a momentum of its own." Rosen has worked in government and knows his way around the corridors of power. He also served time in a Virginia prison, teaching GED courses for 45 cents an hour, while professionals were paid $22 for the same service. His commitment to advocacy arose from seeing too many "broken and damaged people" in prison, trapped in a system that is just an "expensive way to make bad people worse."[67]

Because of the need for bipartisan support, seasoned organizations with credibility inside the Beltway, like the ACLU, Amnesty International, and the NAACP, had to be heavily recruited as partners. However, some otherwise natural allies on the left were seen as a potential liability, such as organized labor. AFL-CIO officials have often acknowledged that criminal justice reform is a "labor issue," though the organization has been mostly silent on the abolition front.[68] Even so, Rosen conceded that support from that quarter might be a "double-edged sword," alienating otherwise sympathetic Republicans. In February 2023, Democratic senator Cory Booker introduced a package of bills that aimed at paying prisoners a federal minimum wage and extending OSHA workplace protections.[69] The bills generated some attention from the labor movement, but Rosen expressed concern that wage measures like this might be a distraction in the tightly focused drive to bring home the amendment measure. Worth Rises's own informal polling has established that public support for prisoner wages registers far below any strong sentiment about abolishing slavery. Additionally, political opponents are always looking for ways of turning the amendment into an economic rather than a moral issue.

Tylek herself has acknowledged that the recruitment of organized labor to the movement has not occurred yet. She is confident that the right conversations will make that happen down the line. One concern that she had heard from incarcerated people is that "prison jobs might be lost to union members if fair wages had to be paid," and so any such conversation would have to prioritize unionization on the inside to ensure that the jobs are not taken by outsiders. As for ASNN's strategy of isolating the moral message of anti-slavery from the messy discussion about wages, she believed that "the cat was out of the bag" after California's infamous $1.5 billion fiscal note and the publicity generated by the Colorado lawsuits. "There is no dodging the fact that ending slavery would have a financial impact," Tylek said. Pretending that the amendments are purely "symbolic measures that would only make change on paper" or are simply "a moral compass that won't change lives," is not a good message for funders, or for those behind the wall. Never theless, Tylek reported that "one of the most common things we hear from people on the inside about ending the exception is that it would bring humanity to the incarcerated; this is an impact that happens immediately—without any lawsuits—and it comes from the acknowledgment that you have the same human rights as others and that you too are owed a protection from this act. Even if nothing else changes, it has that impact."

Acknowledging that the fiscal costs had to be addressed, Worth Rises commissioned an economist to draw up a cost-ben-efits breakdown that would help lawmakers see the advantages of paying fair prison wages.[70] Even if authorities tried garnish as much of the wages as they could, increases in remuneration would still create many benefits for communities, reducing the costs for families of keeping their loved ones alive in prison, and generating a remittance flow from inside to outside. But Tylek also saw an advantage in being able to present an honest estimate: "Let's not make it a secret anymore, let's just say 'here's what it will cost.' Then we will know how much of our economy is based on slavery . . . with that number in your face, do you still say slavery is fine?" As for legislators who demurred at the price tag, she was tempted to respond with "Finish this sentence, 'Slavery is OK when . . . '"

Labor is Labor

May Day, or International Workers Day, originated as an effort to commemorate the martyrs of the American movement for an eight-hour workday. Though it is not officially recognized in the

U.S., it is still a significant date on the labor calendar. The 2023 rally and march in New York to mark the occasion was a lively affair, bringing together hundreds of members of alt-labor groups on the margins of the labor movement's mainstream. These included domestic workers, sex workers, street vendors, freelancers, laundry workers, trans workers, fast food workers, and a variety of precarious immigrant workers who performed "essential jobs" during the pandemic. The collective demand of the loose coalition gathered on that day was for an increased minimum wage and for the Secure Jobs Act, a bill prohibiting employers from firing workers for no cause.

Strewn among the colorful array of banners and logos in Washington Square Park were signs that said "Fair Pay for Incarcerated Workers" and "Abolish Slavery in New York." They were held aloft by green-shirted members of 13th Forward, New York's coalition of advocates, grassroots groups, and justice-impacted people who are organizing to end the exploitation of prison labor.[71] No one questioned their participation in the rally. Like the other ASNN state operations, 13th Forward's members are pushing to end the exception, but they do not shy away from putting labor rights at the front and center of their campaigning. Nor do they regard the right to organize as an insurmountable obstacle to getting legislation passed. Unlike in many other states, organized labor has bipartisan political support in New York. And there is a history of interest in prisoner unions on the part of organized labor that spans more than a century in New York, from the first efforts in 1916 in Sing Sing prison. A 13th Forward flyer circulated before the rally explicitly and pragmatically made the case to unions that, in pushing legislation that "would allow incarcerated workers to unionize. . . . we are creating more potential union members."

Jacalyn Goldzweig Panitz, a paralegal with the Legal Aid Society and a core 13th Forward organizer, helped coordinate the group's participation in the March and Rally for All Workers. Although 13th Forward is aligned with other criminal justice groups (in the Justice Road Map),[72] she emphasized that it approaches prison abolition from an unashamedly "workers' rights perspective" and its "campaign comes out of the labor movement." As if to underline the point, the coalition's original name was LaborIsLabor. The cluster formed after a bill was introduced in the New York legislature in February 2019 calling for a $3 prison minimum labor wage. Carmela Huang, an attorney at the National Center for Law and Economic Justice who represents worker centers and other alt-labor groups, told us that the $3 figure raised some eyebrows "in the worker rights community." The number, she recalled "seemed so arbitrary." Huang quizzed Harvey Epstein, her former colleague at the Urban Justice Center and who is now an Assembly member for Manhattan's Lower East Side: "Wouldn't the minimum wage make more sense?" He vowed that "if you can get people organized behind it, then I will sponsor that bill" (as he subsequently did). Huang joined forces with Bianca Tylek (who had also worked at the Center) and they decided to form a coalition to respond to Epstein's challenge and "figure out what the law would look like." LaborIsLabor was launched in September of that year with a handful of groups including Worth Rises and Legal Aid Society.

After Worth Rises took on the federal campaign for ASNN, the remaining LaborIsLabor partners re-formed as 13th Forward (the authors of this book are active participants in its efforts), and built a broad coalition led by Citizen Action of New York, Color of Change, The Legal Aid Society, the New York Civil Liberties Union (NYCLU), and A Little Piece of Light. The steering committee brought on more than 50 partners, including the New York State Council of Churches, Correctional Association of New York, New York Communities for Change, Vocal New York, Center for Popular Democracy, Bronx Defenders, Latino

Justice, the Vera Institute, and the Fortune Society. A handful of labor groups are among them: Workers Justice Center, Laborers International, Flushing Workers' Center, and a couple of UAW locals. Eventually, the UUP (United University Professions)—SUNY's employee union—also joined the coalition, and, in March 2023, passed a resolution calling on the state system's chancellor to prohibit SUNY's non-state funds from being used to purchase prison-made goods.

Lisa Zucker, a NYCLU representative on the steering committee, acknowledged that unions still need to be recruited to this cause: "it's on us to show why this is an important for organized labor, because this really is a labor issue, and not just a criminal justice issue." On the face of it, she asked, "why should workers be asked to compete against a captive labor pool being paid penny wages?" Previously active in the farmworker justice movement, which secured the right to organize in New York in 2019, her experience in getting labor bills through the state legislature has helped to shape 13th Forward's approach. As in other states, the coalition initially committed to winning a constitutional amendment through the *No Slavery in New York Act*. But it also decided to push a wages and conditions bill, *The Fairness and Opportunity for Incarcerated Workers Act*, that contains a raft of measures: minimum wage, workplace safety, the right to organize, the right to sue based on violations, the removal of Corcraft (the state's prison industry company) as the preferred vendor for government agencies, and the establishment of a Prison Labor Board to determine wage scales and to ensure that work assignments provide quality vocational and occupational training. There were also limitations placed on what the state could garnish from higher wages: child support is allowed, but not court fines or a range of other fees and surcharges.

The two bills were introduced as a package in the 2023 legislative session, and they had the same sponsors in both chambers of the legislature.[73] The amendment bill quickly picked up co-sponsors on both sides of the aisle—50 in the Assembly and 25 in the Senate by the end of the session. After weeks of vigorous lobbying, and after rousing rallies and speeches on the "million-dollar staircase" of the state capitol building, the bill passed in the Senate. But Albany's notoriously compressed window for legislating, compounded with a delayed budget agreement, prevented the measure from coming up for a vote in the second chamber before the session's end. It would have to be reintroduced in 2024 and would have to pass in both chambers twice into order to finally get on the ballot in 2026. In the meantime, the coalition has started soliciting city councils as a means of leverage. In May 2023, Rochester's city council became the first in the state to pass a resolution calling for Albany to approve the 13th Forward bills.

After the close of the 2023 legislative session, 13th Forward was faced with the arduous challenge of maintaining the coalition's momentum for at least the next three years of the amendment process. Instead, in the summer of 2023, the coalition decided to pivot and pursue a different route—trying to pass the No Slavery in New York bill into statutory law instead. Enforcement language in the revised bill would be beefed up, making it clear that COs who ignored the prohibition on forced labor would be held legally accountable. Passage of the bill would also automatically change correctional law. Huang described this approach as "more complete, more holistic, more direct, and more immediately effective" than the amendment route, but acknowledged that there were strong arguments for the latter approach. Inclusion in the "moral document" of the state constitution would be more permanent and it would have engaged public sentiment through the referendum ballot process, but the downside included the high cost of a successful amendment campaign (upwards of $50 million, according to some estimates, for public education alone) and the demoralizing impact of a potential failure to get onto the ballot in a timely fashion. The legislative route would be much quicker, given that the bill has proven support from lawmakers, though it could still face a potential veto from the governor and could always be overturned later by a less sympathetic legislature.

By November, it was clear that the Democratic leadership in Albany was not going to back the statutory bill in the 2024 session. Facing an election year when Democrats are especially vulnerable to charges of being "soft on crime," it was reasoned that any "law and order" reforms would be seized upon by the opposition, and so lawmakers advised 13th Forward to stick to the amendment process. With little choice but to revert to the original plan, the coalition obliged. Bearing in mind the lessons from other states, the coalition has tried to craft amendment language that yields a morally simple proposition for the public to consider but which also ensures that the bill would be implemented. The latter would make the amendment a solid source for legal action and rights enforcement. Without it, any claims against forced labor arising from the amendment would be weak. Having rejected language that would have clearly established the right to action, the Senate rapidly passed the bill in February 2024, but it generated unexpected resistance in the Assembly. Some steering committee members privately expressed dismay at the reluctance of Democrats—who held a super-majority in the Assembly—to move on the bills.

If the anti-slavery amendment act passes, the companion *Fairness for Incarcerated Workers* bill would be the next step, with a hard fight expected over at least three of its provisions: the minimum wage, the oversight labor board, and the right to organize. Lawmakers would undoubtedly push back over the fiscal costs, and it is likely that they might try to exclude one or more of the provisions in order to ensure passage. In addition, our interviews showed that there was a discrepancy between the *maximal* position held by advocates for the state minimum wage who want to start from a high bargaining position ($15 for upstate workplaces in 2024) and the sentiment of incarcerated workers, many of whom told us they were skeptical about the prospects for a minimum wage, and that they would settle for much less in the knowledge that even a few dollars more would make a huge difference in their daily lives. However, as a point of principle, Zucker and others in the coalition initially all agreed that "when you talk about wages, no matter where the work takes place, it should be worth the same amount."

Besides, she argued, "there's all sorts of reasons why higher wages would benefit individuals, their families, and the communities at large . . . which is why we have been saying this is a public safety bill, because by giving people fair wages and a proper job, they are less likely to engage in behavior you don't want to see on the street." Naila Awan, who took over Zucker's NYCLU place on the steering committee, agreed on the pragmatic need to do so, especially in an election year, though she confessed: "I hate that being where we end up, because we should be talking about what's humane and just." Yet the second bill, on wages and benefits, is where she believed that "public safety, post-release, becomes a real talking point because of the bill's likely impact on reducing recidivism—people having skills that transfer to jobs, having money in their pocket and being set up for success, and so on."

One of us participated in some of the initial lobbying for the second bill, and encountered queries, from lawmakers' aides, about its cost.[74] According to Goldzweig Panitz, 13th Forward had commissioned an economist to come up with a figure for New York State, but it proved worthless to offer an estimate without factoring in the money that would be saved from families and kinship networks who supply the funds to keep people alive in prison. "Estimating a fair wage over a 5-day week," she said, "doesn't get at the savings from communities not going into extraordinary debt from supporting loved ones." In addition, "it doesn't get at reduced recidivism," or the fact that "over 40 percent of people coming home to New York City go into a shelter bed—what if they had enough money saved up for a security deposit?" Other factors on the benefits side of the balance would include all of the earnings lost to individuals due to underemployment, under-payment, and lack of social insurance benefits.[75] But these are more difficult to quantify—and some are what economists call "externalities" because they involve third parties. Lawmakers pre-fer hard numbers that compute more readily.

The 13th Forward leadership team is tilted toward legal advo-cates who get excited about opportunities for lawcrafting, but there is a balance between their expertise and the experience and desires of justice-impacted members. As Awan, an attorney with a career record in criminal justice reform, put it, "we need to take the cue from people who are directly impacted, and act in a service capacity to give shape to what they want by putting it into legislative language." First and foremost among the latter group was Wilfredo Laracuente, who sits on the steering committee and brings the experience of his twenty-year stint in Sing Sing, where he developed his advocacy skills on the Inmate Liaison Council, holding administrators accountable for their own rules and reg-ulations. His own familiarity with the conditions of incarcerated labor is a clear asset when it comes to lobbying legislators: "I am able to point to their office chairs and tell them that they are made by prisoners forced to work for 40c an hour." He knows that few members of the public, let alone lawmakers, are cognizant of the vast range of products manufactured through Corcraft, the state prison industry company that generates roughly $50 million in annual sales, and employs prisoners on the cheap in high-skilled trades such as carpenters, electricians, plumbers, and welders.[76]

Some awareness about the scope of the industry trickled up during the pandemic, when it was revealed that incarcerated workers at Coxsackie were making NY Clean hand sanitizer which they themselves were not allowed to use.[77] At the peak of the death toll from the coronavirus, demand for coffins made by Green Haven's prisoners was so acute that an additional production line was started in Auburn.[78] Meanwhile, mask production at Clinton and Coxsackie correctional facilities was also ramped up. As a result of these revelations, the circle of public empathy for "essential workers" was widened to include incarcerated workers for the first time. Knowledge even began to circulate about the hazardous nature of prison labor under "normal" circumstances, when these workers are forced to perform removal of asbestos, lead-based paint, and mold.

Questioned about the apparent disinterest of organized labor, Laracuente's response was quite blunt: "they will never recognize us as workers," he snorted. "I've been on Zoom calls where I try to speak about us and the conversation is diverted smoothly back in to the preferred agenda." On the other hand, he is optimistic about the direction of prison reform in the state. In his view, the fact that "crime is on the rise in urban areas that are depleted of funding, jobs, and services" ought to be seen as a silver lining. "As long as that's on the five or six o'clock news," he pointed out, "people should understand that things will be worse in the next five or ten years, given the mental state of incarcerated men when they return to society." His solution aligns with what 13th Forward is fighting for: "if you increase wages in prisons to $220 a week, that will allow guys to purchase more to improve their overall quality of life, they will care more about themselves and partake of education and voluntary therapeutic programming and lead to less violence—and it will change public safety because when they get out they will know how to be productive people in society. That's a win-win all across the board."

The legislation being pushed by 13th Forward comes on the back of a long wave of penal reform in the New York. The

Rockefeller drug laws that helped to instigate the era of mass incarceration were finally dismantled in 2009. The state's prison population declined by half between 2008 and 2021, as 20 facilities were shuttered. The 2016 Criminal Justice Reform Act led to a 90 percent drop in criminal court summonses issued.[79] A 2019 law eliminated the use of cash bail for most misdemeanors and some nonviolent felony charges.[80] In 2021, the legislature passed a bill limiting the use of solitary confinement to no more than 15 consecutive days,[81] and in 2023 the passage of the Clean Slate Act resulted in the automatic sealing of criminal records three years after sentencing for a misdemeanor and eight years after release for a felony conviction.[82] These measures, among others, represent a step back from the runaway penal growth of the decades of privatization. For the first time since the 1970s, advocates elsewhere were looking to New York to take a lead in changing some of the rules of incarceration. Yet, as Awan noted, "some states that are much more right-wing than New York considers itself have moved faster. New York tends to lag behind, a lot of times—not what I would have expected coming from the Midwest."

If properly implemented, 13th Forward's legislative efforts would have a far-reaching impact. The advent of a voluntary work environment that upholds labor rights equivalent to those enjoyed by free world workers would be a momentous shift in the conditions of incarcerated men and women. Would mass incarceration as we know it survive if those who are caged had the free choice to earn fair wages for a job with an occupational future after their release? Or would the wage increases simply "feed the system" with more dollars, as prison abolitionists in Critical Resistance have argued, rather than to "shrink and starve it?"[83] It is difficult to imagine lawmakers not pushing hard to garnish as much as they can to subsidize their prison systems, but it is also just as likely that they will draw down the incarcerated population if it suddenly costs much more to keep them locked up.

Many of our interviewees said that even slightly higher wages ($3 an hour was often cited)—combined with the right to choose work—would have had a significant impact on their circumstances. In that same spirit, we believe that wherever labor rights and fair compensation replace punishment and exploitation, the cause of freedom advances. However meager the "take-home" pay after deductions—potentially including taxes, Medicare, and social security payments—the recipients would no longer be "slaves of the state." A standard paycheck for work undertaken without duress is not a death blow to incarceration as we know it, any more than the repeal of the constitutional Exception Clause would be. But, in step with Du Bois, we think these are *necessary* if not *sufficient* moves on the road to an abolition democracy.

CHAPTER 2

The Yankee Invention

"The program which we are submitted to under the façade of rehabilitation is relative to the ancient stupidity of pouring water on a drowning man, inasmuch as we are treated for our hostilities by our program administrators with their hostility as medication."
—"Manifesto of Demands," Attica Liberation Faction

The movement to end the penal exception is relatively recent, but the abolition of prison labor conditions described as "slavery" has happened before. The biggest knockout punch came from the same state that pioneered the employment of incarcerated men and women for private profit. A series of laws passed by the New York legislature—beginning in 1884 and ending with a state constitutional amendment in 1894—put an end to the system of prison contract labor that had proven lucrative to penitentiary officials and capitalist entrepreneurs since its establishment much earlier in the century. Versions of the New York laws were subsequently passed throughout the Northern states that had embraced the contract system, and the reforming zeal even spread into the Deep South where it hastened on the demise of convict leasing in the ex-Confederacy.

It is surely this latter system that dominates images of prison labor in the public mind: Black men in striped outfits, chained together and toiling by the side of a highway or in the rows of a plantation field, while a white man with a shotgun oversees their drudgery. A hot Southern sun in the sky adds to the tableau of hard labor and suffering. There is nothing fictional about this scenario, but its prevalence in popular culture helps to uphold a view of the South as uniquely backwards and barbaric in its treatment of confined Black people for so many decades after chattel slavery ended. Yet all of the elements present here—the demeaning stripes, the hard-core overseer, and the shackled work gang—actually originated in New York state. In fact, the practice of making prisoners available for labor to private businesses was known as the "Yankee invention" before it became indelibly associated with the Southern system of convict leasing.[1]

At the time it was introduced in New York's Auburn prison in the 1820s, the adoption of hard labor as the preferred form of punishment was seen as an evolutionary step in penology, a humanitarian substitute for the corporal and capital punishments of the colonial era. The new focus on productive labor promised a way for penitentiaries to be economically self-sustaining, and to redeem prisoners from the presumed evils of idleness. The promotion of a wholesome work ethic among their ranks was intended to contribute to the general goal of their reformation. The Auburn System, as it became known, was closely studied, appreciated, and emulated by administrators in other states and other countries. Yet the scheme, undertaken at the dawn of U.S. manufacturing, quickly segued into an arrangement geared to generating as much revenue as possible, by any means necessary, for those at the top. Fourteen-to-sixteen-hour workdays with minimal breaks and rest days were routine, harsh forms of torture were applied to meet production quotas, surveillance was ubiquitous, and brutal punishments were doled out for any rule-breaking, all of which resulted in high rates of injury and death.

The new prison labor regime's grisly methods of discipline and its pitiless regimen of productivity were a more inhumane version of the workplaces in the New England mills established after the War of 1812. Auburn's immobile, unpaid workers were prototypical of the cheap and docile labor force coveted by early industrial capitalists. Indeed, when the Auburn model was more widely adopted, it became known simply as the *industrial system*. But these extreme workplace conditions, combined with the stark reality of confinement, also lent themselves to comparisons with plantation slavery, especially when the same cruel methods of labor enforcement were deployed.

Though it had given birth to this system, the Empire State was also the origin of the effort to eliminate it. Although this reform initiative ran parallel with the civic energy generated by the Abolitionist movement, it was not inspired by the belief that prison labor in and of itself was an unjust form of servitude. Instead, it was primarily driven by the belief that the livelihoods of free world workers were threatened by being forced to compete unfairly with the ultra-cheap source of prison labor. The abolition of New York's private contract system was a milestone win for the cause of organized labor, and the feat would be reprised, in the following years, by the "eradication" of the sweatshop in the garment industry. But this weighty achievement did not dent the rule of forced labor inside prisons. The unfinished business from abolishing involuntary servitude *for all* would endure for another 120 years before it was taken up by action groups, coalescing as ASNN, who began to push for state constitutional amendments.

The Lash and the Paddle

The first model for American corrections was introduced at Pennsylvania's Walnut Street Prison (which opened in 1790), and was then later replicated at Eastern State, Pennsylvania's second and more expansive penitentiary. Walnut Street's Quaker governors decided that solitary confinement was the most appropriate mode of penance (hence the penitentiary) for those found guilty of wicked conduct. Silence and isolation from others were seen as the key to redemption, along with religious instruction and the provision of some handicraft work in the cell.[2] According to this model, prison labor was limited, and it was wholly attached to the ideal of personal reformation. In Newgate—New York's first prison (opened in 1797)—wardens experimented with Pennsylvania's "separate system," but were increasingly pressured to produce commodities for the open market in order to offset the costs of prison upkeep. Production quotas were set, which favored the quantity of goods over their quality. By 1815, the Manhattan prison was turning out "brushes, spinning wheels, clothespins, bobbins, spools, butter churns, washtubs, pails, hoops, wheelbarrows, machinery, cabinets, whips, and a variety of woven goods."[3] William Coffey, an ex-con who wrote a highly critical account of his years in

Newgate, recorded at least one glaring oversight on the part of the governors: when the craft of locksmithing was introduced in order to service an outside contract, he noted that "of five hundred and eighty convicts, there were at least three hundred who were anxious to be employed in that way," presumably because it provided a highly serviceable skill for use in burglary after their release.[4] Chronic mismanagement, overcrowding, and a reputation for shoddy goods underscored Newgate's economic inefficiency and led to its conversion into a debtors' prison (a more financially stable enterprise) in the 1820s.[5]

Auburn State Prison, by contrast, would become known all over the world for its ruthless efficiency and discipline, after its doors first opened in 1817 in the upstate Finger Lakes region. Although it is often cited as the antithesis to the Pennsylvania system, Auburn's "congregate" model of group labor was actually a compromise, retaining the solitary segregation at nighttime, and also demanding silence in the communal, factory-style workplace that had been designed with uninterrupted production in mind. But the violence exacted on the workforce during the day shift was a world removed from the meditative milieu of its Pennsylvania counterpart. Elam Lynds—Auburn's sadistic overseer—was a devotee of the lash and paddle, and he took pride in breaking men through humiliation and maximal toil. Dismissive of the Quaker creed of self-reformation, he believed in the innate depravity of prisoners, and his methods were based on deterrence through corporal punishment and fear, among them the use of torture akin to waterboarding, which simulated the experience of drowning. Prisoners wore stripes and were chained and forced to march in lockstep: in single file, with one hand placed on the shoulder of the man in front. So extreme was the discipline that his own staff refused to administer floggings on occasion. Auburn townspeople protested when they heard about the barbaric treatment employed behind the walls.

Not surprisingly, however, Lynds' methods delivered results for the account ledger. Both Auburn and Sing Sing, which he also subsequently ran, produced surpluses. This was what lawmakers had demanded, even though some may have privately balked at the means. The notion that a prison could pay for itself also proved attractive to officials outside of New York who were looking for a correctional model that would not be a drain on their budgets. To ensure that it could compete in the face of evolving industrial specialization in the free world economy, the system of silent factories not only employed advanced machinery and a highly compartmentalized division of labor, but was also flexible in its modes of production. The initial "public-account" model, whereby wardens oversaw all aspects of production and sold the output on the open market, ceded to one in which contractors brought in raw materials to the workshops—along with machinery, foremen, tools and fuel—and then took out the finished goods while paying a below-market charge to the state for the labor. In another system, called "piece-price," the warden had oversight of the workforce whereas the contractor only furnished raw materials and sold the finished goods. In the lease system, a third version which prevailed in the post-bellum South, all of these functions were assumed remotely by the contractor in return for a fee. There were handsome profits to be had for those with access to this dirt-cheap labor, and kickbacks for wardens who acted as entrepreneurs and labor brokers.[6] The return to the state was also considerable. Just before the demise of private contracting in all of these forms in the 1890s, it was generating almost two-thirds of New York's budget for maintaining prisons.[7] According to one federal estimate, prisons nationwide were turning out more than $29 million ($46 billion in today's dollars) of prison-made goods annually by the mid-1880s. Only 15 percent of this output was produced through the infamous Southern lease system.[8]

When Lynds was appointed as the first warden at Sing Sing in 1825, he was able to seamlessly transfer his reign of terror from Auburn. He brought with him handpicked prisoners to build the new penitentiary and they stayed there. Additional members of the construction workforce were conscripted from Newgate, and "sent up the river" (by then, the phrase had entered popular culture) from Manhattan. But the Newgaters, it turned out, were not fit for the hard labor. Those transferred from upstate were much better prepared, both for the construction work and for the relentless production regimen of the new facility. According to the accounts of prisoners who served time in both Auburn and Sing Sing, the conditions in the latter were even more brutal, eliciting condemnation far and wide.[9] Lynds' notoriety eventually led to his removal in 1843, though his successors retained the spirit of his methods, albeit in a milder form of labor discipline.

While reports of these barbaric methods circulated widely— drawing criticism from humanitarians of all stripes—the most sustained opposition came from New York's fledgling labor movement. Prison-made products were decried, as early as the 1820s, for having a detrimental impact on the market for the skills and goods of free mechanics and artisans. Yet efforts to brand the Newgate and Auburn products with the stigma of a "prison-made" label proved ineffective, and the state's legislators showed little interest in applying the brakes to their gravy train. However, there is some evidence that the decision to close Newgate and found Sing Sing upriver was, in part, "because of the 'demand of mechanics that convicts should not be employed upon the manufacture of goods that come in competition' with citizen industry."[10]

In 1834, an event occurred that crystallized the tradesman's hostility to the system, and it concerned the building of New York University (then known as "University of the City of New-York"). The university was founded in 1831 and was initially housed next to City Hall in Lower Manhattan. The new university's governors sought out a more elegant setting on Washington Square for its permanent location and drew up plans for an imposing Gothic Revival building on the square's northeastern side. To construct the building—which would flank the merchants' handsome townhouses on the north side—they were advised by state officials to approve the use of dressed marble from Sing Sing's prison quarries on the assurance that the material and labor would come at minimal cost. Elisha Bloomer, a well-known prison contractor, was given the go-ahead to arrange the supply. The city's stone cutters, who were already active in their opposition to the use of prison labor to underbid the market, saw Bloomer's contract as a provocation and resolved to make an example of him. In August 1834, they marched through the streets with placards and then descended on his Broadway depot, where they threw rocks, swung brickbats, and did damage to the premises. The mayor called out the 27th regiment of the National Guard to suppress the protest and subsequently ordered the troops to camp out in Washington Square for four days to ensure that the cutters did not resume their rebellious business.[11]

Early historians labelled this event as the "Stonecutters' Riot," and over time it got lumped together with other insurgencies under the label of New York's "Year of the Riots."[12] These included violent attacks on the meeting places of Abolitionists (the "Abolition Riots"), and a stand-off between Whigs and Democrats during the city's first direct election of a mayor (the "Election Riot" or "Tappan Riot"). Yet the only thing these events really had in common was the mobilization of the regimental troops to restore order, a step that had never been taken before.[13] It would be more appropriate to see the stonecutters' protest as the culmination of the foundational year of the American labor movement.[14] In August 1833, the General Trades' Union (GTU) had been formed to unite all of New York's trade guilds and societies.

The GTU was founded, in large part, in response to concerns that the new generation of industrial capitalists wanted to reduce the independence of artisans by bonding them to the requirements of wage labor. Craft workers would no longer have control over their time and product—they would instead be considered hired men and women who were working at the discretion of an employer.

Opposition to prison contract labor was a central element of the agitation behind the GTU's formation. A union petition to the Albany legislature in 1833 complained that the contract system—which potentially affected all trades—was "taking bread out of our mouths."[15] The grievance went unanswered. In the months leading up to the stonecutters' action, a labor coalition made up of mechanics of many trades passed another joint resolution condemning the "state prison monopoly," and agreed not to work on any marble that had been dressed at Sing Sing. Notably, the proponents were not up in arms about how badly prisoners were being treated in Auburn or Sing Sing. Instead, they were outraged by the unequal competition with their own labor. To strengthen their case, however, they seized upon damning reports about the brutality of the overseers and were suddenly willing to hear agitators describe prison labor as a form of slavery. But they did not dispute the right of the state to force these prisoners to work.

Nevertheless, the stonecutters were most certainly aware that the state's decision to build Sing Sing (from the Wappinger placename, *sin sinck*, or "stone upon stone") on the banks of the Hudson River was due to its adjacency to ample limestone deposits and marble beds, and also because it afforded ready access to barges for transporting this stone downriver. Indeed, the location was approved by the legislature in 1825 for the very purpose of stone quarrying and stone cutting. The stone was quarried initially to build the massive walls of Sing Sing's original cellblock (destined to be known as "The Big House") which enclosed the world's largest penitentiary at the time. But it was destined for use in other significant buildings, including the New York State Capitol itself.

Likewise, a chief factor in the choice of Auburn's location had been its close proximity to the transportation corridor of the Erie Canal. The location of other prisons in New York would also be determined by their capacity for industrial production. Clinton Correctional Facility, built in 1844, was sited in a remote area of the Adirondacks so that prisoners could extract iron ore from mines in Dannemora and Lyon Mountain (at the time, iron was mostly imported and so domestic competition was not a concern for the unions).[16] Convict labor would be routinely used to build infrastructure in the Adirondacks region. Much later, during the prison building boom of the late 1970s and 1980s, other penitentiaries in the North Country were approved explicitly to provide a labor force for the construction of roads, ski runs, hiking trails, and park landscaping to facilitate area tourism.

By the 1840s, the agitation of New York's unionized mechanics had begun to produce results. The Albany legislature passed measures to ensure that convicts were not employed in some trades which would compete with free world artisans. In response to these restrictions, administrators only employed prisoners in occupations not practiced by mechanics, restricted the use of advanced machinery, placed limits on working hours, produced goods that were more typically imported, and began to make products for sale exclusively to state-owned enterprises. The latter "state-use system"—more fully under public control—would eventually replace private production after the abolition of the contract system and it would flourish in the course of the twentieth century.

The stonecutters' targeting of Bloomer in 1834 had been a tactical move, but it was also a response to the GTU's principled assertion of the "natural rights of free artisans" in its founding constitution. The new confederation initiated some strikes and won some pay raises for members and would eventually unionize most of the city's male artisans. The GTU spread to Boston and other cities over the course of the next year, and the first nationwide body—the National Trades Union (NTU)—was created in December 1834. Membership would grow rapidly until the financial crisis of 1837. The ensuing depression and mass unemployment put an end to this first version of a national labor organization.

The root sentiment about the economic independence of workers survived the NTU's demise, and animated the efforts of its successors: the short-lived National Labor Union in 1866, and the more successful Knights of Labor, formed in 1869. By the time that the more resilient American Federation of Labor was founded in 1886, industrial specialization had taken a further toll on workers' autonomy, but the prison contract was still being cited as a powerful "menace" to the rights of free labor and an expression of disrespect for these rights on the part of the state. In more radical quarters, the spectacle of a wholly captive workforce being treated as mere automatons was seen as the most logical extension of the capitalist factory's perverse organization of human labor. After the overthrow of the private contract system, the sweatshop—already established in the garment industry's model of subcontracting (known as the "sweating" system)— would take its place as the curse that had to be lifted for labor to be free. The elimination of both of these afflictions was touted as proof of the growing power of the movement. These successes were each widely promoted in order to spread organized labor's influence and reach.

Organized labor's persistent voice of opposition, and its eventual capacity to elect workingmen and their advocates to the legislature, resulted in the laws that ended the contract system in New York and elsewhere. The decades-long campaign produced a monumental win, but it had not been undertaken out of solidarity with prisoners being forced to toil for nothing under the most oppressive circumstances. Labor leaders ceaselessly villainized the contract system, just as they called out industrial capitalism as a system built on "wage slavery." The preamble to the 1878 constitution of the Knights of Labor included, as a central goal, "to abolish the system of letting out by contract the labor of convicts in our prisons and reformatory institutions."[17] But the organization, which coined the slogan "an injury to one is the concern of all" and which fought hard against convict leasing in the South, did not clamor for the abolition of involuntary servitude in prisons. Barring goods made with convict labor from the open marketplace was not at odds with the accepted view that forced work in Northern prisons was a morally legitimate punishment for crime, as long as it did not serve private profit. The wardens continued to assume they had the customary and legal right to force prisoners to work, regardless of whether a sentence committed offenders to hard labor, and so this became a normative presumption even among trade unionists. To this day, the AFL-CIO inveighs against unequal market competition from the exploitation of prison labor, but the federation has not added its voice to the movement to end the exception.

The consistent primary concern of trade unionists has been to prevent prison labor being deployed to compete with or underbid "honest" workers on the outside. In the nineteenth century, this meant loudly protesting that the contract system depressed free market wages and that it provided employers with a scab workforce to thwart workers' organizing or strike efforts. They petitioned their representatives to pass laws that protected their position within the free market, and to outlaw, or minimize, the displacement of citizen labor. For much the same reasons, the Knights of Labor supported the Chinese Exclusion Act of 1882, and the Alien Contract Labor Law of 1885, which barred companies from bringing unskilled laborers into the United States to work under contract.

Just as the labor movement's agitation eroded support for the contract system, proponents of rehabilitation also pushed back against the legacy of Lynds' punitive model of penal servitude. In its place, they promoted a scientific or medical approach to the goal of reform, centered around the individualized "treatment" of prisoners and the provision of benefits and rewards for good behavior. The most influential prototype was established by Zebulon Brockway at the Elmira Reformatory, which opened as a model of the new penology in 1876. Brockway introduced indeterminate sentences and parole (thereby extending penal supervision into the community), as well as programs of education, vocational training, and recreational culture. Courses in industrial arts were taught along with fine arts, and elementary training was offered in as many as thirty-six trades. These innovations were presented as ways to incentivize prisoners to seek early release, but they were also aimed at producing "Christian gentlemen," obedient to the Protestant work ethic. To emphasize this underlying discipline, prisoners were subject to a rigorous military regimen, comprising daily marching in uniform in a rough imitation of West Point drills. [18]

After the contract system was abolished, and for the first time in New York, Elmira's prisoners were personally compensated for their labor and good behavior (though most of this wage was garnished for room and board). Like Lynds' industrial system, Brockway's methods of "prison science" were closely studied and copied by penal reformers nationwide and by prison inspectors from overseas. Adopting and customizing them was central to the reform credo of rehabilitation for the better part of the next century. Yet the glowing public relations profile enjoyed by Brockway's Elmira was quite at odds with the cruel reality of the prison's daily operations, as Alexander Pisciotta has shown. He found that whipping, shackling, solitary confinement, and other forms of "benevolent brutality" were all too common, albeit "scientifically" administered.[19]

The Osborne Effect

California was actually the first state to abolish the contract system in its 1879 constitution, but New York was a much bigger prize for reformers. The electorate voted overwhelmingly for abolition in November 1883, and lawmakers began to dismantle the system through statutory legislation. Other Northern and Western states followed. In 1887, Congress outlawed the leasing of federal convicts to farmers and manufacturers, and finally, in November of 1894, New York's voters ratified a state constitutional amendment banning the use of private contract.

The amended constitution now read: "no person in any such prison, penitentiary, jail or reformatory shall be required or allowed to work while under sentence thereto at any trade, industry or occupation wherein or whereby his or her work, or the product or profit of his or her work, shall be farmed out, contracted, given or sold to any person, firm, association or corporation." But the amendment also explicitly directs the legislature to "provide for the occupation and employment of prisoners" while noting that the ban should not be "construed to prevent the legislature from providing that convicts may work for, and that the products of their labor may be disposed of to, the state or any political division thereof." In other words, producing for the open market was now prohibited, but prisoners would still be required to work and they would do so under state supervision and for the purpose of making and supplying goods for purchase and consumption by state vendors and agencies. A new government entity, the Division of Industries—later to be branded as Corcraft—was set up to administer and operate the workshops.

At the same time that they eliminated one system of penal servitude, politicians and voters legally enshrined a new one. The amendment presented the use of prison labor for public use as an *obligation* on the part of the state. Since the profit from that labor would go to the state and its agencies, this enterprise could now be recast as an acceptable public benefit. Prison labor would still be a compulsory part of incarceration (as part of repaying a prisoner's "debt to society") but the result would contribute to the welfare of the general population rather than the bank account of a venal capitalist.

The elimination of private contracting dealt a huge blow to prison budgets and delivered a pressing challenge to wardens, who were now confronted with a sharp increase in idleness at their facilities. The frenetic pace of industrial production had served as an effective mode of everyday discipline by and of itself, and now this regimen was gone. But the obligation to provide employment presented officials with a new opportunity to promote labor as a virtue of great redeeming value to the individual, now that the financial interest of private firms had been eliminated. According to this new gospel, the cultivation of industrious work habits could now be framed as a builder of wholesome character and would therefore be even more central to the therapeutic rehabilitation of the prisoner. If the state had an obligation to provide work, it would do so as part of a more ethical effort to properly reform and prepare the incarcerated for a life of obedient employment after release. That was the new creed of progressive penal reform and was firmly aligned with the moralism of the Protestant work ethic. Once again, New York led the way nationally, taking cues from Brockway's Elmira prototype.[20] The lawmakers who deliberated over the language of the amendment at the 1894 Constitutional Convention were heavily influenced by this doctrine. They therefore viewed the injunction to labor not as a retrograde form of

"involuntary servitude" but as a humane and progressive measure, aimed at the self-redemption of prisoners. In discussions
about the amendment, there was also moral cover for the more
practical need to "reimburse the taxpayer" by generating revenue for the state. The capacity to go on subsidizing the expendi-
tures on prisons and reformatories was a paramount concern
of legislators.[21]

Other states like Massachusetts and Pennsylvania initially held
on to remnants of the old order, in the form of the state-account
system where prisoners produced goods entirely under state auspices for the open market. Others took advantage of the rights
of interstate commerce to freely sell prison-made products in
other states, until further lobbying from organized labor resulted
in the outlawing of such practices under the Hawes-Cooper Act
of 1929 and the Ashurst-Sumners Act of 1935. But New York
went exclusively into production for state-use, hoping that a
monopoly on the closed market of public producers and buyers
would be large enough to offset the costs of its prison system. It
never came close to doing so, and unions made it their business
to further limit the reach of the state-use system. Nevertheless,
the New York prison system was now a *planned economy*, where
officials sought to oversee a division of labor between skilled
and unskilled prisoners, and to oversee the distribution of specialized workshops to different facilities. To more fully demar-
cate the state-use system from the old slave-like one, the 1896
Prison Labor Law established pay for labor, "at a rate of up to
ten percent of the total value of goods produced at the institution (approximately 2¢ to 5¢ per day)" to be collected on release.[22]
State-use, of course, proved to be a flexible rubric that could be
extended far beyond manufacturing, to road building (under the
Good Roads Movement) and other kinds of infrastructure construction or public service beneficial to residents of the region
hosting a prison facility.

As the Progressive era took hold in the early twentieth century, many states followed New York's example, even though the reduced revenues from state-use meant that taxpayers were eating more of the costs of keeping their prisons open. Criticism of penal servitude took on a new dimension. Influential reformers like Stagg Whitin, chair of the liberal National Committee on Prisons and Prison Labor, argued that the new state-use system was still akin to slavery and that only the provision of a free world wage and withdrawal of the compulsion to work could redeem it.[23] By 1913, the Quakers were calling for a "new abolition movement" to overthrow the deployment of "convict slavery" for state use.[24] In response to this disapproval, New York officials pushed their reforms even further. Education in particular would soon be competing with, and in some facilities supplanting, productive labor as the central component of welfare rehabilitation.

The early heyday of this reform phase occurred in Auburn and Sing Sing from 1914–1916. Lynds had made these prisons a byword for brutal discipline in the 1820s, but Thomas Mott Osborne, a businessman, the mayor of Auburn, and the warden of both facilities, presided over their transformation into experimental models of prison democracy. After he was appointed chair of the new State Commission on Prison Reform, Osborne famously spent a week in Auburn in 1913 as a prisoner ("Tom Brown") in order to experience conditions from the inside. He then published *Within Prison Walls*, a widely read and mercilessly critical report on the wretched state of the cells, sanitation, and food.[25] Appointed to chair of the New York State Commission on Prison Reform, and then briefly as Auburn's warden, his main achievement was to institute a Mutual Welfare League as an exercise in prisoner self-management. It allowed prisoners to plan events, channel grievances, adjudicate internal disciplinary matters, propose internal policy changes, and assist in preparation for re-entry. The result was akin to a bloodless revolution, overturning almost a century's observance of the customs of tyrannical administration set in place by Lynds. Not surprisingly, the prisoners took advantage of their new privileges to make a world where they could feel like humans in control of their lives who had lessons to offer their jailers. Or, as Rebecca McLennan puts it, "in a reversal of the fiction of rehabilitation whereby the state undertook to reform convicts, the prisoners of Auburn attempted to reform the state—and its courts and prisons— by demonstrating that indeterminate sentencing, probation and parole, and healthy prison conditions would effectively rehabilitate prisoners who had transgressed the rules."[26]

News about Osborne's experiment travelled far and stoked speculation about which prison would be next on his list to overhaul. Many of his supporters advocated for him to be assigned to Clinton—the "Siberia" or "Klondike" of the system—where the most hardcore prisoners were sent and where his innovations would be truly put to the test. But he was instead offered the wardenship at Sing Sing the following year. He only accepted on the condition that the prisoners approved his appointment.[27] There, he installed a Mutual Welfare League, to which delegates were elected, and an executive board of prisoners which oversaw all its divisions and committee appointments. He gave its inmate court broader powers over all disciplinary matters, withdrew guards from many of the common spaces, introduced an honor system (under which a runaway famously returned weeks later to complete his sentence), and eliminated striped clothing, lockstep, shaven heads, and other vestiges of the dark Lyndsian past. The League spawned numerous committees to oversee all aspects of the institution—sanitation, visitation, finance, recreation, education, entertainment, religious services, mail and communications, the kitchen, and re-entry employment.[28]

Other innovations included a choral society, a prison band, a knitting circle, movie screenings, baseball, and a wide range of educational classes.[29] In addition, prisoners received a minimum weekly wage of $9 in token money for their labor, from which they paid for their room and board and other services.[30] A commissary was set up for the scrip to be used to buy goods, and a self-managed bank was founded to handle savings and offer health and accident insurance. AFL officials were even invited to decide if prisoners could become dues-paying members. They did so, although the initiative did not get very far.[31]

Under the new rules, the League was responsible for maintaining order and discipline, while guards functioned as security cadre rather than as much-hated "screws" with full police powers. The rate of incidents of assault and violence plummeted, and Osborne was wildly popular among the general population. From all accounts, Sing Sing operated more efficiently and with much less strife than anyone had ever imagined possible. Consider that the year before Osborne took office, an uprising had occurred in response to appalling conditions in the facility. As is often the case, the action—which involved hundreds of prisoners— began in the places of labor, when workers went on strike at the shoe, knitting, and clothing shops and set fire to several of them. Osborne, in other words, arrived in the wake of a violent mutiny at the Bastille-on-the-Hudson. His "Republic of Sing Sing" was a paragon of decorum by comparison.

Were there any changes to the world of prison labor under the Mutual Welfare League? The mode of production was not touched, nor was the compulsion to work. But guards were removed from the workshops, leaving only civilian foremen in place. Discipline was placed under the jurisdiction of the inmate court, which meant that anyone who refused to work or went on strike was punished by the court—usually, by stripping him of membership in the League. And, of course, the $9 pay packet was introduced. Not surprisingly, productivity improved at Sing Sing under the new order,[32] previewing a lesson that capitalists would learn in the course of the 1920s when they discovered that employees worked harder and better when they were treated like humans and not machines.[33]

The overall goal of Osborne and his supporters was for Sing Sing's population to emulate, and even elevate, the best practices of society on the outside as much as possible rather than serve as a sequestered enclave where obedience was learned and punishment administered. When people say that "the inmates are running the prison," they typically mean to suggest a state of chaos and disorder. Osborne's Sing Sing gave quite a different gloss to this phrase. It demonstrated that prisoners, given the opportunity and the resources, could run their sectors of the institution tolerably well. Nothing like it had ever been seen before, nor would anything come close in the century to follow.

Not surprisingly, Osborne's reforms nettled powerful interest groups. These included the established prisoner elites (the "highbrows"), the state system's senior bureaucracy, an assortment of political patronage machines, a new Republican governor who was a former prosecutor, and an army of public opinion-makers opposed to the notion that incarcerated people should enjoy any privileges, let alone the "reward" of self-government. Osborne soon faced a trumped-up legal challenge to his conduct, based on charges of sexual relationships with prisoners (a common mode of defaming prison reformers). He was acquitted in a much-publicized Grand Jury trial. However, facing duress from the new superintendent of prisons, he moved on from Sing Sing after only 16 months, and continued his work at Portsmouth Naval Prison in New Hampshire. In accord with the now established tradition of New York leadership, various versions of his self-management model were adopted in other states.

Over the next several decades, the cause of progressive penology would occupy one pole of the pendulum of change that seemed to swing so insistently between compassion and repression. Or as David Rothman shrewdly put it, "reform is the designation that each generation gives to its favorite programs."[34] By the 1920s, criminological theories about the innateness of "born criminals"—who therefore could not be reformed—had established deep roots in the popular mind, yielding support for tougher sentencing policies (the Baumes Law of 1926) and retributive punishment behind bars. But humanitarian reformers pushed back, fighting for programs and pathways more conducive to returning prisoners to productive lives. Sing Sing's brief Osbornian moment in the sun—demonstrating that prisons could actually be run by the incarcerated without the bullheaded policing of guards—lay at one extreme end of the spectrum. As an ideal, it bears some comparison with the more recent call to abolish or "defund" the police and to replace their functions with community-based alternatives.

After Osborne left, the pendulum swung to the other extreme at Sing Sing. A hardliner from Atlanta was appointed warden and he eliminated many of the League's activities including a raft of privileges associated with membership. Subsequently, under the long tenure of Lewis Lawes (1920-1941), the League was protected and maintained to some degree. Over time, however, Lawes—a manager rather than an innovator in the Osborne mold—dismantled the League altogether in recognition of his conviction "that there can be no democracy with prison walls."[35]

We think Lawes may have been correct. Democratic forms of self-rule are an illusion in places of total confinement where the incarcerated are essentially powerless, isolated, poor, and sorely lacking in resources and rights. Their liberty has been taken away. They are "wards of the state," or, in some legal versions, "slaves of the state." They share the institution with guards, often referred to as "police" by our interviewees, whose authoritarian customs and routines are resistant, over the long run, to changes imposed from the outside and even from their own superiors.[36]

Above all, the unpaid, compulsory labor that keeps the operation running, and—at times—profitable, is at odds with any vision or practice of self-rule. The inclusion of prisoners in managerial decision-making might result in a more efficiently and peacefully run facility, as it surely did in Osborne's Sing Sing. But that veneer of civil decorum could also mask the vengeful design behind the establishment and maintenance of the prison as a colony for poor people who are either shut out of, or unwilling to participate in, the wage labor market.

However, we cannot discount how changes in a prison's "culture," including alterations of its rules of operation or improvements to its physical infrastructure, can provide real humanitarian relief (not to mention hope) for those who are locked up and who have lost faith that there might be a light at the end of the carceral tunnel. Nor can we ignore the possibility that such changes might, under some circumstances, shift the balance of power within the prison, laying a pathway toward the abolition horizon.

The Educational Turn

When he died in October 1926, Osborne's coffin was carried back to Auburn prison, where fourteen hundred men attended a mournful but appreciative funeral service for their former warden. It was an unusual, and surely unique, event in American penal history.[37] The attendees had reason to be sorrowful. Their League had been under threat for several years and had been undermined by the new warden's effort to make delegates into "under officers," beholden to him as opposed to serving as representatives of the men. The recently enacted, tough-on-crime Baumes Laws (including a "fourth strike" policy that mandated a life sentence for anyone convicted four times) were beginning to fill the prison well beyond its design capacity. A major strike in 1929 at the equally overcrowded Clinton would be followed by two well-coordinated uprisings at Auburn in July and December of that year. The latter resulted in the hostage-taking of the warden and other guards, the destruction of buildings and workshops, an armed face-off, and several escapes and deaths. The insurgencies were blamed on the League, and the League was dissolved. It would take four decades for the spirit of the League to revive, and then only in a much weaker form, when Inmate Grievance Resolution Committees were created at various New York prisons.

Austin MacCormick, one of Osborne's most loyal acolytes and the DOC Commissioner from 1934 to 1940, wrote of the League that "the primary aim and result of this method of prison organization is to transmute the 'gang' spirit, whose essence is loyalty to the local group, into a spirit of loyalty to the larger group which constitutes the prison community."[38] Yet this brand of loyalty could also be transmuted into the spirit of solidarity behind strikes and uprisings. Instead of self-pacification, it could lead to revolt. Indeed, in 1970, as we will see, another more consequential uprising at Auburn would provide the spark and inspiration for the landmark Attica rebellion.

While the local impact of the 1929 Auburn riot was one of retrenchment, the reformers within the bureaucracy doubled down, and a state-wide initiative for rehabilitation was launched under Governor Franklin Delano Roosevelt and his Lieutenant Governor, Herbert Lehman. Adult education was at the heart of this reform, to be administered by a new Division of Education within DOC.[39] One of the inspirations was the example set by reformist warden Katharine Bement Davis at Bedford Hills women's prison. She had made it a priority to center education and job training, especially in domestic science, while also introducing nurseries and other family-friendly programs.[40] In the overcrowded men's prisons, mass idleness and underemployment (accounting for more than half of the national prison population, according to an Attorney General's survey in 1935–36)[41] had deprived administrators of the pretext that they needed to justify reforms i.e. the argument that steady work habits had a redeeming character. It was also clear that the state's prison industry work-shops were doing little to prepare those who toiled in their work-places for reentry to society. Instead, the reformers began to push for more vocational or trade schools. MacCormick, the incoming commissioner, had done a comprehensive study of existing penal education and found it wanting.[42] His preference for general—as opposed to utilitarian—education was also an influential factor in the introduction of new educational programs at Elmira and three new prisons: Wallkill, Coxsackie, and Woodbourne. These prisons had been established to relieve overcrowding.

Wallkill, which today hosts NYU's Prison Education Program, is the institution in which the authors came to know each other and collaborate. Our program, through which NYU offers a four-year B.A. degree, is in direct line of descent from the initial plan for Wallkill to offer a range of quality educational programming alongside its vocational workshops. The new facility, 75 miles north of New York City, had no surrounding walls or fences and it boasted a spectacular view of the Shawangunk Mountain Ridge. It was designed by Alfred Hopkins in the neo-Gothic collegiate style. Indeed, today's casual passerby might still mistake it for one of the pastoral liberal arts colleges that dot the New England countryside, except that its mountain views are now marred by the neighboring Shawangunk Correctional Facility, which was designed and built in the maximum-security Gulag style in 1983.

When Wallkill opened in 1932 on its picturesque 950-acre rural site, it was supposed to be the prototype of a new welfare-ori-ented phase of rehabilitation. Its vocational curriculum offered training in 24 trades, and its academic curriculum led to either a Regent's diploma or a high school equivalency diploma.[43] Ech-oing the elitist message of its Oxford-style architecture, administrators were allowed to choose whomever they wanted to be transferred from other facilities, and so they selected those who were most likely to succeed academically. Wallkill was intended to be an experimental place where the combination of model prisoner-students, handpicked personnel, and a congenial environment would yield proof that the reformers were on the right track. Farmland on the property was worked to provide healthy, fresh produce for the facility and for Sing Sing across the Hudson River. The galleries in each housing wing were communal in nature, with a shared bathroom and a recreational room in the manner of a college dorm. Cells were not locked, unless by the occupant. The workshops were organized around specialized crafts. Even though prisoner self-governance—the stand-out feature of Osborne's Sing Sing—was not any part of the pilot phase, Wallkill was far removed in feel and purpose from the "dark Satanic mill" of Lynds' industrial system.

The same architect designed Woodbourne and Coxsackie in the Anglo Collegiate style as "prisons without walls" that looked nothing an old-line penal institution. Housing prisoners who were judged to be less academically capable than those at Wallkill, they served as reformatories for young—or first time—offenders who had a maximum of three-year sentences. By far, the majority of prisoners in each of these three facilities were enrolled in educational programs, in contrast to the existing Big House prisons which were largely bypassed by the new wave of education-based rehabilitation. But how would guards be trained to react without resistance or rancor to a novel milieu engineered to facilitate learning and self-development?

One answer came in the form of a Central Guard School, established at Wallkill in November, 1936. This was another first for both New York and the nation. Fresh recruits, enrolled at the school for eight-week sessions, were instructed according to the reformers' scripture, i.e. to show humanitarian respect to prisoners, rather than to swing a stick. They also received three hours' daily training in military drills, calisthenics, boxing, and jiu-jitsu, as well as in the use of gas and firearms.[44] Who knows whether the lessons in restraint and de-escalation stayed with them when they were placed on duty in the tougher prisons? Perhaps they found the martial arts training more applicable. In any event, a large portion of the correctional workforce recruits went through this school until it was shut down—under war-time conditions—after 1942. As for the prisoners, the Wallkill ethos was to nurture their development on an individual basis, in keeping with the progressive reform philosophy. A specific set of programs was assigned for each prisoner, coordinated with parole staff. This "Wallkill Approach" was adopted as state-wide policy, and Wallkill continued to be the New York facility where new services were introduced. The first Alcoholics Anonymous program was introduced at Wallkill in 1945, and in 1976, the first overnight Family Reunion Program.[45]

A college of any kind inside a prison is full of contradictions, as we ourselves have found. How can a curriculum geared to opening the mind of students truly thrive in such a closed, authoritarian environment—especially within neo-Gothic architecture where the cathedral windows have grills instead of leaded glass and panes and where the heavy oak doors have steel security bars? There is a deep irony attached to teaching a degree like Liberal Studies—which our NYU program offers at Wallkill—in a place where only the instructor is at liberty to leave the classroom and walk out of the facility.[46] On the other hand, our students seldom miss an opportunity to tell us how valuable the experience of learning is to them. Most of them leave with a degree in hand or are able to complete the B.A. requirements at NYU in New York. Unlike many colleges that offer stand-alone classes, we decided that we needed to offer a credential that might be useful to students entering the employment market. Arts classes, by comparison, which have become more common in prisons since the 1970s, are often presented as therapeutic in nature.[47] But they too have a hard time fostering self-transformation in a milieu that, even with the most uplifting architectural trappings, is still set up to discipline and punish. As Nicole Fleetwood argues, they have been used by countless prisoners as a tool for liberation but they are also favored by administrators as soft instruments of pacification and control.[48]

In the early decades, the educational offerings and the workshops at Wallkill, Coxsackie, and Woodbourne were primarily focused on skill-building or work experience that might give prisoners an edge in the free world labor market. Accordingly, none of these facilities had industry shops churning out furniture, clothing, license plates, or beds for state agencies. Vocational work was unpaid because it was seen as educational in nature. Even so, many of the shops were still producing for the institutional needs of the state's prisons, and so they too required the application of routine labor. In addition, prisoners, as always, were still doing the bulk of the maintenance work: cleaning, cooking, laundry, and landscaping.

The more idealistic reformers who helmed the experiment believed that the vocational shops offered some stability for building a new life on reentry, and they assumed that there would be jobs at the end of the line. Was that the case? Thanks to the assistance of advisers and teachers from Columbia Teachers College, the more proficient students at Wallkill did better overall, but the evidence collected over time showed that vocational training—especially at the other facilities—produced meagre outcomes. In his study of Coxsackie's history, Joseph Spillane notes that most alumni who found employment in a trade attained the rank of "helper" rather than advancing to the more skilled levels.[49] For one thing, they were marked with a scarlet letter as felons, and access to skilled jobs was even more difficult for applicants of color. As one Coxsackie graduate put it, "us Blacks and Puerto Ricans in prison took our courses and studied our brains out, but without much hope of ever really working at the trade outside, we were the wrong-colored race and now we were also ex-cons."[50]

In the 1960s, Wallkill introduced an optics manufacturing program—the first in the nation. Initially operated on a specialized craft basis, the contractor taught optical theory and the art of grinding optical glass by hand to a few apprentices. Rudimentary manufacturing technology followed in the 1970s. In 1992, Corcraft adopted the shop into its industry program, producing eyeglasses for New York's Medicaid recipients among other public clients. The shop still thrives, producing hundreds of thousands of glasses annually. Yet in our own, more recent, experience, it is still proving difficult for graduates—even those who have earned trade certificates—to find jobs in the field on release. They may get callbacks, but then their criminal record presents an obstacle to getting any further. We know of only one Wallkill alumnus who succeeded in setting up his own optics business.[51]

These less than stellar outcomes were not systematically reviewed until 1966, when New York's governor ordered a commission to evaluate the programs and determine whether education-based rehabilitation was delivering results in the form of job placements for parolees. The preliminary report was generally critical of the reformers' efforts. One of the commission's researchers in particular, the criminologist Robert Martinson, would go on to put the decisive nail in the coffin of penal reform. His subsequent, more exhaustive, study of evaluation reviews looked exclusively at whether vocational programs reduced recidivism, and he found no evidence that they had done so. In a series of follow-up articles and comments, he infamously concluded that "rehabilitation is a social myth," or in a more quotable form, that "nothing works."[52] Martinson's comments, bolstered by the authority of his empirical study, were catnip to the advocates of

classical, custodial punishment, and so they received a broad air-
ing on TV and in print. He himself believed that the liberal "myth
of correctional treatment" had been used to prolong the existence of prisons, which he thought should be torn down, but that
was not the view taken up by the popular media which amplified
only his criticisms. He later recanted his reported conclusions, but
by then it was too late. The pendulum was swinging again toward
the pole of punishment.

The Punishment Turn

In 1971, New York's correctional and parole agencies were
merged into the new Department of Correctional Services (later
renamed the Department of Correctional and Community Services, or DOCCS). An incoming administration began to push
the remaining reformers out. They upgraded the security levels
on their model institutions like Wallkill, Elmira, and Coxsackie,
and called for stepped–up production in the state industry shops,
reducing spending on programs. This new direction reflected a
national popular mood that had begun to shift toward the law-
and-order politics espoused by Richard Nixon's 1968 presiden-
tial campaign. As the 1970s wore on, the much-analyzed profile
of mass incarceration began to take shape, as harsher sentencing
rules, habitual offender laws, and new crime classifications drove
a wave of prison expansion. The blunt protocols of tough-on-
crime policies would soon supplant the reformers' talk about
rehabilitation and reeducation. The new prisons (New York alone
built 53 between 1970 and 1995, increasing the population five-
fold)[53] served to warehouse the surplus fractions of the working class that had been abandoned by deindustrialization and
forsaken by a rapidly shrinking welfare state.[54] But 1971 would
be remembered in New York's correctional history for another,
more inflammatory reason. The Attica Rebellion in September

of that year—the bloodiest in the nation's history—brought the prisoner rights movement to a head, offering a dramatic lesson in the politicization of the long history of prison revolts.

Like all workers under a harsh regimen of discipline, prisoners had always found ways to resist and protest. In his study of the early Pennsylvania prisons, Michael Meranze details many of these incidents, accompanied by demands for fair wages and labor rights.[55] Rebecca McLennan describes how the incarcerated men in Walnut Street Prison regularly stopped work on "Blue Mondays" in the late eighteenth century.[56] This was probably a version of what free workers called Saint Monday—an unofficial holiday observed in defiance of industrial employers for more than a century.[57] So, too, she records the persistent incidence of "theft, sabotage, arson, and self-inflicted injury" during the last several decades of the private contractual system, which culminated in a series of labor strikes and slowdowns towards the end. These strikes occurred during the era of the most intense Gilded Age conflicts between capital and labor.[58] They challenged the perception that prisoners were helpless cogs in the industrial machine. "In their collective acts of defiance, McLennan writes, "prisoners realized—and caused contractors to recognize—that far from having an entirely free hand within the prison factories and camps, contractors were subject, if only in some small degree, to a relation of dependency."[59] This everyday dependency hardly needed to be pointed out to incarcerated workers toiling on the job every day, but the escalation of these scattershot tactics into a unified program of action required some degree of organization and solidarity. Each renewal of the prisoner rights movement has made conscious and explicit use of the recognition that the carceral system is acutely dependent on the labor power of those it locks up.

In the late 1960s, a new prisoner rights movement began in California's Folsom and San Quentin prisons, and its organizers seized on unpaid labor as the central theme. Among the list of prisoner demands in the much-circulated Folsom Prisoners Manifesto of Demands (1970) were calls for a labor union, union scale wages, compliance with federal workplace standards, worker compensation insurance, and the abolition of forced work.[60] When the prairie fire that had been lit on the West Coast reached New York, these items were still priorities. On July 29th, 1971, workers at Attica's metal shop went on strike over their low wages (they were paid between 6 cents and 29 cents a day). Initially punished with lockdown, the organizers were supported by their peers through a show of shop-wide unity which resulted in a pay raise to between 25 cents and a dollar a day.[61] That metal shop would be used as an arsenal for making makeshift weapons during the subsequent uprising.[62]

The wage hikes won at the shop inspired the belief that further gains could be achieved by stopping business as usual. Sam Melville, a white anti-war radical who had been arrested for bombing corporate, bank, and court buildings in Manhattan, circulated a pamphlet entitled, "Anatomy of the Laundry," which broke down the economics of how the state profited from penal servitude. Melville wrote: "How does the pig exploit the laundry slave? How does the pig profit? Like so: The average wage of a unionized dry laundry worker on the outside is $3.50 per hour; whereas the average wage of a laundry slave here is 25¢ per day. The laundry slave works 3 1/2 hours per day for 25¢; an outside unionized worker would earn $10.50 for the same work. Projected to a monthly basis, the slave gets $5.50, while an outsider gets $231.00."[63]

Melville was soon joined by Black Muslim radicals and Black Panthers who were transferred from Auburn after they organized a labor strike and an occupation that led to the hostage-taking of guards.[64] The militants formed an Attica Liberation Faction, penned their own version of the Folsom Manifesto, and presented their grievances to prison and state administrators in July.

Their "Manifesto of Demands and Anti-Depression Platform" included reasoned demands for prisoner unions, workers comp programs, workplace safety standards, and the application of federal and state minimum wage laws.[65] Foremost among the conditions for releasing the hostages taken at Attica was the call to "apply the New York State minimum wage law to all State Institutions"—a demand repeated in further iterations.[66]

These labor-based demands cannot be separated from the heightened understanding among Black prisoners in particular about the role of race within the prison system. The Nation of Islam had been a presence in prisons since the 1940s, most famously in the Massachusetts maximum-security facility of Charlestown, where Malcolm X served his sentence from 1946 to 1952. The Black nationalist creed of the Nation of Islam was reformulated by Malcolm and by imprisoned California radicals like George Jackson into a forceful doctrine that all Black people in the US were, and still are, a "captive nation," and that their incarceration was an illegitimate act of violence on the part of a white supremacist state. This ideology helped to shape the consciousness of prisoners of color who had long struggled to survive under the informal, but rigidly observed, racial divisions and hierarchies among the prison population. This racial order was reflected in almost every aspect of carceral life, from pretrial processing, to work assignments, to cell placements, to early parole, and it was enforced by the brutality of white officers, often from rural backgrounds and with no prior experience of contact with nonwhite people. The discrimination would be amplified, during the 1980s and 1990s, through the warehousing of mass populations of Black and Brown people arrested under the new sentencing laws, as Michelle Alexander showed in her analysis of post-civil rights "color-blind racism."[67]

Racial conflict was a significant factor in a number of New York uprisings in the 1950s and the 1960s, especially at

Great Meadow, designated an "end of the line" facility for the unreformable and ungovernable, where prisoners of color and gang members were disproportionately transferred. By the time Attica blew up, most of the Black members of the prison population had been exposed to some degree to the nationalist argument about captivity, and, in particular, by the notion that unpaid or underpaid prison labor was a vestige of slavery. Acceptance of the theory of a direct line of descent from the plantation to the modern penitentiary became more widespread as the number of facilities multiplied and filled up with young Black and Brown men displaced from urban employment markets and forced into the illegal underground economy. By 2018, the numbers still told a stark story: Black people constituted 15 percent of state residents, but 43 percent of people in jail and 48 percent of people in prison.[68]

The trigger-happy suppression of the Attica uprising (best recounted in Heather Ann Thompson's book, *Blood in the Water*) was ordered by Governor Rockefeller after consultation with Richard Nixon in the White House. But the brutal massacre of prisoners, and the violent recriminations that followed, were not just a heavy-handed command from the highest levels of state power to restore order. The offensive (which included New York State troopers, sheriff's deputies, and correction officers) channeled much of the pent-up rage and resentment of custodial and policing employees. These were working-class agents of state power whose customary and discretionary use of force had long been devalued and downgraded by reformers. They were not just taking back control of a prison. They were reclaiming what they considered to be the proper functions of discipline and security in a prison, functions that were central to their sense of professional identity and purpose. Osborne's Sing Sing had imagined a prison that did not need guards, whereas the retaking of Attica was a blunt reassertion of the desire for guards to be in fully-armed control. This also served as a grisly reminder of the cold-blooded expression of their authority on the job. In addition, there was a palpable racial element to the onslaught. In their reforming zeal, administrators had not only overlooked the persistence of racial persecution and conflict among the general prison population but also the racially edged appetite for retribution on the part of predominantly white guards.

As part of this drive to reaffirm their professional livelihood, correctional officers were bolstered by their own history of efforts at labor organizing. They had every reason to form a union, since they performed an underpaid and dangerous job, which came with high levels of overwork, stress, and low social status. The American Federation of State, County, and Municipal Employees (AFSCME) began to organize at Sing Sing in 1953 and soon won a forty-hour workweek for its members. Over the next two decades, guards staged intermittent pickets, sick-outs, lock-ins, walk-outs, and wildcat strikes at a variety of facilities to address their chronic underpayment and other areas of neglect, like lack of promotion, retirement benefits, health insurance, vacations, and seniority privileges. Alongside their class-conscious demands for better pay and conditions, they developed a more informal critique of overly-lenient wardens.[69] Could the CO unions play a role in adjusting the balance of prison power in favor of their members? In April 1979, they pulled off an unprecedented sixteen-day stoppage, which affected the whole system. The state pulled in the National Guard as scab labor and fined the union for violating New York's law against public sector strikes. But the COs won considerable gains in pay, pensions, and grievance procedures. They also bolstered their authority in the workplace as the default say-so on the job.

Over time, a phalanx of powerful unions emerged: the New York State Correctional Officers (the guards' union), the Police Benevolent Association of New York State (representing state police) the Correction Officers' Benevolent Association (the municipal jailers' union) and the Police Benevolent Association of New York City (the NYPD officers' union). As in other states, these unions have become a formidable political force, much more effective in their lobbying influence than the prison superintendents or DOCCS itself.[70] Their control over personnel decisions and their fierce resistance to internal investigation—let alone reform—has allowed them to preside over a culture of callous brutality within the ranks of the NYPD, in addition to at the notorious Rikers Island jail (likely subject now to a federal takeover) and in many of the state's tougher, upstate prisons.[71]

Return of the Private Contract?

The decades since the 1970s have seen a steady decline in the density and political influence of organized labor as a whole. Among the exceptions are the police and correctional unions, which have expanded and deepened their power. This is no coincidence. The decimation of public services and the widening of class inequality during these years have been accompanied by a steady increase in funding and reputational status for the law enforcement, custodial, and security sectors of the economy. Consequently, the mentality of control and armed response has established deep roots in the popular mind. The result is the growth of a *carceral society* where techniques of surveillance, discipline, and punishment have extended far beyond the sprawling archipelago of prisons, jails, and other institutions of state supervision into the domain of civic life.[72]

By the time of the watershed 1979 guard strike, prisons were already filling up with new offenders of the draconian Rockefeller Drug Laws, another New York innovation that was emulated elsewhere. The national prison population would swell from 330,000 in 1973 (when the laws were passed) to a peak of 2.3 million in 2009 (or one in every 100 adults in the U.S.)[73] Correctional officers found themselves in a growth occupation. Their mass hiring was part of the lifeline extended to rural communities who were assured that hosting a prison would be the key to their economic survival. This promise of regional development turned out to be a mixed bag—and most prisons are environmentally toxic to their hosts—but the provision of well-paying union jobs has been a tangible benefit.

For most of the 1970s, New York commanded the penal limelight, as had often been the case for the previous century and a half. The shock impact of Attica reverberated around the nation, generating a two-sided response. On the one hand, it sparked a wave of reforms and an expansion of prisoner rights in state after state, including—for a brief period—a flowering of prisoner union organizing through the United Prisoners Union and the Prisoners Labor Union.[74] For decades after, the uprising was memorialized by prisoners. One of our interviewees, who had served a long sentence, recalled that, at the beginning of his bid:

> The biggest thing in prison at one time was Attica. Because Attica changed everything in prison. And every year, we kept Attica holy in our way—and the COs knew it—and they respected it. We would go to the mess hall, and they wouldn't even cook that day because they know no one's going to eat. So we go into the mess hall, get a tray, our silverware, and we sit down. You won't hear a thing—that will be the only day you'll never hear a fucking word or sound in the mess hall. And we'd sit there for ten minutes. The CO would come over and hit the desk, the table. We'd all get up, put our silverware away, and march out. Some guys even fasted for those three days or whatever. These days, you ask some of these inmates, "Yo, what are you doing for Attica?" They'll say, "Attica? What are you talking about?"

Fear of "another Attica" haunted prison administrators, and so the uprising (which was blamed on militant revolutionaries) also generated a sharp and effective pushback on a wide front by anti-reform advocates of law and order. The Rockefeller Drug Laws (mandating 15-year minimums for possession of four ounces of narcotics—the same as for second-degree murder) turned out to be the progenitor of nationwide "tough-on-crime" measures that put two generations of nonviolent offenders in cages on long sentences. And the 1979 guard strike sent a loud message that the clout of custodial interests was a force to be reckoned with. But after these three consequential moments in penal history, New York relinquished its role as national leader. Henceforth, the trends would be set elsewhere, in the South and West, especially in the business of prison labor.

The government-owned Federal Prison Industries, which had formed in 1934, underwent a rebrand as UNICOR in 1977 and expanded its industrial operations across the country. Today, UNICOR operates a manufacturing empire (with business units in clothing, textiles, furniture, and electronics) along with a wide array of services. It nets almost half a billion dollars annually, selling mostly to government agencies (50 percent of its sales are to the Department of Defense) but also to select corporations. Federal prisoners are paid between 23c and $1.15 per hour, but up to 50 percent of these earnings are subject to mandatory deductions. The state-run prison industries generate more than a billion dollars in sales nationally, from manufacturing a broad variety of goods, and providing services through call centers, logistics, and digitization.[75] New York's Corcraft, which operates in 14 facilities and turns an annual profit of $30 million, produces state license plates, soap, street signs, eyeglasses, janitorial supplies, school lockers, metal crowd-control barricades used by the NYPD, wooden benches used throughout the state court system, and furniture purchased by local school boards.[76] The state's monopoly power requires local government agencies to "look to Corcraft first" when they are in the market for such items. Hourly pay in Corcraft's prison shops ranges from 15 to 65 cents and has not budged since 1993.[77]

But it was the return of private contracting that promised to alter the landscape of prison labor most decisively. As union power faltered over the course of the 1970s, the private sector lobbied hard to roll back the New Deal regulations against contracting for profit. By the end of the decade, corporate America had begun to abandon its domestic workforces for cheaper labor south of the border or overseas. Lawmakers were advised that re-opening prisons to private industry might help to stem the out-flow. The lobbying paid off in 1979 when Congress authorized an exemption under the Ashurst-Sumners Act to pass the Justice System Improvement Act, thereby creating the Private Sector/Prison Industry Enhancement Certification Program (PIECP). Under this law (and others that would follow), prison administrators were encouraged to partner with companies to produce for the open marketplace. Once again, capitalist employers would have access to a vast and literally captive pool of laborers who could be forced to work. The firms would have to pay the local prevailing wage for the labor, but all other production costs came free of charge or were minimal. PIECP also allowed UNICOR, along with state industry programs, to expand into the realm of private contracts. To sweeten the pot for the employers, officials offered a variety of additional subsidies, free industrial space, and tax breaks. In return, PIECP allowed states to garnish up to 80 percent of wages for room and board, victim compensation, and family support.[78]

As marketization picked up pace, the logical next stop exploiting private prison labor was to privatize prisons themselves.[79] Several states sought to slice costs during the prison boom by contracting the building and operation of their penitentiaries to companies like Corrections Corporation of America (now CoreCivic) and Wackenhut Corrections Corporation (now the GEO Group). The major players in this new for-profit sector feasted off PIECP contracts. They also generated unsafe sweatshop conditions in their facilities because prison workplaces are not governed by federal occupational safety standards. Prisoners as well as guards were put at grave risk from the dangers of handling toxic material and operating unmonitored machinery. Injury rates increased.[80]

The prospect of such a cheap, immobile labor pool in close proximity to domestic markets was enticing to the private sector. In the 1980s, many corporations were shifting production to Central America or overseas, but the new prison workforce on tap offered a competitive alternative, and some of the top brands initially jumped at the chance. Whole Foods, Boeing, Target, Starbucks, Texas Instruments, IBM, McDonald's, Nordstrom, Intel, BP, Nike, Honda, Sprint, and Macy's have all allegedly used prison labor. Over time, other employers who went offshore considered moving some of their operations back in order to take advantage of prison labor. Ironically, they would be employing the same workers who had been abandoned during the first wave of deindustrialization in the mid-1970s. As Steve Fraser and Joshua Freeman put it: "Those back home—disproportionately African-American workers—who found themselves living in economic exile, scrabbling to get by, began showing up in similarly disproportionate numbers in the country's rapidly expanding prison archipelago. It didn't take long for corporate America to come to view this as another potential foreign country, full of cheap and subservient labor—and better yet, close by."[81]

Access to this labor boosted profit margins at the same time as it took away employment from free world workers. It further stifled the efforts of workers to organize because the threat to move production into a prison was deployed as a union-busting tactic. In the most perverse way, it even provided some corporate politicians and state legislators with a talking point about how they were keeping manufacturing in the U.S. or helping to bring it back onshore. Ironically, for some workers, they stood more chance of being employed in prison for a wage than they did on the outside.

Stories about the corporate super-exploitation of prison labor can easily trigger public outrage, and these stories make for sensational headlines—Victoria's Secret Bras Are Being Made by Convicts! But the portion of prison production claimed by private contracting proved to be relatively small. Less than 1 percent of incarcerated people are employed today by private companies through PIECP.[82] Why not more? One factor is unreliability. The efficient operation of a workplace depends on the consistent availability of workers, and prison security priorities will always override an employer's desire for ready access to the work site. A lockdown, however temporary, can block workers from being able to show up or shift goods out. Another factor is brand exposure. Companies risk harm to the reputation of their brand when it is tainted with the stigma of prison labor. And it is difficult to get rid of the stain. Victoria's Secret, for instance, suffered the consequences of relying on a vendor who employed prisoner labor in the 1980s. Although the corporation broke off the relationship in response to adverse publicity, the damning charge is still in circulation today.

Bad press is also directed at the private prisons themselves. Yet only 7 percent of the national incarcerated population is currently housed in privately-owned or -run facilities, and these tend to be concentrated in a few states, such as Texas, Florida, Arizona, Tennessee, Georgia, and New Mexico.[83] The vast majority (approximately 80 percent) of prisoners nationwide serve their sentences in state-owned institutions.[84] Most of those who produce goods and services are working in state correctional industries, and this worker population still only accounts for 6 percent of people incarcerated in the state prisons. Everyone else is assigned maintenance work, which is by far the most common kind of labor done by prisoners.

In 1998, DOCCS commissioned an internal study of Corcraft, New York's state-use industry program, to do something about its "marginal or negative operating results." The authors of the report acknowledged the "increased inmate populations" without explaining how and why they had increased, and blamed "substantial inmate idleness" on the overly regulatory constraints that had been placed on the use of prison labor during the New Deal era. They recommended that New York look into "enhancing" its program by joining the thirty other states that had partnered with private industry through PIECP, producing in such diverse sectors as brand clothing, metal work, telemarketing, mapmaking, electronic cables, and computer networking. The report cited several advantages: 1). the additional revenue would reduce the burden on taxpayers; 2). the state could extract more taxes and restitution fees; 3). prisoner idleness would be reduced; and 4). businesses would be retained in New York. On the downside, the report recognized that PIECP contracts could result in the displacement of local workers.[85]

PIECP participation requires the payment of prevailing local wages and also that states consult with organized labor and local industry to ensure that employment of free world workers is not threatened or terminated. In some states where these stipulations were not followed, contracts were contested by unions and discontinued. The authors of the 1998 report acknowledged that New York's strong labor movement would have a large say in any effort to reinstate the private employment of incarcerated labor. The AFL-CIO's official position, at that time, was that it "supported efforts to provide training opportunities for prisoners to help in their rehabilitation and to reduce recidivism, but always with the caution that prisoners should never be used in competition with free labor or to replace free labor."[86]

The 1998 DOCCS internal recommendation did not get much traction initially. It would take more than twenty years for the initiative to work its way up the political ladder. By then, Kathy Hochul, the state's incoming governor, was ready to overturn the ban on private contracts, Her call for the repeal arrived in Albany at the same time that 13th Forward's Campaign to End Prison Labor was launched. Hochul declared her interest during her 2021 run for the governorship, and she floated a proposal in her first "State of the State" speech in 2022. Labelled as "Jails to Jobs," it bundled the "opportunity" to perform an in-prison private sector job alongside other reforms aimed at facilitating re-entry, such as vocational training, career planning, job placement educational release, transitional housing, eliminating parole fees, restoring the Tuition Assistance Program, and sealing certain felony and misdemeanor records.[87] Some lawmakers were eager to back a measure that would allow the state to garnish up to 50 percent of the PIECP earnings. Critics of the plan argued that a high rate of deductions would be an impediment rather than an aid to a successful reentry. In addition, the governor's proposal included no guarantee of basic labor protections against punishment for refusing to work in dangerous or unsafe conditions, nor any provision for state oversight of wages and hours.

In the face of strong pushback, the governor dropped the plan, which would have overturned a prohibition that had stood for almost 130 years. Her climb-down gave some momentum to 13th Forward's bill, the *No Slavery in NY Act,* and also to its *Fairness and Opportunity for Incarcerated Workers Act,* which incorporates all of the labor-related demands laid out in the bill of rights issued in Folsom and Attica. Yet nothing in the governor's Jails to Jobs proposal—nor in the DOCCS report that launched the initiative back in 1998—suggests that anyone in the state bureaucracy had stopped to consider what New York's incarcerated men and women thought about these plans. In fact, the state has never gathered testimony about the daily work performed in its prisons, either in the Corcraft shops, or through the household work assignments that keep these correctional institutions running. Fortunately, we did, and in our interviews with men and women who had been housed in prisons all over the state, we were able to build a picture of the complex world of work behind the walls.

CHAPTER 3

From State to State

From the mid-1970s, the punitive turn in criminal justice and corrections policy combined with the rise of neoliberal ideologies to reshape the conditions of life—including with respect to the organization of labor—inside U.S. prisons.[1] This paradoxical combination of the neoliberal faith in "small government" with the building of the largest prison system in history resulted in what legal scholar Hadas Aviram called "mass incarceration on the cheap."[2] At the same time as incarceration rates exploded, most correctional systems also slashed quality-of-life budgets for these incarcerated populations.[3] When it came to prison labor, that meant squeezing as much profit as possible from the system's captive pool of workers.

Having spent over 35 years in New York prisons, Jim Hatton had a long-term vantage point on this historical shift. He was able to experience, at close quarters, the transformation of living and working conditions inside the state's correctional facilities. Jim first arrived at Sing Sing in the summer of 1985, and—like other interviewees who had spent decades in the New York prison systems—he remembered with some fondness the food that facilities used to serve in the "old times" before the Department of Corrections and Community Supervision (DOCCS) centralized all food production in a "cook chill" facility in the early 2000s.[4] Many of the training and educational opportunities introduced in the course of the reformers' efforts at prisoner rehabilitation had disappeared by the turn of the millennium. Jim was instead assigned to a multitude of maintenance and administrative positions, most of them paying less than 30 cents per hour.[5] This was the case for most of the formerly incarcerated people we interviewed in New York, who reported working in their facilities' kitchen and laundries, mopping floors, repairing electrical systems, mowing grounds, shoveling snow, and everything in between—doing their part to keep the system running for a few pennies an hour.

In New York prisons, incarcerated people get their first job assignment from their facility's Program Committee, which usually includes a Corrections Officer, a counselor, and the deputy superintendent. The committee is supposed to take into account both the facility's needs and the person's preferences and skills, and therefore assign people accordingly. In practice, we learned that almost everybody starts off in custodial maintenance, working as a "porter" to keep hallways and other common areas clean. At a rate of 10 cents per hour, porter positions are among the worst paid—just above the "idle pay" received by prisoners for whom no work assignments can be found. After three months on the job, workers are supposed to go back to their Program Committee to be assigned to a new position, although most have told us that the ability to leverage their personal networks—with other prisoners or with COs themselves—was usually much more effective if they wanted to land a better job inside the facility.

We found a consensus about which assignments were to be avoided, but not everyone had the same notion of what constituted a good job. Nor was there much agreement on the best strategies to secure them. Dylan Cameron, who shared a cell block with Jim, recounted how and why he spent his entire bid working as a porter in various facilities. Had it been up to him, he would not have worked at all. When he arrived at Auburn in 2004—his first adult sentence, after a few brushes with the law as a juvenile—his plan was to "sleep away" his 14 years. With solid financial support from his family, and with his own ties to active prison gangs, Dylan saw no reason why he should work for the system for a few dollars per week. "Listen," he told members of the Program Committee, "I am not working. Throw me to the box, do whatever you like. That is just not happening." That was when one of the counselors took him aside to say: "Let me give you some advice: become a porter. It's a very simple job—everybody is a porter. They probably won't even call you out of your cell, you have to do nothing. Just take the porter position."

It turned out to be sound advice. "Every single jail I went to," he bragged, "I made sure that I was a porter." And the counselor was right: the porter assignments were indeed quite lax. On a regular day, Dylan said, he would only perform actual work—sweeping and mopping floors—for about an hour or so in the course of a five-hour shift.[6] On top of that, as a porter he had greater freedom than most of his peers to move across different housing units. To him, this was even more valuable in a maximum-security facility like Auburn: "[When you are] in maxes, it's all cells, so being a porter allows you to be out, to be mobile. It allows you to take a shower every day, to pass things along. It allows you to get cool with the other officers, which in turn allows you to do more things."

A few other interviewees recounted following the same strategy as Dylan, doing their best to stick to porter jobs throughout their incarceration. Most of them had alternative sources of income, either from their families or from the informal prison economy, and so the opportunity to make a few extra cents per hour doing a more taxing job was not very attractive. Some valued the relative freedom afforded by porter positions for its own sake and decided that this sense of independence was worth going without any commissary money for weeks. Juan Lopez, for example, did not get regular financial support from his family or friends on the outside, but he still figured he would rather go hungry than "slave away"—as he put it—in a more demanding if slightly better paid position. He had not always felt that way. For the first few years of his sentence, Juan did go after higher pay, and even landed an "industry" position, making mattresses at Eastern. At 65 cents per hour, or about $70 per month, this manufacturing job was easily one of the highest paid jobs in the New York prison system, though it was still barely enough to purchase food and other essentials at the bi-weekly commissary. The pay bump came at a steep cost, however, because he found that the shifts were oppressive and that the work conditions were "dreadful": "I was just making mattresses, every day all day, five days a week. It was very repetitive, and I wasn't getting anything out of it."

After a few months of this grind, Juan decided that the exhaustion from working eight-plus hour shifts just to help Corcraft turn a profit was not bringing him any closer to his goal—namely being able to support himself *after* his release from prison. He quit the job at the mattress factory, asked to be transferred to a porter position, and started taking college classes—first at Eastern and later on as a student in NYU's college-in-prison program at Wallkill.[7]

Minimizing their involvement in labor assignments worked out reasonably well for Dylan and Juan, but that was not a viable path for many formerly incarcerated men and women we spoke with in New York. Most of them did not have the same level of family support as Dylan, or else they had no easy access to lucrative hustles in the prison informal economy. Some were older, facing lengthy sentences, and did not feel that they could eke out their survival on a porter wage inside prison, as Juan opted to do in order to pursue a college education. Whatever the reason, their porter assignments were just the first step in the quest for more remunerative positions.

After working as porters for a few months, those people leveraged their networks to get pulled into better assignments—or else tried their luck going back to the Program Committee. Theresa Morrison, for example, quickly realized that she would not be able to afford even the basic necessities on 12 cents per hour, the wage she received for her first assignment as a dishwasher at Taconic Correctional Facility. In those early days, Theresa (who was twenty-one years old and facing a nine-year sentence) was making $28 every two weeks, but DOCCS was garnishing half of that in order to pay off a $375 court surcharge. Like most of the formerly incarcerated women we interviewed,[8] Theresa received almost no support from her family and friends on the outside, so she was left with $14 to spend at the commissary store every other week. This was barely enough to buy a bar of soap, toothpaste, and some oatmeal. Given her limited options, it is not surprising that her priorities were quite different from the likes of Dylan, for instance, when it came to job assignments:

> I didn't have any support from outside, I didn't get any packages sent in. Every dollar that I earned was precious to me, so I had to work. I was working in the mess hall for shifts that I wasn't even supposed to be there for, and I was on the schedule for five days a week but I was working all seven. I mean, of course if I had gotten a porter job I probably would have less hours to work, but I needed the money, I wasn't really in a position to bargain.

After about a year, Theresa secured a slightly better-paying position in the mess hall, earning about 25 cents per hour. Once she was transferred to Bedford Hills, she was able to double that, working at the DMV call center.

We interviewed many people like Theresa who recounted their relentless quests for "better" jobs as they tried to make ends meet inside prison and ease the financial burden on their families and friends on the outside. More often than not, what people looked for in job assignments wasn't just a higher wage but was also the "perks" that came with a position. These benefits, for example, made mess hall assignments particularly desirable for those who needed to get their hands on more resources during their bid. For sure, the wages were slightly higher than in most lower grade maintenance jobs but what was even more important was gaining access to extra food, for both direct personal consumption and for trading on the black market. The ability to take advantage of this access allowed people like Julio Suarez to sustain himself in prison even after his family support had dried up.

When we talked to him, Julio had already been home for more than two years, but he could still vividly recall how hungry he had been in his seven years inside New York prisons. The way he saw it, the extra food he bought every other week at the commissary store was not a "plus," but rather a vital nutrition source he depended on to avoid starvation. Mess hall meal portions, he explained, were always insufficient. The food was of poor quality and unhealthy, when not altogether inedible. During the first years of his sentence, his family had rallied to send him regular financial support, but that stream of funds slowly dried up, as his loved ones struggled to make ends meet in their own household economies. Once Julio realized he couldn't count on outside funds, he requested a transfer to the mess hall, and then he worked his way up to become one of the head cooks at Eastern. In addition to making about $80 per month—one of the highest wages incarcerated workers can make in New York outside of the Corcraft industry jobs—Julio had access to more substantial food portions, and to surplus supplies he could sell to others. Pretty soon, Julio had developed an additional stream of income based on "contracts" with regular customers who ordered specific food items that he could smuggle out of the mess hall.

Climbing the prison employment ladder in this way had its benefits, including slightly higher wages and access to perks. For Julio, Theresa, and others, this combination could make all the difference between extreme deprivation—including acute hunger and malnutrition—and being able to cover at least their basic needs without constantly relying on supplemental funds from their families. However, as both Dylan and Juan explained, such benefits did not come without costs: in the mess hall (as in most of the other better-paid positions) the shifts were much longer, more grueling, and often dangerous. Discipline in the workplace was also more tightly enforced: when working at the mess hall or in other positions that had a critical role in facility maintenance, there was no equivalent to "just sweep and look busy," which was how Dylan described his responsibilities as a porter. Those on assignment to the mess hall reported doing twelve-hour shifts with little time to rest. "Mess hall will push you hard," as Jim put it. Porters knew that COs did not care whether they were doing their jobs properly, and so they could get away with neglecting to properly clean the cells and bathrooms, but the COs knew much bigger trouble could be in store if a meal was not served on time.

Industry

The reported revenue for Corcraft, the New York correctional industries program, in FY2020-21 was $42 million, with almost $30 million in sheer profit.[9] In the previous three fiscal years, Corcraft made a total of $152 million in profit.[10] These returns go into the state general fund, financing everyday operations in New York.

Some of our interviewees recounted seeking out Corcraft jobs during their incarceration. The hourly wages were still insultingly low, but generally much higher than any other prison assignment. With bonuses—which doubled the pay if you hit the production quotas—some reported making almost $1 per hour, or about $100 per month. This would be just enough for a full commissary buy every other week. For those with little or no financial support from the outside—or those who were not cut out for hustling—an industry job assignment was the most effective way of trying to make ends meet inside prison.

And yet, despite these higher wages, it was Corcraft work that formerly incarcerated New Yorkers most frequently associated with slavery in the stories they told us about prison labor. After reporting that his earnings topped $100 per month—a wage that "makes you rich in prison"—Jim was quick to add that "it was still slave labor." He pointed out that an income of "$100 or even $200 a month, when you don't have nothing, is a lot of money. But then just look at how much money New York State makes off license plates. So even though they are paying one schmuck $200, if he is lucky, they are making thousands."

When asked what was different about the Corcraft workplace, several mentioned the harsher discipline and tighter surveillance that they experienced. Nate Blakely, who had worked as a porter, a clerk, and in lawn maintenance during his five years, reported that none of these assignments were anywhere near as arduous as toiling in Eastern's Corcraft mattress shop:

> You tend to work more hours than you would on other jobs. It can be exhausting at times, especially if they feel that you aren't keeping up with their demand of what needs to be done. You know they will wake you up long before, so you will get up early, and go back to your cell late. If you refuse to work within the industry program, that department takes it very seriously. That's an example of something within the system they tend not to play with, because it's money.

Jim had a similar observation to share about his time working for Corcraft at Clinton:

> [In industry], you are not sitting around. If you work in Lawns & Grounds, you might work for maybe 15, 20 minutes, hang out, smoke a cigarette, bullshit, and just walk around the facility. You do whatever the hell you want to do, because basically you're not doing anything.

In industry, you're either working a machine, or you're putting stuff together, so there's no lollygagging. They have got a quota, and if you are not making it, you are not getting your bonus.

Nate said that the pressure to work harder and to maximize profits would sometimes mean that people were forced to work in hazardous conditions, with little in the way of protection for their personal safety:

In Eastern's mattress shop, they would use a hot wire cutter to cut foam. You are cutting with something hot, so obviously smoke billows up, and you can breathe that stuff in. So they provided what they felt was an appropriate respirator, meaning one of those construction paper masks. But when it comes to that particular kind of vapor, you are supposed to use an actual respirator that actually filters everything out. And they didn't provide it, they felt it was too costly. Oftentimes, they don't provide the right gloves, cut-proof gloves, safety glasses, or steel-toe boots.

Even more than the tighter discipline and the risky conditions, the Corcraft jobs got singled out because incarcerated workers could so clearly put a finger on their own exploitation. For sure, people on maintenance assignments—cleaning, cooking, shoveling snow for a few cents per hour—are also being openly exploited by the prison system, since the same work would cost DOCCS many times more if performed by non-incarcerated staff. Yet Corcraft made the naked extraction of profit so much more palpable. People knew that the desks they were manufacturing were being sold for several hundred dollars each, while they were only being paid cents per hour.

Probably because Corcraft encapsulated the exploitation of prison labor best while also evoking the historical and moral ties with slavery, derogatory stories about the state-owned company seem to circulate widely inside New York prisons, especially among those who never set foot in its shops. Many of our interviewees would routinely bring up how Corcraft made handsome profits on the back of its incarcerated workforce. Indeed, analysis of Corcraft's economy was such a staple feature of prison gossip and folklore that it was not uncommon for people to greatly exaggerate the company's profits or the power of the Division of Correctional Industry within the prison system. Jim, for instance, was convinced that Corcraft was traded on the stock market—likely confusing it with CoreCivic, the world's largest private prison company. His former cellmate Paul believed that Corcraft managed and set the wages for all prison job assignments, including maintenance and administrative positions.

The fact that these and other misconceptions sounded credible to many inside the prison tells us something about Corcraft's central role in the New York carceral labor regime. Though it employs less than one tenth of the state's incarcerated workforce (less than 2,000 by some estimates),[11] the company is a powerful symbol of the dynamics of exploitation that operates throughout the system.

The Violence Behind the Labor

Our interviewees had their reasons for seeking out specific prison job assignments and avoiding others. Some were after higher wages in the industry program, while others were attracted by the perks of working in the mess hall or the laundry. But a few confessed that they worked just to kill time or to seize an opportunity to get out of their cells. Whatever their motivation, no one doubted that coercion underpinned the entire system and made it function. While people could try their best to avoid an undesirable job, refusing an assignment was not an option. The consequences of refusing to work ranged from losing commissary and other privileges to being placed in solitary confinement. And if you challenged the guards' authority long enough or with the wrong attitude, then a beating would surely be coming your way, especially in facilities like Attica or Clinton, which were known for rigid and often vicious enforcement of the rules.

Mark Dollimore learned that lesson right when he turned 18 years old. In the fall of 2013, he arrived at Upstate, a maximum security facility just a few miles from the Canadian border. There, he was assigned to work as a porter, bringing food trays to people in the Special Housing Unit (SHU). "They didn't have any educational programs in the facility, they didn't have nothing but work for you," he recalled. "And, you know, I had just turned 18, so this is a time where it is right for growth, the things you do in that time will determine who you are. And I was like, why do we have to be working here while I could be learning something that could benefit me?"

Still, Mark knew better than to turn down that assignment, since most of the cell occupants to whom he was delivering trays were in there for refusing to work themselves:

> When I was on my way up there on the bus, there was people with me who were going to the SHU. So they were people who had been around prisons for 10, 12, 15 years, and they are telling me: "Listen, you get there, try to get this job, this is a better job. They are probably going to stick you in the mess hall or make you a porter, but if you refuse, you are gonna get 30 days in the SHU." And, then, right after they told me that, I saw it happening.

Built in 1998 as the first supermax facility in the state, Upstate was specifically designated for solitary confinement. While a few hundred prisoners like Mark were sent there to work maintenance jobs, most were in Upstate as punishment for "violent or disruptive behavior" which could include assignment refusal:

> People were coming from [facilities] downstate all the time, they refused to work and they were sent to the SHU. So, you go to the SHU for 30 days, and when you come back out they send you back to your old facility, and if you refuse again, they send you back. Like that cycle happens about three times, so you'll end up in a SHU for 90 to 120 days. That's assuming you don't get write ups while you're in the SHU.

In solitary confinement, violence from COs was a routine part of the equation. "Especially in a SHU," he explained, "people get assaulted all the time. You'll hear the porters coming back talking about how they heard a guy in his cell screaming, and they beat up a guy because he wouldn't give his tray back, or because he was complaining that he didn't get a tray."

Elijah Trudeau, who had served twelve years in New York prisons before coming home to Brooklyn in the spring of 2022, confirmed Mark's account about being forced to labor under pain of solitary confinement, which is considered by the UN to be a form of psychological torture.[12] The punishment for turning down an assignment, he noted, often depended on which CO was on duty and on the victim's reputation for disobedience. "They might begin by giving you a ticket," he explained, "or suspending some 'privileges' such as commissary or rec time, but locking you up in your cell for the entire day was the usual next step." Those who were seen as "repeat offenders" would get thrown in solitary in places such as Upstate or would be assaulted by COs. As he put it euphemistically, "some guards like to demonstrate their authority in different ways." Elijah saw this happening often enough that he got "desensitized" to the omnipresent violence. "That's what you have to do, for your own sake," he reported, "just to get through the times, like you have to normalize some of the stuff that's going on, otherwise you'll be in there in a heap of emotions and it'll make your time harder."

Violence wasn't just present in forcing people to work: it was also a crucial tool of discipline in the workplace itself. Every direct order issued on the job was backed by the CO's absolute authority over the workers. Several interviewees told us that not all guards were the same, and that they had experienced reasonable supervisors on their job assignments who treated them "as human beings." But no one could doubt that an order from even the most congenial CO was ultimately backed up by the threat of potential violence. Such orders might involve performing dangerous tasks, or pressure to come to work while sick, or even while mourning the loss of a loved one. Theresa witnessed the latter while working in the mess hall at Taconic, when the CO in charge ordered one of her co-workers to "get out of her cell" and to come to work the day after losing her mother, even though someone else had offered to cover her shift. When something like that happens, incarcerated workers have no recourse. Nate described the futility of filing a complaint through the "inmate grievance system":

> I have seen pushbacks occur, but I have never seen a successful one. I have seen people demanding protective gear, or pushing back against abusive correctional officers, who treated them like slaves. But we are talking about a system that protects the individuals who work there before anything. While working for Corcraft, I have never seen an abusive staff member who got disciplined,

or removed. But I have seen instances where COs who didn't engage in that behavior, who did not see themselves as slave masters, would say something to abusive correctional staff. And they ended up being reprised for their conduct, rather than the abusive ones.

On the Side

When we asked about their experiences with work, our interviewees were encouraged to describe not only their formal job assignments but also the various activities they performed in the prison informal economy. Only a handful of people reported receiving enough financial support from their families to meet all their basic needs during incarceration. Everybody else needed to find a hustle in addition to their jobs. For the majority, this did not come as much of a culture shock: growing up in segregated and impoverished urban neighborhoods, most had learned at a young age that formal employment was rarely a pathway to financial security, or even survival for that matter.

Elijah, for instance, recounted taking up a number of "random jobs" in his youth. He did not have much trouble finding employment in East Brooklyn, where he lived with his family, but almost every position he could find was temporary and badly paid. Thus, while he aspired to "transition out of the drug trade," he ended up staying involved throughout most of his youth. Once he arrived at Wallkill, Elijah quickly realized that the "hustle mentality" he had learned in the street was going to serve him well there, too. "There is a whole other economy that's happening," he explained, "among the inmates themselves. To be honest with you, if you're not in a facility that offers any kind of industrial work, then survival solely based on what the prison has to offer is not really survival at all." Elijah ended up selling drugs again and gambling on the side in order to make a living at Wallkill, then in

Eastern. But he also developed a reputation as a writer, and so fellow prisoners started hiring him to help them with their letters—and even school assignments—in exchange for a small fee.

Unlike Elijah, Mark made a point of staying away from the risks and violence associated with trading contraband. Instead, he did a bit of everything—from tailoring clothes to selling birthday cards. While at Franklin, he even had a small bakery operation, with donuts, ginger and banana cakes as his best-selling goods. Mark witnessed people providing all sorts of services and goods inside prisons:

> There were some phenomenal hustlers in there. People sold t-shirts they bought from outside, others were knitting hats, gloves, and scarves, and they sold them. People drew artwork, like I used to get portraits drawn up of people and send them home for $25, $30, I mean like phenomenal portraits. People did Paper Mache, you could get cards drawn up, some even played 1-on-1 basketball for money.

The hustles listed by Mark were just a few of the many we heard about in our interviews: people cooked meals, washed clothes, cleaned and even repainted other people's cells, in exchange for food, cigarettes, or stamps. They also bartered and traded pretty much anything they could put their hands on, including both goods they received from outside and those they were able to skim off the prison. The most successful traders were sometimes able to set up and operate "inmate stores" from their cells. Often referred to as "juggle men," the store owners let people borrow cigarettes, food, and other commissary items, which they would then have to return with interest (usually double the amount) at the next commissary cycle. If (as was common) their financial support from the outside dried up, they could rely on making enough of a profit from the store to be able to regularly shop at the commissary.

Nearly all these hustles are considered violations of the prison disciplinary code which forbids individuals from selling, exchanging, or even gifting their possessions. Yet such activities have a vital role in the daily life of the prison. If they were to suddenly cease, the institution would not have enough resources to feed, clothe, and care for its population. When he was smuggling food out of Eastern's kitchens, for instance, Julio was not only earning some additional income for himself, he was also liberating institutional goods for collective use and therefore injecting additional resources into a communal economy that was starved of them. For some of Julio's customers, the cans of beans, apples, chickens, and other items that he extracted from the mess hall pantry made all the difference in staying healthy and resilient. For those who received no outside support and could not afford to shop at commissary, trading with people like Julio was their only chance of getting extra food in exchange for goods or services such as cooking or cleaning up after a meal. From the perspective of collective survival, many of the other hustles had a similar social function as Julio's trade—namely augmenting, stretching, and redistributing the scarce resources available to the general population.

After four decades of budget cuts and austerity-driven reforms, it is hard to imagine how prison facilities could stay afloat if not for all the ingenuity and tireless labor—both formal and informal—of the incarcerated. Several of our interviewees had come to the same conclusion about the social function of the informal economy and they believed that all but a few COs had realized this fact as well. That is why, they observed, regulations against trading and bartering were very rarely enforced. Julio, for instance, said that most of the mess hall guards knew very well what he was up to, but they decided to let it slide: "Nine times out of ten you just tell the officer that the food was for you and they are going to let you go, if you are not a troublemaker."

That said, overzealous COs would occasionally ticket people for gifting away some of their food or would shut down a store. Julio himself was eventually kicked out of the mess hall. However, the more experienced COs knew better than to get involved in that kind of micro-management. The institution itself had a vested interest in preserving those practices. If they were to close down all the stores and stop all the informal trading, then they would end up with much bigger troubles on their hands.

The Hoe Squad

Of the four states where we conducted interviews, Texas stands out for the pride its prison administrators take in being "tough" and committed to clinical, economic efficiency though profit-seeking policies of austerity.[13] Even when civil pressure mounted to relax harsh sentencing laws in 2007, the state asserted its fiscal conservatism through launching its Right On Crime campaign.[14] Yet Texas's efforts to turn its prisons and jails into self-sustaining institutions have generally not been successful. As in other states, especially in the South, its lawmakers have been reluctant to reduce prison beds or lay off guards and other staff, but are quick to cut spending for basic services inside prisons and jails.[15] For instance, when faced with a budget shortfall in 2011, the legislature eliminated lunch for some prisoners on weekends. "If they don't like the menu, don't come there in the first place," said State Senator John Whitmire, a Houston Democrat who pushed the measure.[16] The same year, the legislature also drastically cut education programs in state prisons, slicing their budget by over 25 percent.[17] To further reduce spending, Texas Department of Criminal Justice (TDCJ) also ramped up its agricultural operations, putting prisoners at work without pay to grow and harvest their own food. While this push towards food autarchy did not result in any meaningful savings for the public (with TDCJ's operating budget remaining well over $3 billion per years between 2010 and 2015[18]), it still helped officials look good to their hard-right electoral constituencies. After all, nothing conveys toughness and frugality like the spectacle of prisoners toiling without pay to feed themselves and their peers, albeit with substandard rations.

Agricultural labor played a central role in nearly all the conversations we had with formerly incarcerated men and women in the state. When asked about their experiences with prison work, most of them would begin by telling us about the months, and sometimes years that they spent picking up cabbage heads or pulling weeds in facilities with large farms. Working in the "hoe squads" of Texas opened people's eyes to the brutal coercion undergirding the entire labor system. As elsewhere, the threat of violence was omnipresent for those assigned to maintenance jobs or to the private industry sector, but nowhere was it deployed quite as unabashedly—and as routinely—as in the fields.

TDCJ makes sure that every incarcerated person in the state learns that lesson early on in their sentence. While incarcerated New Yorkers start their employment careers in custodial maintenance as porters on "easy street," the first and most arduous assignment for most prisoners in the Lone Star State is a stint on the hoe squad. Donna Fairchild, one of the first Texans we interviewed in the Fall of 2022, described what it had been like for her to start working in the fields at the Dr. Lane Murray Unit, one of five women's facilities clustered around the town of Gatesville in Central Texas. Just a few weeks after being sentenced to serve ten years in state prisons, Donna appeared before her facility's Unit Classification Committee. One of the officers there told her, "you look young enough and healthy enough, we are going to put you in the fields." Donna, who was in her early thirties at the time, had worked in human resources before getting arrested and had little experience with manual labor, let alone agricultural work. Still, she was informed that work would start at 6am the following day. For the next 18 months, she was one of approximately 200 prisoners assigned to work in one of six hoe squads at her facility.

Donna, who is white, described the field labor that she performed as "plantation work." Led by armed officers on horseback, squads went out every day from 6:00 am to 11:00 am, and then again between 12:00 pm and 4:00 pm. While in the fields, there was little to no downtime, and discipline was tightly enforced. On her first field assignment, she was pulling weeds by hand for hours at a time in the heat of a Texas summer. There were specific rules about how that task should be performed: "you were supposed to stand up and bend at the waist, you could not squat, and you could not stop. Anything longer than a short pause to stretch your back, and you could be in trouble." If an officer thought you were stretching for too long, working too slowly, or failed to complete your work assignment for the day, they could write you up. In a squad of about 30 workers, Donna estimated that at least three or four people would get disciplinary cases every day. Punishment for such infractions usually involved a 30-day suspension of phone or recreation rights. If you racked up three of those, this was considered a major infraction. For one of these infractions, Donna lost her contact visits for four months.

Rules about time-wasting even extended to using the bathroom. For the entire time that she was working in the hoe squad, relieving herself while on the job was seen by officers as a privilege and not as a basic right:

> So, let me explain how the bathrooms worked. When the tractor [with porta-potties] comes, the field boss will say, from horseback, "Deuce it up." And that means stop what we're doing in the field and come to the front and get in lines of two. But they are only going to choose

four or five people to go . . . They can't monitor the fields and the bathrooms at the same time, and they are not going to waste the time of everybody not working for everyone to get a chance to go in the restroom.

While disciplinary rules were strictly enforced, Donna said that officers seemed more than happy to cut corners when it came to regulations to protect the safety and health of incarcerated workers. Her first summer on the job, Donna found herself picking corn with temperatures rising to more than 100 degrees. In the winter, her squad was often forced to go out in freezing weather:

> TDCJ has a policy that inmates don't work outside if it's below freezing. Texas inmates aren't provided with things to keep them warm, because we just don't have that many cold months, right? We have a jacket, it's very lightweight. So we were at the back gate, and it was all six squads lined up, and we heard on the radio, the prison would do a temperature check every half hour and it would come across the officers' radios, and we heard that it was 31 degrees. And the ladies were cheering, like we were fixing to turn around. We were lined up at the back gate to go out to work. The sun was not even up yet, and we were thrilled. But the lieutenant that was in charge said, "I didn't hear a thing." That was my first experience in there, and I remember thinking, "They don't really care what happens to me."

Several of our interviewees confirmed Donna's account of how discipline was meted out on Texas hoe squads. Simone Washington, for instance, who served more than 10 years in Texas state prisons, worked in the fields around Lane Murray Unit between 2012 and 2013. Like Donna, the hoe squad was her very first job assignment, despite having no prior experience of working outdoors:

> My body went through such trauma that first couple of days that I was not prepared for. I couldn't even walk or bend or sit because on the hoe squad it's a lot of farming, and you're not allowed to stoop down. You have to be bent over for four to six hours picking weeds, or planting, or weeding, or stepping in pig shit, cutting down trees, baling hay.

During one particularly hot summer spell, she reported, it was only after several people passed out in the fields that the field boss agreed to establish an additional water break. And on the job, pretty much any deviation from regulations was cause for an officer to write you up:

> The bosses, they're not nice, man. To them we're all bitches and hoes. There's no talking, no eating, nothing. Sometimes we would sneak little stuff out there to eat. And if they catch you with it, it's a case. Or, say you and me are walking two by two, you are my deuce, but you are not paying attention, you are not in sync with me. You get an out-of-place case, and I get one too. That sucked. We could be working, four-stepping, my breast would be on your back, your crotch would be on my tail. We'd be literally working, don't bend over because I'm gonna be with my butt in your crotch. So we'd have to be straight and hitting an aggie [fellow field worker] in sync. Everybody. And if not, you get a case.

Field labor is almost always the first assignment for incarcerated men, too, said Damien, who was nineteen years old in the late

1990s when he arrived at the Dolphe Briscoe Unit, which was 70 miles south of San Antonio. "It was an initiation to slave labor," he explained, talking about his early months on the hoe squad. Anyone who was not physically fit had a hard time keeping up, and those who lagged behind risked being punished, not just by field bosses but by other workers too:

> You would have guys on the line saying to you: "you're not cutting, you're not chopping your grass, you're making us look bad." And those things would lead to fights out there in the fields. Sometimes correctional officers would encourage that. They would let that happen, and not intervene when fights broke up.

Juan, whom we interviewed in the summer of 2023, estimated that he had worked nearly 50,000 unpaid hours on behalf of TDCJ during three different bids. Many of these hours were spent in the fields or doing other demanding physical labor. The last time Juan was assigned to work on the hoe squad was in 2008, after being transferred to the Ramsey Unit. He was almost 50 years old and a few months short of being released. Like Damien, he also regularly witnessed field bosses inciting fights among prisoners to enforce collective discipline or simply for their own amusement. Chantal, who had barely turned 18 when she received a sixteen-year sentence, reported the same tactics while she worked alongside Donna at the Lane Murray Unit:

> I've seen people use the restroom on themselves because the officers refused to let them use the restroom. They would say: "Oh, this offender is walking too slowly and holding the line up." Or: "This offender didn't cover all their potatoes, or didn't hoe fast enough, or didn't do something the way that the officer wanted it, so everybody else

had to suffer for it. So, no, you're not getting that water break, or, no, you're not getting the restroom break because such-and-such didn't do this." So, now everybody's mad at that one person, and you've basically put a target on this person's back, because they didn't do something to your liking. And then there goes a fight. So, they'll sit there and start a fight. Then after the fight, they will lock you up. A lot of the fights out there were caused by officers starting it.

In Texas prison fields, violence—or the threat of violence—is routinely deployed to drive productivity. Donna, Simone, Damien and others had seen plenty of that. The profit motive, however, did not come close to explaining the callous cruelty of field bosses. It did not explain the gratuitous punishments and the everyday indignities to which workers were subjected. The same officers who didn't seem to think there was enough time for everybody to take a bathroom break did not hesitate to order entire squads to complete the most futile tasks, just to make a point about their absolute authority. Donna, for instance, described one occasion when her squad was ordered to spend an entire day moving rocks across hilly terrain around Gatesville. The day before, several members of her unit had submitted formal grievances against their field boss, and that was his vengeful way of showing them who was in charge:

> Once all those grievances came in, we got punished as a unit. We had to go to what we called "the mountains," the big rolling hills around Gatesville. So, we are on one side of the mountain and there is a pile of rocks, or I should say boulders, because it's something that you're picking up with your whole body and holding close to you because it's so heavy. And the officer is having us haul these boulders up on one side of the mountain and

pile them up. And then you have to run down the other side of the mountain, go back, and pick up another boulder. And when they all got to the top of the mountain, he had us pick them up from the top, and run them back to the hill. And then he saw that some of us were moving quicker, so he's like: "if you lap somebody, you can stop." So, I ended up lapping somebody, and he has me at the top of the mountain with him. While I was up there, he was telling me, "that's one of the bitches that wrote the grievance." So that was our punishment.

Damien and Jorge were also regularly ordered to perform "make-work," such as pulling weeds or digging up tree stumps in untended fields. In all those instances, correctional officers didn't seem particularly concerned with productivity. Damien thought that was no mistake, but was instead a deliberate punitive tactic by his supervisors. When he was working on the hoe squad, he said nothing made him feel quite as helpless and humiliated as being forced to perform taxing but utterly useless labor. That lesson stuck with him for the rest of his incarceration.

The strip searches to which women were subjected twice a day were another example of the "degradation ceremonies" which punctuated their working lives.[19] Simone described how most women looked "shell-shocked" after the first time they were forced to go through such searches. As with the futile make-work tasks, it was clear to them that the point of strip searches had nothing to do with security but was all about their public mortification.

On these prison farms, carceral violence is deployed with an especially cruel kind of candor. Field bosses use violence to drive productivity, but also as a rite of initiation—a way of conditioning new prisoners to the discipline they will face in facilities over the course of their sentence. And even as Donna,

Simone, Damien and others moved to their next job assignments, they knew that the fields were never far away: a small disciplinary infraction, or just getting on the wrong side of a correctional officer, was often enough to land someone right back on the hoe squad.

Leaving The Fields

According to Simone, most of the prisoners at the Dr. Lane Murray Unit spent between 12 and 18 months on the hoe squad before moving to a new job. Like most prison rules, however, there were always exceptions. No matter how many times they requested a transfer, some people could not get a new assignment. Often, transfer refusal was the punishment for crossing a lieutenant, or for racking up too many disciplinary tickets. But in some cases, nobody seemed to know why transfers were being denied. Simone had witnessed how some would go as far as injuring themselves in order to get out of field work:

> I have seen people getting chemical burns, or breaking a wrist or a foot, just not to work [on the hoe squad]. They'll slam their wrist or their ankles in their lockboxes or break them with the shower brush. Have your home girl hit your ankle two, three, four times. It's painful, but they get off whatever job duty they have for about six months, until you had to break something else.

That was the decision Chantal faced. As an "outspoken person," Chantal got in trouble with several officers on the hoe squad, and she figured her lieutenant was not going to let her off the squad easily. After several years in the fields, she had reached her breaking point:

In my head I was like: "I'm never gonna go home, I'm never gonna make it out of here if I don't get off the hoe squad." Because I'm getting written up every day. I don't have no privileges. I can't have a contact visit. They were preventing me from doing stuff. I mean, this was something I needed for my mental state.

So Chantal did what she saw other women doing before her: she asked a friend to slam her finger in a locker enough times that she broke it. That got her transferred to the laundry, an assignment that she was able to keep even after her finger healed.

Simone was lucky not to have to go to the same lengths. When she put in her transfer request after about a year on the hoe squad, the lieutenant agreed to "release" her. While that was a relief, there were still many undesirable assignments she wanted to avoid, starting with the kitchen, where people worked 10-hour shifts preparing thousands of meals each day. Donna, who did end up there, confirmed Simone's fears. While the bosses there were "less harsh" than the ones in the fields, and while there was a little bit of downtime here and there to socialize with other workers, working conditions were not that much better than in the fields. "I hated being inside that dish room in the summer," she recalled. "It's a closed dish room with two big, huge, industrial dishwashers, and it's hot and humid. There is no air conditioning, so it was miserable, miserable."

Simone was glad when she heard that she was being trans-ferred to the commissary room. She ended up working there for the next four years, unloading 18-wheelers that were deliv-ering commissary products to the facility. As far as prison jobs go, that was a good one, she explained. Officers treated work-ers there "right," or at least "normal," especially when compared to what she had experienced in the fields: "they treated us as human beings, for the most part." While she wasn't getting paid there either, she could at least get some lunch leftovers from the officers' refrigerator every once in a while. Even so, the job didn't come without its risks. Officers still held absolute authority to do as they pleased with their workers. Less than a year into the job, Simone got injured while unloading a truck: she was trying to pull a pallet off the truck by herself, lost her balance, and hurt her ankle and foot. When she reported that to the officer, she got a case for performing an "unsafe act." After that, she knew better. "Whenever stuff like this happens," she explained, "when you get cut, or you fall down, you just don't tell nobody. You don't report it, don't go to medical. You eat it. Because if you report it, you get a case."

While both Simone and Donna felt fortunate to get off the hoe squad, neither of them ever got to the point of earning wages for the labor that they performed on behalf of the Texas prison system. In Texas, the only paid assignments are those for private company contracts through the Prison Industry Enhancement (PIE) Certification Program, and those positions are few and far between. In 2019, less than 1 percent of the incarcerated population in the state participated in that program.[20] Donna and Simone's applications to join the PIE program were repeatedly denied, and so the two women had to find other ways to cover their basic needs. Donna was able to get some regular financial support from her family, while Simone turned her hand at a variety of prison hustles, from washing clothes to cooking for others, to even writing letters to single men on the outside in exchange for money.

Damien was one of the few people we interviewed in Texas who worked for a wage while under TDCJ's custody. Approximately five months after leaving the hoe squad, corrections officers woke him up in the middle of the night to tell him that he was "catching the chain," which is what both prisoners and guards call the prison bus:

> We called it the chain because you are shackled on the
> bus with everyone else. I had no idea about where I was
> going, and why. The bus stopped by several units, pick-
> ing up additional inmates along the way, and we even-
> tually landed in Huntsville, in what's called the Walls
> Unit, which is like a central classification unit. And then
> I ended up going from Huntsville to Lockhart, which
> is about 30 miles southeast of Austin. And I still didn't
> know what it was until I started talking to other inmates
> and realized that this was a private prison run by Wack-
> enhut, which later became The Geo Group.

To this day Damien does not know why he was transferred, but
that move came with a couple of perks: the private facility had
air conditioning and it participated in the PIE program, allowing private companies to employ incarcerated workers. It took
Damien two years of unpaid jobs in maintenance at Lockhart
to work his way up to a paid position with an Austin-based tech
company. He told us there was a lot to like about that job: there
was a wage, for a start, although after what TDCJ garnished for
room and board, Damien was only getting about $2 per hour.[21]
He was also acquiring new skills rather than wasting time performing futile tasks in the fields. As much as he appreciated
that, it was not long before he realized that even though $2 per
hour was much more than what any of his incarcerated peers
were making, the company was making millions of dollars selling the circuit boards he was assembling to large corporations
such as Dell and IBM. Workers performing those same tasks
on the outside were earning many times his wage. "The peak of
the hypocrisy," Damien added, was that those same tech companies that were eager to employ him at Lockhart, wouldn't
even call him for an interview once he came home in 1998,
despite the abundance of jobs during the Austin tech boom.

After a couple of failed attempts, his caseworker bluntly let him know that "those spaces are just not going to hire you." A few days later, Damien got a job doing data entry for a local staffing agency.

The Paradox of Forced Idleness

Starting in the early 1980s, legislators and correctional administrators in Alabama were facing similar budgetary pressures as their colleagues in New York and Texas. Their recipe for fixing the problem wasn't particularly original. While the Department of Corrections operating budget kept growing year over year—nearly doubling between 2010 and 2020[22]—austerity cuts targeted basic services for the incarcerated population, including food services and healthcare.[23] What was different about Alabama was the lengths to which officials were willing to go to make their overgrown prison system look cheaper. As in other Deep South states,[24] the result has been widespread violence and a humanitarian crisis inside prisons and jails.

Several of the people we interviewed on our field visits had spent decades in the state prison system because they were convicted under Alabama's Habitual Offender Law.[25] Passed in 1977, at the dawn of the tough-on-crime era, the law mandates longer sentences each time someone commits a felony, regardless of the time between offenses. Long-timers like Liam Braxton, who was paroled only recently, still remembered what it was like to work in Alabama's fields in the late 1970s. When he first arrived at Draper Correctional Facility at age eighteen, Liam experienced the same mix of disciplinary and sadistic violence described by many of our Texan interviewees. While the hoe squad was first and foremost a punitive assignment, back then Alabama DOC was still hoping to turn a profit from its farmlands. Supervisors behaved accordingly:

When you first get to prison, they are going to put you on the farm, most likely. Then you can move up, from there you might get an institutional job working in the infirmary, or in the laundry, the kitchen, or something like that. We used to go out on the farm and pick cucumbers, and pick potatoes, and cotton too. An officer would take out 15, 20 guys, and he'd ride a horse while you were working in the fields. If you refused to work, they put you in lock up. Back then, they also had what they called a hitching bar: they would handcuff you to the bar outside until that evening, and then let you go back.

By the time Don arrived at Draper—some 20 years after Liam—Alabama DOC had given up all hopes of turning a profit from its farms. Some of the lands had been sold and the remaining ones were largely left unattended. People coming into Draper were still assigned to 90 days in the fields, but—as Don explained—it wasn't much of a farm anymore: "during all the time I was there, I didn't see any crops, it was just make-work." With the profit motive gone, delivering harsher punishment was the only reason to force people to work on hoe squads:

A horse-mounted officer would walk you all the way out in the field. Once you got out there, they literally lined you up in a row all the way down. And then you just take the hoe and knock it down to the dirt. And just keep going backwards until they'd say stop. And then you'd move to another section and do it again, and that was what you did for eight hours. That was pretty much it. There was no real purpose, the grass was gonna grow back anyway. You would still get in trouble if you didn't do the work, even if we weren't really doing anything.

It wasn't just the farm work that was pointless. By the early 1990s, Alabama prisons had become both overcrowded and understaffed,[26] leading to a state of almost permanent lock-down for prisoners, as the few remaining officers manning facilities gave up on running programs, including most of the labor ones. That resulted in a paradoxical combination of forced idleness and forced work. After being transferred from Saint Clair to Donaldson Correctional Facility early 1990s, Liam had a hard time getting assigned to just about any job. Those who didn't work had no other option but spending most of the day locked in the barracks style dorm. He described how being locked down all day in a closed environment like that, "you have a lot of tension, a lot of violence. There were a lot of fights, a lot of stabbings and killings, I just wanted to get away from that." Even when violence wasn't rampant, Robert said that doing nothing all day was enough to "deteriorate" you. As he put it, "Boredom will run you crazy in prison, you know, the monotony of doing the same thing every day."

When Robert first arrived at Donaldson in 1988, jobs were already hard to come by. Things only got worse over the next two decades that he spent in Alabama state prisons. It got so bad that people were competing for—and fighting over—unpaid work assignments, just to have something to do. Officers were quick to exploit that labor surplus and would recruit a few prisoners as their personal "runners" in exchange for cigarettes or leftovers from their meals. At some point, Robert said, he got so desperate to get away from his dorm that he accepted the role of runner for one of the officers before finally being able to get a job at the prison infirmary.

While getting a job, even if unpaid, was described as a privilege of sorts by many of those who had spent time in Alabama prisons, that didn't mean that work conditions were any better or that people could freely leave their assignments. Marty Brown, a native of Lowndes County, observed the same odd mix of compulsory labor and chronic idleness. When he arrived at Donaldson, he could easily avoid getting any job, since there were not nearly enough to go around. Yet, once he was assigned to one, he found that it was not possible to quit. "Basically, you have a choice not to work," he reported, "but if you started working and then you didn't go to work, you would get written up on disciplinary, which hurts your visitation and phone privileges, or worse."

Prisons like Draper were already in bad physical shape when Liam first arrived there in the late 1970s. Twenty years later, under the concurrent pressures of overcrowding and underfunding, they were falling apart. Liam witnessed the progressive deterioration of prisoners' life conditions during his 40-year sentence, from food services to the crumbling infrastructure. At Donaldson, where he spent the last 25 years of his sentence (and which housed approximately 1500 people), plumbing repairs had been neglected for so long that bathrooms were barely working: "You got two or three sinks working out of eight or nine, for an entire block. The showers are constantly running over because the drains are clogged up, messing folks' feet up, and so they ended up putting portable showers in the block, and a lot of times you ain't gonna get hot water."

Things were even worse in the housing blocks, where as many as 200 people lived in dorms designed to accommodate half that number. "Conditions were inhumane, for real," according to Robert, who acknowledged that it was hard for him to figure out whether this living hell was due to lack of funding or a result of the belief, ingrained in the Deep South, that wretched living conditions should be part of criminal punishment:

> They run these prisons like modern day plantations. We had people who were going to help us build a library and everything, pushing for even a computer room, but they

kept blocking it. Let's say, I could make a phone call now to the University of Alabama and offer to have a book drive. Alabama won't take your books. They're not concerned about you being educated, or about the amount of guys that should be in mental health classes. You've got 1,500 or 1,700 guys in a prison, and they have only spots for 50 of them in mental health classes each year. I was talking to a guy the other day, asking about what he'd been doing and stuff, and does he have his G.E.D. He said, "Nah, they wouldn't let me take the G.E.D." They honestly wouldn't let this guy take a G.E.D. class. That should be against the law.

In such circumstances, just staying fed and healthy was a constant challenge. With the state progressively foregoing its responsibilities to maintain its carceral infrastructure and to care for the general population, it was up to prisoners to make repairs and to maintain essential services. In New York, we found that prisoners' informal labor has increasingly been filling the gaps left by dwindling state provisions, but in Alabama it has all but replaced the responsibilities of the state.

In recent years, several Alabama sheriffs made headlines for pocketing unspent money from their jails' food budgets. Over time, one of them was able to save enough off the $1.75 per day officially allocated to feed each inmate to buy a $740,000 beach house.[27] Another sheriff invested $150,000 in a used-car dealership from the proceeds.[28] Marty, who worked in the kitchen at Donaldson in the early 2000s, reported that—even when there was no skimming going on—just witnessing how the food was prepared was enough to convince him to avoid mess hall meals at all costs. Instead, he took advantage of his position in the kitchen to steal whatever ingredients he could get, bringing them back to the housing unit to cook his own meals or sell them to others. Everyone we encountered was involved in similar exchanges, even more than in New York. As Robert explained, most of the officers who ended up staying on the job for more than a few months, despite the low wages and unsafe work conditions, did so because they had found lucrative hustles, usually involving dealing drugs or smuggling phones into the prison. According to Don, approximately half of the officers working at Draper in the early 2000s were involved in some illegal scheme to generate extra income. While the active participation of COs in the drug trade and other illicit activities is certainly not exclusive to Alabama, the extent of their involvement seems to set the state apart.

In addition to hustling to stay afloat, long-timers like Robert and Liam would also take it upon themselves to provide other essential services to their peers, such as mental health support and other educational programs. "Because the prison ain't trying to rehabilitate you," Liam said, "you have to try to do it yourself." He ran several formal and informal therapeutic groups during his time, trying to motivate his peers to remain active, to read the news, and to stay connected with the outside world. Similarly, while officially working as a barber at St. Clair, Robert was also doubling up as a therapist of sort for many fellow prisoners, who had no access to mental health services:

> Being a barber is like being a therapist. Guys, they'll give you their stories. And then when I'm cutting their hair, I'm like, "Oh, how did you get this wound? How did you get it? Who tried to cut you around the neck?" And so, you just see a lot of that. [Years later] I was back in the same dorm where I used to cut hair, and the guy behind me said: "Man, you don't remember me? You taught me how to do this, how do to that." A few weeks after I walked into chow, and I heard these two guys talking.

"Man, when you come in, don't be so trusting, just have little circles around you, don't let guys into your environment because not everybody is your friend." And then he said: "You know who taught me that? That dude right behind me." I didn't remember that, and so, it just surprised me how much the guys would listen to what I said while I was cutting hair.

The chronic lack of officers and, more generally, the diminishing capacity on the part of the state to effectively manage and govern its correctional facilities, meant that prisoners increasingly had to take personal safety into their own hands. When he first arrived at Draper in 2005, Don was quick to figure out that he could not rely on the guards to ensure his safety:

I never felt just completely safe. You've just always got to be aware of your surroundings, so I pretty much always kept my head on a swivel. The best thing you could do was always try to see trouble coming. If something was about to happen, you need to be aware of it before it just happened. That's what Draper was like. You know the way it is set up, there are no single cells there, it's giant concrete-walled two-story dorms, with usually over 200 people sleeping in each dorm. So there is basically no place at Draper where you are safe, if somebody wants to get you.

Things only got worse over the years, as fewer guards were assigned to watch over a growing incarcerated population. Eventually, it wasn't just individual prisoners, but entire dorms that would try to get organized to maintain some semblance of order and to curb violence. By the time Liam left Donaldson in 2022, it got to the point that prisoners were being informally recruited to perform even some of the COs' duties:

I got some friends that I left behind at Donaldson. Matter of fact, my oldest son is there, he was staying in the same dorm with me for a while. The other day he told me: "Hey man, they're so short of officers, they got inmates doing the count. You got inmates walking around unlocking the door and locking them back." Right before I left, he and I worked in the laundry together. One day, he had to go to another block to pick up some clothes, and the lieutenant told him: "Hey man, you gonna have to come back after they change shifts, ain't nobody in the [officers] cube, nobody can open the door." So, you've got guys on the block who are completely unattended, no roll was on the floor, no officer in the cube. They are just there by themselves, locked down. You got one police, they are trying to put him in the shack on the south side, or on the east hall, they got him working two, three spots at the time. So, something is always unattended.

This scenario—where the dereliction of duty means that prisoners are forced to self-manage the institution in order to protect themselves from harm—is one endpoint of the austerity policies advanced under neoliberal capitalism. Loïc Wacquant has argued that the modern penal state is a *centaur*, with a liberal head mounted on an authoritarian body.[29] Upstream, the state has ceded authority to the invisible hand of laissez-faire economics, while, downstream, it has only tightened its brutally punitive grip on socially marginal populations. The application of this "iron fist" helps to explain how so many poor people end up in cages, but, inside Alabama's rudderless prison system, our interviewees saw more evidence of abandonment than any heavy-handed exercise of control. Like them, we could see no reasoning behind it, only the grisly spectacle of a punishment machine, running on empty.

CHAPTER 4

No Shame in Alabama

"If you wear these overalls to jail, they're going to work
you real hard over there."
— George Wallace to Rev. Fred Shuttlesworth Jr.

Sixty years after the "events of Birmingham" brought the civil rights movement to the boil, we drove into the mineral-rich Jones Valley immortalized by the folk ballad "Down in the Valley" (otherwise known as "Birmingham Jail"). Passing the rusty hulks of the Sloss Furnaces, a vast landmark from the industrial past, we slipped into town below the Southern Appalachian ridge of the Red Mountain, whose rich reserves of iron ore fueled the valley's transformation after the Civil War into the South's premier manufacturing center. The smokestacks of the foundries and rolling mills in a city once known as the "Pittsburgh of the South" have ceded the skyline to the banking and corporate towers rising above Birmingham's central business district. They are flanked by the big boxy buildings of the sprawling medical complex that drives its economy today. The old industrial warehouses are now pricey lofts for young professionals who dine at the upscale bistros and tequila bars in the downtown area.

Despite this affluent urban footprint, Alabama itself ranks near the bottom of most national measures of quality of life—in education, health, and economic well-being. It is one of the country's poorest states, with a child poverty rate of 24 percent. Its rock-bottom ranking in medical care also means that it has one of the nation's worst infant mortality rates.[1] It incarcerates 938 per 100,000 people (including prisons, jails, immigration detention, and juvenile justice facilities), trailing only Louisiana, Mississippi, Georgia, and Arkansas for the percentage of its people that it locks up.[2] Conditions in its prisons, where the death rate is four times the national average, are arguably the worst among this same cluster of Deep South outliers.[3] There were 325 deaths reported in Alabama's prisons in 2023.[4] The in-custody homicide and suicide rates are by far the highest in the nation. In fact, the state's correctional facilities, grossly overcrowded and understaffed, have been the target of federal investigations for more than a decade. Alabama is facing a Department of Justice lawsuit over the "violent, cruel and unconstitutional" condition of its prisons.[5] This isn't the first time that the state's penal system has been threatened with a federal takeover.

But a series of labor strikes, beginning in 2014, have produced a rare unity among the prisoner population. The Free Alabama Movement behind these events has attracted solidarity actions in other states and has prompted advocates to ask whether the outcome might lead to a resurgence of the prisoner rights movement from the 1960s and 1970s. Three months before our first visit, voters in Alabama—along with Tennessee, Oregon, and Vermont—passed an amendment to the state constitution banning slavery without exception.[6] Involuntary servitude in prisons is no longer legal. However, as is the case in other states that updated their constitutions in this way, little has changed inside Alabama prisons. If this measure is to prove anything more than symbolic, then the agitation inside prisons and the vigor of public support on the outside will be key, not just as far as legally enforcing the changes, but also to making sure that they are observed on the cellblock.

Our first stop in town is a support group meeting hosted by the Offenders Alumni Association (OAA), an influential organization of formerly incarcerated volunteers who assist in reentry. Three elderly Black men, newly released after almost a century of time served between them, are being welcomed back to the free world. Others in the room who have gone through this experience are there to help them readjust and to show that a compassionate community already exists for them. After an opening prayer, everyone introduces themselves. Several voices find different ways of saying "we are here for you." The air is thick with therapeutic advice and love. One female veteran in the group makes a frank observation: "You are seventy years old, you are not the twenty-seven-year-old man you were before prison, and your loved ones are not the same people they were either." Discharged after thirty years, with nothing more than $10 gate money and a bus ticket, it is a blessing to be given such a warm reception. "It's good," ventured one of the men at the end of the meeting, "to be among people who aren't tripping when you talk about your feelings."

When we meet with her later, Dena Dickerson—the organization's charismatic COO—wants to impress on us that *postincarceration syndrome* is a very real thing for those re-entering the free world, with a range of symptoms that she has seen close up. "Freedom doesn't happen right away," she tells us, "people are very vulnerable for the first ninety days, and sometimes for 3 to 5 years afterwards." Her peer-supported group has done the work, assisting six thousand clients in a little over eight years. OAA now operates out of six branches in Alabama and Georgia. Her phone is blowing up as she talks to us. Although she describes herself as an "out-of-the-box girl," Dickerson sees her role as that of a "quiet advocate" who nonetheless "speaks up when called." Among a multitude of other activities, she teaches much-needed classes in life skills at one of the state's men's prisons. Typically, the newly released men and women whom OAA welcomes back have received no such preparation. If they are able to avoid reincarceration on release, they often become homeless and destitute. Having been convicted herself on a 114-year sentence for dealing cocaine (for which she only served 10 years), there is not much she hasn't seen, both on the inside and through serving those who are coming out to face a "second incarceration" in a society that wants to forget they exist. "Punishment comes from the bench," she declares, "and then Alabama's prisons are all overkill after that."

The day after the OAA meeting, we met with some of the newly released men at the offices of Alabama Appleseed, a legal nonprofit that works to release inmates with long sentences, many of whom have been inside for decades for nonviolent property crimes when they were teenagers. The number of elderly prisoners has also exploded in recent years, and now accounts for a quarter of the state's incarcerated population. These are inmates who are especially vulnerable to the poor medical care available inside.[7] Seventy-year old Chris Washington had been locked up continuously since the 1970s, and so he had seen the prison system go through several phases. In the early portions of his sentence, some of the facilities still had working farms. "We picked cotton, cucumber, and potatoes," he recalled, "in a squad of fifteen to twenty guys and the officer rode a horse with a shotgun and a side pistol. If you refused, you were handcuffed to a hitching bar, or you were beaten up, or put in the hole, literally underground, where you could stay up to 21 days, and you only got bread and water . . . it was real bad back then." Farm labor was usually the first assignment, "just as a punishment" and "then you got moved up to infirmary, laundry, or the kitchen." Like everyone else, he found his hustle to stay alive. The best hustle was in the laundry, where custom wash jobs could earn him six or seven packs of cigarettes, which, on very good days, could add up to $70. Almost every job had a perk, even working on the highways on the chain gang. "People would throw you a carton of cigarettes or food or money from their cars, or show their titties," he remembered, "and so some guys without any support from their families wanted to go on the gang to make some money that way."

Like everyone else we interviewed, Washington had stories about the appalling conditions in the facilities where he had been housed. "You wake up in the morning, and someone next to you might be dead. There will be roaches in the bed, rats all night long, and even snakes. Spider webs fall on your face. You might only get one or two hours sleep with the guys fighting and fussing all night." At Donaldson, his last facility, "the inmates are running the place, cos there are no officers to be seen some days," and the plumbing has all but given up: "only two toilets and sinks working for 150 guys, with the drains blocked up and overflowing. It's chaos in there." He only survived by taking tips from the other old-timers, like Floyd Coleman, a one-hundred-and-two-year-old man who was still inside Donaldson, about how to avoid the "tension and stabbings and killings" that were an ever-present part of daily life.

Brian Whitler, a younger man, served his time more recently. Alabama prisons had gotten out of the increasingly unprofitable plantation business, and so his experience of labor on a non-productive "farm" was quite different from Washington's. "You wear shackles on your ankles," he recalled, "though not your wrists because you were gonna work. So you had to walk with shackles on your feet. Let's just say when they walk you out in the field you no longer saw the prison. And, basically, we were just out swinging blades and backhoes to keep the grass from getting too tall." In other words, it was make-work. "Their objective was to get you out of the camp and to get you tired, so you couldn't come back in and make no fuss with nobody, no officer, or inmate, or anything. That's why the walk was so long because by the time you get out there, you're gonna be tired, and not want to do nothing." But, he reported, "you got to work—otherwise, you'll get disciplinary action for refusing to work."

No doubt the prison administrators approved this work regime in order to stave off trouble by keeping the men busy and exhausting them in the process. But in Whitler's experience, idleness was not what generated unrest and violence: instead, it was the dynamic between men packed in like sardines and the fact that some "people who are gonna get in trouble are troublesome, no matter what." He had also done time for a year in a Mississippi prison. How did it compare with Alabama? "On a scale of one to ten, it was a ten," he replied. "Instead of the open bay dormitories here, with 200 to 300 men, you had pods, with two people to each room, so you had some privacy. The staff was not as aggressive, and my family didn't get any hassle when they came to visit. In Mississippi they treat you like a human being, no matter what your crime was, no matter what you were locked up for." We asked him why he thought the conditions were so much worse in Alabama. "Because nobody cares," he replied. It was a phrase that came up repeatedly in the dozens of other interviews that followed.

Just as common was the charge that Alabama officials and their correctional employees flagrantly neglected their own laws and rules. Leah Nelson, senior researcher at Alabama Appleseed, summarized this point when she told us that "the Alabama Department of Corrections, for whatever reason, will not do what it takes to have anything like the rule of the law within its prisons. They don't follow laws that are made to govern them, and they don't impose a society where normal rules apply . . . it is just lawless in there." It was the height of irony to see these managers of an overloaded system built on the back of "law-and order" rhetoric show such little regard for law or order behind the walls.

In the course of our conversations, we were able to form a damning picture of life inside what advocates call the state's "death camps," and what the courts refer to, more clinically, as "deliberate indifference" on the part of Alabama Department of Corrections (ADOC) officials who are responsible for the deplorable conditions.[8] The malpractices include parole being systematically denied, inhumanely long sentences for nonviolent offenses, dangerous overcrowding, omnipresent violence, brutality and sexual abuse, facilities in states of advanced decay and sanitary crisis (with a contaminated water supply), rising death rates from drug overdoses and homicide, a chronic shortage of guards that have rendered prisons ungovernable, and a Death Row filled with men who would not be there in any other state.

Before we traveled to Alabama, we had been warned by a local abolitionist that the forced work assignments were a low priority problem for those locked up in the state's penitentiaries. "Don't be surprised," she said, "if the people that you interview don't place too much importance on the work they have to do. They've been through much worse things." She was right. We knew, going in, that things were bad, but many of the stories we heard about the daily struggle for survival were downright chilling. Was it possible to separate these conditions from the labor that kept the system running? In all their wretchedness, the prisons were the product of that labor. And when the labor was withdrawn—as happened during the strikes that had rocked the system—the prisons, along with their supply of goods and services to the state of Alabama, almost stopped functioning.

Ball and Chain

Hearing about these appalling conditions reminded us that Alabama's correctional policies have roots in the calcareous, clay soil that made its Cotton Belt plantations so productive to their owners and so baleful to those forced to toil on those lands. To understand the full meaning of that legacy of racial bondage and terror, we need to revisit the era of convict leasing that began immediately after chattel slavery officially ended. In Alabama, that system began earlier and lasted longer than anywhere else in the nation. Some hardened cynics insist that its racial spirit lives on in the mass criminalization of people of color that overfills todays' penitentiaries.

As in other states, Alabama's prisons were seen, from the outset, as a ready source of unpaid labor. The first was Wetumpka, just north of Montgomery, which was founded in 1841 and which hosted the light manufacturing of saddles, harnesses, and shoes.[9] This supply, produced by a predominantly white inmate population, became quite profitable after 1861 in the form of war goods made for the Confederate Army. But Union troops destroyed the existing penitentiaries during the war, along with the existing industrial base of forges, mills, foundries, and arsenals, and so prisons had no part to play in the labor-intensive task of Reconstruction. Instead, the much more efficient convict leasing system was concocted to provide the cheap manpower necessary for the post-bellum effort to modernize the South.

In some respects, convict leasing was a variant of the prison contracting pioneered in New York's Auburn and Sing Sing. But in the Southern states, all of the work was done outside prison walls, largely because the prisons were now in ruins. In effect, the penitentiary was relocated to a private employer's workplace. In the case of railroad construction, mine extraction, logging, or turpentine distilling, the labor camps were mobile iron cages with shackles. Unlike in the slave market that had supplied the plantations, the new workers were akin to "slaves of the state," hired out by judges and other government officials to planters, industrialists, and any kind of employer in search of the very cheapest labor.[10] Contractors who bid for the leases had absolute control over the workforce, and there was almost no state oversight.

In 1866, Alabama's lawmakers seized upon the Exception Clause to pass into law their version of the notorious Black Codes.[11] Like other laws hastily passed in Southern states, the Penal Code of Alabama allowed county authorities to arrest formerly enslaved African Americans for vagrancy or debt forfeiture and lease their labor to private contractors. In practice, "vagrancy" could mean almost any kind of loitering or idleness, and included such misdemeanors as speaking too loudly, drinking, and gambling, or simply being in the wrong place at the wrong time.[12] The routine sentence for these manufactured crimes was hard labor. Large blocs of prisoners were then leased out as unpaid labor to be exploited for the duration, though many died before the end, of their "sentence." State revenue from the lease system soared. By 1883, this income accounted for about 10 percent of total state revenues, rising to nearly 73 percent by 1898.[13] Indeed, of all the Southern states that adopted the system, Alabama made it the most profitable.

Another route to Southern servitude was through the surety system. Local judges intentionally set court fees higher than anyone who was swept up in the dragnet could afford to pay, and so the "offenders" had no alternative but to hire themselves out to local employers willing to assume the court debt through a surety bond payment. The judges took a cut from the surety. Farmers—small and large—could basically purchase workers from county sheriffs and other traffickers who made a good living out of the convict trade in a system that was all but indistinguishable from peonage. Faced with the choice of being sent to timber, mining, and turpentine operations (where the high mortality rates in chain gangs and labor camps were equivalent to a death sentence),[14] Black men and women accused of trumped-up infractions chose to sign a "confession of judgment" and to be bound over to landowners who offered to cover the fines. Many had been tenant farmers and were now private peons, held in servitude to pay off a debt held by the employer. They could be resold if they escaped. More often than not, they worked on land where they had once been freedmen. Through this surety system and the more informal network of trafficking, white planters availed themselves of the same unpaid labor force as they had under slavery.[15]

As for the lease system, the state was the broker of these contracts through a formal bidding process that involved larger corporations, especially in the business of heavy manufacturing, and the system consigned convicts to inhumanly hard labor in the most gruesome conditions. The capitalists' new mines, furnaces, and factories lay in the emergent industrial belt that ran from Knoxville, Tennessee through the northwest corner of Georgia and down into the Jones Valley, where there is an abundant mix of bituminous coal, iron-ore deposits, and limestone flux.

The Birmingham district was the only place in the world where these basic ingredients of iron-making could be found in close proximity, and so the new city was founded in 1871 to prosper from the profitable extraction and processing of such minerals. Despite this bounty, however, the deposits were buried deep beneath the mountain slopes. As a result, the ore had a lower metallic content than ore mined in the Great Lakes region. Rock-bottom labor costs were therefore the only way for Southern capitalists to compete in the marketplace with the Northern powerhouses of iron and steel, and so they relied heavily on the state's provision of unpaid labor through the convict leases. Depending on the workers' physical fitness, the firms paid from $9 to $18.50 per month for their lease, incurring minimal costs to house and feed them.[16] As with the planters, the industrialists had at their disposal exactly the same unpaid Black workforce that had formerly supplied war materiel in their capacity as enslaved workers.

The big firms in Birmingham's industrial complex—such as the Tennessee Coal, Iron, and Railroad Company, the Pratt Coal and Iron Company, and the Sloss Iron and Steel Company—employed white ethnic immigrants for more skilled positions in the smelters and foundries while reserving the Black convict workforce for the mines and the most punishing tasks. Below ground, work discipline was administered by the whipping boss and by foremen skilled in water torture techniques. Forced to toil from dawn to dusk, shackled convicts rarely saw even a ray of sun. The mortality rate soared. According to one estimate, by 1870 over 40 percent of prisoners had died while working on Alabama leases.[17] Some historians have cited these statistics to argue that convict leasing was "worse than slavery," or at the very least, "slavery by another name."[18] Unlike in the chattel system—where slave owners had some self-interest in looking out for the health of their workers and could also use them as collateral for loans—the convict lease carried no such benefit or obligation. If a prisoner died, it was very easy to "get another."[19] Suicides and self-mutilation were desperate, but they were logical responses to the reality of being forcibly worked into an early, unmarked grave. State inspectors made periodic visits and issued reports about the appalling conditions, but there was too much profit at stake for any reforms to take hold, at least in the short term.

In industrial workplaces where unions such as the United Mine Workers were increasingly active, the advantage of a captive work force was crystal clear. These were not workers who could ever go on strike and they could be easily recruited as scabs to replace those who did. The only danger posed by this system was the prospect of Black and white workers sharing a workplace—a fundamental taboo according to the Jim Crow racial order of the South.

In the waning years of the century, a wave of reformist energy from the North reached Alabama and the other rebel states. Organized labor brought down the system of private labor contracting in New York, and neighboring states followed suit, switching to the public-use system of prison labor. Rehabilitation was in the air. The horrors of convict leasing in the old Confederacy had gotten public media exposure as the worst of the worst. Southern progressives and radical agrarian populists were about to have their moment in the sun, as state after state moved to end the lease, beginning with Tennessee in 1896. Alabama was the very last to do so, in 1928, though it was not fully stamped out at the federal level until 1941. This was seventy-five years after the onset of the system, when U.S. Attorney General Francis Biddle's "Circular 3591" instructed federal attorneys to aggressively prosecute cases of peonage and involuntary servitude.

The path toward abolition was hardly smooth, however. At the dawn of the Progressive era, Teddy Roosevelt authorized the Department of Justice and local U.S. attorneys to investigate the peonage system in rural Alabama and other Southern states. Grand juries were empaneled in 1903 to take testimony about the extensive trafficking rings, including sexual slavery.[20] But the memory of federal orders during Reconstruction was still fresh enough to fuel a vicious backlash—including a long season of lynching and the resurgence of the Ku Klux Klan. This stymied the momentum of reformers, reinforcing a pattern of fierce local resistance to federal intervention that continues to the present day.

One of the legacies of convict leasing was a conspiracy of silence about the forced labor behind the fortunes, both big and small, that were amassed during this period. Douglas Blackmon's 2001 article in the *Wall Street Journal* caused a stir. He wrote about the mass graves of leased convicts that were uncovered beside a mine owned and operated by U.S. Steel, revelations that sent shockwaves all the way to the executive suite of the corporation itself.[21] The African Americans who wrote to him described:

> . . . how the article lifted a terrible burden, that the story had in some way supplied an answer to or part of one to a question so unnervingly few dared to ask aloud: If not racial inferiority, what explained the inexplicably labored advance of African Americans in U.S. society in the century between the Civil War and the civil rights movement of the 1960s? The amorphous rhetoric of the struggle against segregation, the thin cinematic imagery of Ku Klux Klan bogeymen, even the horrifying still images of lynching, had never been a sufficient answer to these African Americans for one hundred years of seemingly docile submission by four million slaves freed in 1863 and their tens of millions of descendants. How had a such a large population of Americans disappeared into a largely unrecorded oblivion of poverty and obscurity? [22]

But these Americans hardly just "disappeared" under Jim Crow. To cite three well-documented examples of resistance, there is the remarkable account of Communist organizing by Black sharecroppers in rural Alabama that Robin Kelley offers in his book *Hammer and Hoe*. Additionally Sarah Haley explores the opposition and sabotage of Black women under convict leasing in *No Mercy Here* and Steve Hahn has chronicled the history of Black political struggle in the rural South in *A Nation Under Our Feet*.[23] Nevertheless, Blackmon's and other historians' investigations of the brutality of the lease have helped us understand how profiteering from the criminalization of Black Americans not only survived the formal abolition of chattel slavery but thrived in its aftermath and endures today as a central component of racial capitalism.[24] Then as now, the abuses are deeply rooted in the belief that penal confinement should be an instrument for conscripting the unpaid black labor that Emancipation had taken away from white employers.

In that regard, Alabama, along with many other states (including in the North), barely skipped a beat when convict leasing was abolished. The business of exploiting prison labor was simply taken over by the state itself, albeit concentrated in sectors where organized labor could raise no opposition. A suite of federal legislation—Hawes-Cooper Act (1929), the Ashurst-Sumners Act (1935), the Walsh-Healey Act (1936) and the Sumners-Ashurst Act (1940)—forbade the sale of prison-made goods on the open market or through federal contracts, but states were still at liberty to utilize prison labor for the benefit of their own institutions and agencies.

As a result, the chain gang and the labor camp continued to thrive under direct state control and for the use of specific agencies, like the Department of Highways. Four-walled penitentiaries were still few and far between. In the Southeast, road building—under the aegis of the Good Roads Movement—became a favored way to use workers. Reformers heralded the shift away from private profit to public benefit, and extolled the health value of sunshine, fresh air, and exercise for the road crews as a more wholesome form of penal labor. In some states like North Carolina, prison funding was entirely dependent on the work of these road crews until the 1970s.[25] But a larger pool of Southern prisoners labored on state-owned agricultural enterprises, some of them vast, infamous penal farms like Parchman (Mississippi), Angola (Louisiana), Cummins (Arkansas), Eastham and Sugar Land (Texas)—places that had been taken under public ownership in the early decades of the twentieth century.

Well into the twentieth century, four-walled penitentiaries were few and far between in states like Virginia and North Carolina, while general conditions on the road crews and on the farms' hoe squads were appalling, and indeed had changed little from the days of slavery.[26] On former plantation lands, Black workers picked cotton and cut cane under the scrutiny of high-riders: white guards on horseback with Stetsons, shotguns, sidearms, and bloodhounds at the ready in case of escapes. The field bosses looked and behaved the same as they had for decades. The centuries-old rhythms in the fields were undisturbed over time. While the public chain gangs were promoted as more humane than their predecessors, media exposés of abusive treatment—including beatings, malnutrition, overwork, and the lack of medical care— led to their demise by the mid- to late 1950s (though, in South Carolina at least, they were not abolished until the 1970s). Warner Brothers' influential 1932 film—a version of Robert Elliott Burns' memoir *I Am a Fugitive from a Georgia Chain Gang!* (1932)— spurred popular revulsion. This would be followed by *Chain Gang* (1950) and *Cool Hand Luke* (1967). Public distaste was no doubt reinforced by the spectacle of white actors playing the leading roles of prisoners in each of these films, just as the 1924 report of a white worker drowned in a laundry vat in Birmingham for working too slowly helped to turn popular sentiment decisively against convict leasing in Alabama.

As with the death of convict leasing, abolitionists claimed they had vanquished the "last vestiges of slavery" with the elimination of chain gangs and the humiliating striped uniforms associated with them. But these signature features of penal servitude were destined to re-surface during outbreaks of tough-on-crime rhetoric from lawmakers and judges running for re-election and eager for photo ops.

Alabama led the way for one such revival in 1995, when Ron Jones—a hardcore prison commissioner—reintroduced the chain gang as "a cost-effective" response to shortfalls in the state budget. Facing down an avalanche of national criticism, Jones appealed to the reliable revanchism of local sentiment: "People say it's not humane . . . But I don't get much flak in Alabama."[27] The experiment barely lasted a year before a federal court took up a class action lawsuit from the Southern Poverty Law Center (SPLC) alleging that the practice was a form of "cruel and unusual punishment" under the Eighth Amendment.[28] A pre-trial settlement with the state put an end to the practice and Jones was pressured to resign, though individuals continued to be chained at the ankles for several years after.[29] So, too, Alabama's example was followed by Florida, Arizona, Wisconsin and Iowa, as well as by sheriffs in several other jurisdictions such as Maricopa County where Joe Arpaio, "America's toughest sheriff," even innovated with female chain gangs.

The same SPLC lawsuit took aim at the notorious "hitching post," another penal institution that was peculiar to Alabama. We interviewed several men who remembered this stationary metal rail to which unruly field hands were chained for several hours and left to roast under the hot sun. According to one of our older interviewees, "it was a special piece of hell for those who refused to work—an iron bar out of the ground, to which you were handcuffed before the sun came up and until the sun set. It was set high enough off the ground so that you could not sit down. No water was given to you. And on top of that they would tape or zip tie the bottom of your pant legs so that if you shit yourself you could not shake it off." This interviewee was a survivor of many spells of solitary confinement (deemed to be psychological torture by the UN) where he had to sleep on concrete slabs, but he assured us that the torment of the hitching post was so severe that he "avoided that at all costs." A lesser alternative, sometimes referred to as the "Mexican jail," was "to put you in a fence inside of a fence, and lock the gate so that you can't get out, and if you climb it, that's considered an attempt to escape."

The hitching post was administered officially as a "correctional tool" but the federal magistrate who ruled against its use described it as "a form of painful and torturous punishment." In her judgment, she wrote that "with deliberate indifference for the health, safety and indeed the lives of inmates, prison officials have knowingly subjected them to all of the hazards of the hitching posts, then observed as they suffered pain, humiliation and injuries as a result."[30]

Fill the Jails

Jones' 1995 chain gang experiment was introduced at the height of the Clinton administration's embrace of the New Right's "law and order" electoral politics. This was a mere six years after Alabama's correctional system was released from a 13-year-long spell of federal oversight. By the early 1970s, the state's overcrowded, understaffed, and brutal prisons had established a reputation as particularly barbaric places. Shocking testimony about the chronic violation of human rights attracted the legal attention of Frank Johnson, a U.S. District Court judge who had made land-

mark rulings concerning desegregation and the disenfranchisement of African Americans during the civil rights era.[31] In 1972,
Johnson—an Eisenhower Republican—ordered comprehensive
changes in the system's health services, citing "knowing and
intentional" mistreatment and "pervasive and gross neglect" of
sick and injured prisoners.[32] His 1976 ruling in *Pugh v. Locke* established that an oppressive "totality of conditions" in the state's
prisons violated the Eighth Amendment's prohibition against
"cruel and unusual punishment."[33] Issuing a far-reaching order of
federal supervision over the entire system, he charged Alabama
with establishing "minimum constitutional standards" regarding
the provision of clothing, diets, living space, and the opportunity
to enroll in educational and vocational training programs. State
officials were prohibited from accepting new prisoners until the
existing population was reduced to the design capacity of their
facilities. A Human Rights Committee was delegated to monitor
compliance with the order.

Given the longstanding hands-off policy observed by federal
authorities in the matter of how states ran their prisons, Johnson's
decree was an explosive intervention into Alabama's affairs. It set
a litigation model that would be followed in many other states. It
was also guaranteed to call forth strenuous forms of obstruction
and resistance on the part of officials. Bear in mind that George
Wallace, the archpriest of segregation, was still governor. Never
one to lack bluster, Wallace declared that Johnson's ruling would
turn prisons into "vacation resorts," and issued his infamous
threat that some federal judges might be in need of a "barbed wire
enema." In response, Johnson calmly pointed out that Alabama
had all but invited the intervention of federal judges because it
had so repeatedly dodged its responsibilities with respect to civil
rights. He wryly described this pattern as "Alabama's punting syndrome," referencing a famous football game between Auburn
and the Crimson Tide in 1972.

The pushback against Johnson's order by officials and guards was strong and multipronged, though it lost some of its vigor over the duration of the compliance period. When the state reassumed control in 1989, some progress had been made in professionalizing prison staff, improving mental and medical care, and establishing more programming. Furthermore, prisoner advocates in more than forty states had followed his legal precedent and succeeded in placing their correctional systems under court orders to improve conditions. But by most accounts, there was little lasting impact in Alabama. When federal officers saw the need to intervene again in 2017, the problems were almost identical, albeit more aggravated in nature. Once again, the sitting governor, Kay Ivey, insisted that "this Alabama problem" should have "an Alabama solution"—implying that the federal government had no business poking its nose into the state's penal affairs.[34] In the interim, the breakneck growth of the carceral population had magnified the scope of the problems. The "solution" that Ivey conjured up seemed well beyond the reach of a legislature whose members the Department of Justice once again accused of "deliberate indifference" to the harms faced by prisoners in Alabama's wretched correctional facilities.

Ironically, one of Alabama's responses to Johnson's 1976 ruling had been to increase its spending on corrections and to build ten more prisons, swelling the caged population by a factor of five. This was an expansion wholly in synch with the nationwide turn toward mass incarceration in the 1970s and 1980s. Because his influential appeal to the Eighth Amendment focused solely on conditions and not on the cause or purpose of incarceration, officials found it expedient to make the case for new prisons to relieve overcrowding rather than to confront the issue of why they were locking up so many people in the first place. Likewise, prison litigation in other states that adhered to the legal reasoning behind Johnson's ruling steered clear of addressing broader penal policies. As Elizabeth Alexander, director of the ACLU's Prison Project, put it, "the history of the Alabama litigation does suggest that for prison reform to have any chance of success . . . it must address the issue of who goes to prison, not just what conditions society tolerates within its prisons."[35]

A less obvious irony relates to the keynote events of the civil rights movement, to which Johnson had made indispensable contributions. Among those, his order to desegregate seating on city buses during the Montgomery Bus Boycott in 1956, his move to legally protect the Freedom Riders from attack, and his overruling of the law obstructing the 1965 Selma to Montgomery March earned him the KKK's moniker of the "most hated man in Alabama." By then, the state had a long record of using its jails to frame up innocent Blacks like the Scottsboro Boys and also to lock up political dissidents. In the 1920s and 1930s, Birmingham Jail was in regular use as a place to incarcerate trade unionists and Communist party activists. A 180-day statutory sentence was put in place to keep them from organizing.[36] In 1961, Bull Connor used the jail to detain the Freedom Riders, along with local civil rights leaders like the Reverend Fred Shuttlesworth Jr.[37] When Shuttlesworth brought Martin Luther King Jr. and Ralph Abernathy—the figureheads of the Southern Christian Leadership Council (SCLC)—to town in 1963, the jail had a pivotal role in the events that led to the dismantling of Jim Crow. King wrote his celebrated epistle in a Birmingham Jail cell, initiating a vogue for martyrs to present themselves for arrest and detention, almost as a rite of passage for people who wanted to be part of the movement. When he and his allies wore denim overalls in marches to identify themselves with working people, Connor retorted: "if you wear those overalls to jail, *they're going to work you real hard over there.*"[38]

The most effective tactic devised by the SCLC's Project C (C for confrontation) was the exhortation to "fill the jails" in order to draw attention to the repressive policies of Birmingham's officials. The explicit goal of Project C was to provoke and expose police violence and subjugation to the watchful media. Seasoned activists obliged, but not in large enough numbers to fill the cells. It was not until the "Children's Crusade"—when high school students joined the street protests and marches and were arrested en masse—that the plan took off. With the jails now overflowing, Connor took the bait and resorted to more public and predictably brutal methods of crowd control. Everyone knows what happened next. The infamous images of fire hoses and German shepherd dogs being turned on children told the story to the world. Within a month, the Jim Crow signs regulating the segregation of public places in Birmingham were taken down.

Filling the jails turned the segregationists' playbook against them. The exposure of so many Black people to incarceration in 1963 transformed the customary fear and trauma of being locked up into a carnivalesque experience. Laughter and movement songs reverberated around the walls of the cells, and the ballad of "Birmingham Jail" was refurbished many times with new lyrics.[39] To be in jail was now a badge of honor and was a pathway not to servitude but to freedom, at least for a brief season.[40]

By the time of Johnson's 1976 court order twelve years later, Alabama's correctional facilities were no longer sites of righteous struggle and they were overflowing for different, and less joyous, reasons. Like some other Southern states, Alabama houses its prisoners in large barracks-style dormitories with single bunk beds close to one another. The proximity of prisoners, the lack of privacy, and the callous brutality of the staff were invitations to mayhem. Johnson's federal mandate to reduce crowding would be undone in the course of the next decade by the fabrication of new crimes and the passage of tougher sentencing laws, especially the 1979 Habitual Offenders Act, which mandates life imprisonment without parole for anyone convicted of a Class A felony after three previous convictions.

By the time that federal oversight ended in 1989, the pendulum that swings unfailingly between reform and retrenchment throughout the history of American penology had decisively veered away from Northern ideals of rehabilitation and toward the harsher pole of Southern punishment. As Robert Perkinson put it in his study of Texas prisons, "we used to think the South would become more like America, but America has become more like the South."[41] In his account, the rise of supermax facilities, solitary confinement, privatized prisons, and rigid labor discipline were policies all aimed at the cost-effective warehousing of prisoners as opposed to their moral reformation. These were trends that evolved organically from the South's long history of racial control and penal profiteering.[42]

From 2007, Texas sought to maintain its leadership in penal policy by pioneering clinical efficiency and fiscal conservatism through its influential Right On Crime campaign.[43] By contrast, Alabama seemed dead set on proving that it had the worst-run prisons, hands down. When federal agents came calling again in 2017 in response to prisoner complaints about civil rights abuses and inhumane conditions, they found "little had changed" since the 1970s. A two-year investigation of men's prisons resulted in a damning and at times horrifying report about the unsafe and unconstitutional state of the system's facilities. Testimony included in the report describes spiraling violence by prisoners and guards alike, rampant sexual abuse, extortion, dangerous drug use, and "horrendously inadequate" mental health care.

Tutwiler, the state's only female prison, was already under federal oversight after an even longer series of incriminating investigations. In 2002, a federal judge found overcrowding and underfunding at Tutwiler to be a violation of the constitutional rights of its prisoners. In 2007, the Department of Justice ranked

Tutwiler as the women's prison with the highest rate of sexual assaults in the nation.[44] In 2012, the Montgomery-based Equal Justice Initiative (EJI) issued a report based on testimony of more than fifty women incarcerated at the facility about chronic sexual abuse on the part of correctional officers.[45] The Department of Justice launched a formal inquiry the following year and corroborated the EJI's findings in a 2014 letter to the governor:

> Tutwiler has a history of unabated staff-on-prisoner sexual abuse and harassment. The women at Tutwiler universally fear for their safety. They live in a sexualized environment with repeated and open sexual behavior, including: abusive sexual contact between staff and prisoners; sexualized activity, including a strip show condoned by staff; profane and unprofessional sexualized language and harassment; and deliberate cross-gender viewing of prisoners showering, urinating, and defecating. The inappropriate sexual behavior, including sexual abuse, continues, and is grossly underreported, due to insufficient staffing and supervision, inadequate policies and procedures, a heightened fear of retaliation, and an inadequate investigative process . . . Officials have been on notice for over eighteen years of the risks to women prisoners and, for over eighteen years, have chosen to ignore them.[46]

The state's own investigators pushed back against the allegations as unfounded and lacking in adequate evidence, but Alabama's DOC had to comply with a settlement agreement filed by the federal agency, mandating more than forty provisions to protect the women from sexual victimization. Among the measures, female guards were recruited, staff underwent gender-specific training, and as many as three hundred cameras were installed to ensure the safety of the women. Slated to close in 2016, Tutwiler was still open in 2023 when we interviewed more than a dozen women who had served time there. In contrast to the stories we heard from Alabama's formerly incarcerated men which all had similar features, the women's accounts of their experiences showed more variation.

Most of the women who had served time before the EJI's report depicted the environment as rife with sexual terror, long after Congress passed the Prison Rape Elimination Act in 2003 (PREA). "Women were dragged around and beaten and raped," recalled one of them. "There were no cameras, and it was just 'everyone for themselves.'" The jobs that required night shifts were the most dangerous and there were other assignments which ensured that male guards would have access to their favorites. The consensus among those who lived through the changes was that the federal intervention was for the better. At least one interviewee who reported being regularly beaten for twenty years for her "defiance" had a different experience. "Before the Feds came," she reported, "the abuse was there, but so was structure and consistency, and things were much more stable. Some relationships of trust came out of interactions with the guards, but there is none now that the guards are not allowed to touch us. It's a mess, the inmates are running the prison, and no one cares if you don't work."

If the most chronic sexual abuse had been eliminated at Tutwiler, abusive work conditions had not. We heard many stories about the appalling state of the cramped and overheated kitchen, which was typically the first work assignment for newly admitted prisoners. Full of gaping holes, the floor was crawling with rats and roaches, and raw sewage often backed up and flowed around the feet of workers. As one former kitchen worker put it, "God feels so far away in that place." Things were so bad that the supervisors—who were described as "slave-drivers"—began to offer rewards like lotions and cosmetics from a "treasure chest" for those who put in a little extra effort on their shifts. Montgomery's work release center was also a much-feared place. "It has a tin roof," reported one survivor, "and is so dangerously hot during the summer that no one wants to move at all, never mind work."

Shortly after Tutwiler fell under DOJ monitoring in 2016, the agency began its investigation of men's prisons. Its initial report was issued in April 2019:

> There is reasonable cause to believe that the Alabama Department of Corrections ("ADOC") has violated and is continuing to violate the Eighth Amendment rights of prisoners housed in men's prisons by failing to protect them from prisoner-on-prisoner violence, prisoner-on-prisoner sexual abuse, and by failing to provide safe conditions, and that such violations are pursuant to a pattern or practice of resistance to the full enjoyment of rights secured by the Eighth Amendment. The violations are severe, systemic, and exacerbated by serious deficiencies in staffing and supervision; overcrowding; ineffective housing and classification protocols; inadequate incident reporting; inability to control the flow of contraband into and within the prisons, including illegal drugs and weapons; ineffective prison management and training; insufficient maintenance and cleaning of facilities; the use of segregation and solitary confinement to both punish and protect victims of violence and/or sexual abuse; and a high level of violence that is too common, cruel, of an unusual nature, and pervasive.[47]

In addition, investigators decided to look into allegations of excessive force and sexual abuse from staff. In July 2020, the DOJ issued its follow-up report, confirming most of these charges.[48] Both reports contain gruesome and damaging details about numerous violations. Unable to negotiate a settlement with Alabama, DOJ officials filed a lawsuit. Among other matters, the lawsuit noted that although it had been several years since the initial notice to ADOC, conditions had only gotten worse. The trial was scheduled to take place in 2024.

In the meantime, U.S. District Judge Myron Thompson (who succeeded Frank Johnson on the district bench in 1980) had been issuing rulings in a 2014 class action suit brought by lawyers from the University of Alabama's Alabama Disabilities Advocacy Program and the Southern Poverty Law Center. The case focused in particular on the lack of mental health treatment in the state's prisons which resulted in "a skyrocketing suicide rate."[49] Thompson's initial ruling, in 2017 (*Braggs et al. vs. Jefferson Dunn, et al.*), put the system under court orders. Four years later—after little progress had been made by ADOC in addressing the conditions—he issued another more scathing 600-page opinion. He gave state officials until July 1, 2025—with benchmarks along the way—to meet new staffing requirements.[50] Revisiting the staffing in February 2023, Thompson noted that, in spite of the court order, ADOC was failing miserably. The system had lost almost 30 percent of its security staff employees over the previous 18 months.[51]

The Ivey administration initially responded to all of the serious legal charges concerning overcrowding by pushing hard for the construction of three new megaprisons. The jurisdictional population was down from its 2013 peak of 32,523, but several prisons had been closed in the interim, so the proposed new facilities would probably expand the overall numbers. It was as if "filling the jails" to more than twice their design capacity had been a strategy all along for securing new and lucrative construction contracts.

The initial plan was to lease prisons to be built by CoreCivic, the industry leader in the private prison business. The plan was abandoned in September 2021 after a coalition that included Alabama Students Against Prisons, Justice Capital, and Communities Not Prisons put pressure on investors to back out.[52] Barclays subsequently delayed its plan to underwrite the lease, thereby dooming the deal. Thanks to the coalition's efforts, Alabama would not be operating a new suite of privately-owned prisons, but its lawmakers were still intent on building their way out of the mess they had created in the old ones, and so they approved a bond issue for the new facilities. In effect, they were committing taxpayer money to pay back investors—with interest—for decades to come. Weak demand from buyers caused underwriters to shrink the offering by $200 million in June 2022.[53]

In the meantime—in a move that inspired public outrage, national ridicule, and some legal challenges—Ivey sought to divert the state's appropriation of COVID stimulus funds from the American Rescue Plan Act to construct the new facilities. The legislation had been approved to help states with health care and economic costs from the pandemic, but the Alabama legislature decided that the business of locking up their poorest citizens qualified. As the cost estimates soared, the GOP lawmakers doubled down, and approved even more funding. Ivey's original proposal was for three prisons at a cost of $900 million. By September 2023—even before any concrete had been poured—the price tag for one of these alone had jumped to more than a billion dollars. According to Alabama Appleseed, this would make it the most expensive prison ever built in the U.S., costing more than $270,000 per bed.[54] Ironically, since several decrepit prisons are going to be decommissioned, the likelihood that the new ones will be overcrowded is high.[55]

Bare Life and Dark Arts

None of the legal interventions by district court judges or government agencies that we summarize above had much, if anything, to say about forced labor practices in the state's prisons. For example, the lawsuit that ended Alabama's chain gang charged that its use was cruel, unsafe, and degrading, but the lawsuit ignored the self-evident fact that the prisoners were shackled together to secure and expedite their hard labor. The reason for this apparent neglect had everything to do with the Exception Clause, according to which it is legally permissible to require prisoners to work for nothing, as is the case for most incarcerated people in Alabama. And yet, as we have argued in this book, involuntary servitude is the irreducible element of prison life, whether deployed as punishment or as an instrument of discipline. Its baleful reach even extends to the withdrawal of labor and to the tedium of idleness. In this regard, it is noteworthy that Johnson's 1976 ruling in *Pugh vs. Locke* cited idleness and the lack of "meaningful work" as contributing factors to the totality of inhumane conditions:

> Most inmates must spend substantially all of their time crowded in dormitories in absolute idleness. Such unbroken inactivity increases boredom, tension and frustration, which in turn promote incidents of violence. The evidence reflects that idleness of this magnitude destroys any job skills and work habits inmates may have, and contributes to their mental and physical degeneration.[56]

Johnson's comments spoke to the fading ideal of rehabilitation through purposeful labor, to which Southern prison administrators had only ever paid lip service. But his subsequent directive—that "each inmate shall be assigned a meaningful job on the basis of the inmate's abilities and interests, and according to institutional needs"—also dovetailed with the high-profile call in the free world economy for more purposeful and fulfilling work. In a time of near full employment at the height of the Fordist model of grinding mass production, labor advocates demanded a redesign of workplaces along more humane lines in response to widespread resistance to boredom and alienation on the job. Absenteeism, sabotage, and wildcat strikes were all symptoms of this "revolt against work." How did these phenomena relate to the prison system's internal labor economy? By the 1970s, the strenuous industrial model of penal labor lay in the past, though the daily grind was still all too apparent in field and road labor. But the program-driven rehabilitative paradigm that was supposed to be the reformers' successor to the treadmill of industry had never been properly funded nor embraced, especially in the South. As a result, idleness was chronic, even before the prison boom, reducing the experience of incarceration to one of bare life.

On the outside, the pendulum would soon swing as a buyers' labor market materialized during the course of the 1970s, due to the first wave of capitalist restructuring that sent jobs offshore and prompted austerity politics at home. Labor unions were thrust into a concessionary mode, desperate now to save jobs as opposed to making them more gratifying. Inside prisons, the push to provide more meaningful work also got sidelined as the incarcerated population mushroomed, yielding a surplus of prisoners with little to do. As a result, Johnson's directive never came close to being followed in Alabama.

By the time we did our interviews, it was difficult to find any evidence that "meaningful work" was even a consideration in the administration of the state's prisons. Educational and vocational programs had been sliced to the bone. Overcrowding meant that, in some facilities, jobs were only available for about one-third of the general population according to estimates of some of our interviewees. In December 2022—just before we began our visits—the overall jurisdictional population was 26,525, but the design capacity of all facilities was only for 12,115.[57] Most of those we spoke to wanted to be occupied in order to achieve some respite from the cramped, unsanitary, and dangerous dorms, where some prisoners may not even have a place to sleep and are effectively "homeless." Yet jobs that taught skills that might be applicable on reentry were few and far between. Some interviewees reported that the mere routine of showing up for and completing a few hours of make-work was a welcome reminder of a regimen they felt they needed for their mental and physical stability. One defined it as a way to "rehabilitate myself." Indeed, *self-rehabilitation* is a passable description of the best they could hope to do under circumstances that did nothing to redeem their spirit or sense of purpose in life.

While most were dismissive of the efforts of administrators to claim they were providing productive work, every so often we came across a potentially rewarding work experience. Jackson Dunbar, a youth counselor in Montgomery, recalled graduating from picking peas and okra on a prison farm to being a cowboy on a ranch formerly run by the state at Atmore near Mobile:

> I started riding horses, doing the cattle on the cowboy crew, to where we did roundups, inventoried the livestock, tagged the new calves and the old cows, took care of the bulls, and broke the horses. I was scared to death of animals before, but there I learned how to rope and how to AI [artificially inseminate] a cow. When you are riding a horse, you have a chance to get your solitude, in the open air, with the trees, and just chill out. So instead of looking at it as being punishment, I looked at it as being, maybe I can get something out of this . . . In prison, down here, you'll get very depressed, it'll take you to the point where you think you don't want to live no more. So, you have to change your perspective in order to survive.

Unfortunately, Dunbar was not destined for that kind of livelihood after he was released. However, the regard with which he
spoke about the opportunity to take on tasks well outside of his
orbit was striking, if rare.

The state's work-release facilities might have offered a more
direct pathway to employment on reentry. Prisoners can spend
the last few months of their sentence in a less restrictive setting,
working in the community for a private or public employer. Occasionally, they are hired at the same job or at the same firm on
release. But the economy of work release is hardly fair to them.
Those contracted for public sector work are paid $2 a day, the
same rate set in 1927. If the employer is from the private sector,
they are paid the minimum or prevailing wage, but ADOC takes
40 percent off the top. Their pay is garnished by up to 25 percent
for court fines and fees and for any restitution bills. Along with
other deductions for laundry, gas, and food, employees might be
left with only 15 percent. Whether they are hired out to public
agencies or to private firms, the state reaps most of the benefits.
Some local critics described this economic arrangement as akin
to convict leasing, and the practice lay at the heart of a major
anti-trafficking lawsuit brought against Alabama in December
2023, alleging that the state profited to the tune of $450 million
annually from this "modern form of slavery."[58]

Most of the useful skills learned in Alabama prisons are for
survival, or they are picked up from hustling, often in highly
ingenious ways, to generate revenue from the underground economy. Some of the income results from offering personalized services. As in other states, informal currency—like tobacco, ramen,
stamps, or real money (transferred to an outside account)—can
be earned by cutting hair, washing clothes, writing letters, cooking
specialized meals, and making cards or porn magazines for someone who is "paying" out of pocket or to repay a debt. Tutwiler
women have a well-developed culture of crocheting and making

custom clothes, including knock-off designer wear. The state also runs an official hobby craft program, in which applicants learn how to work leather to make items like wallets and belts that can be sold on the outside through their families. However, in some facilities guards control this sub-economy, reaping the profits from markups on items that they purchase from prisoners.

The more lucrative hustles are predatory or exploitative, including the operation of price-gouging "stores" or the sale of drugs, weapons, phones, and other kinds of contraband. Trading sex, we found, is often used to settle debts or for protection from harm. The internal black market is an inflationary version of the free world informal economy, and it often involves outside actors in street organizations. Like the formal work assignments, these activities are governed by force and threats of physical harm. As in all prisons, most of the assigned institutional jobs carry some ancillary advantage or perk. A job in the mess hall offers handy access to food—especially healthy raw produce. Working at the commissary affords control of the queue: people will pay to be allowed to cut to the front of the line. Jobs that allow for mobility have many potential benefits. But sometimes these perks are downright demeaning. For example, Alabama's prisoners are often assigned as "runners" to administrators or senior COs, a job that is basically akin to a personal servant and sometimes referred to as a "houseboy" or "house negro" job. The reward for cleaning their stuff, shining their shoes, or doing errands is to be thrown leftovers from a lunch, a few cigarettes, or a bag of chips.

For some, the art of the hustle carries over from illicit activities that led to their incarceration, especially if it involves contraband and organized coercion. In addition, what they have to do to survive behind bars will extend to "the street" upon their return. In that respect, a term or two in prison will not have differed much from how they eke out a livelihood in the neoliberal shadow economy on the outside. Others will become newly tutored in the dog-eat-dog world behind bars, and the dark arts they learn there will be rooted in mistrust, manipulation, and plunder—not in mutual aid. Nor is this education optional, since, in Alabama's prisons, it usually proceeds under the imminent threat of violence at all times of the day and night.

One interviewee told us that his "head was always on a swivel, constantly looking out for danger." Jackson Dunbar, the quondam cowboy, offered an example: "When you use the bathroom, and go to have a bowel movement, you had to pull one of your pants legs off, and hold it to the side so if anybody bothers you, you're ready to get up and fight." He also explained the dynamics of nighttime: "If you're a stand up guy during the day, and you got your people, then you really ain't gotta worry about night because y'all watch each other. But if you're an asshole or whatever and you have enemies running around, then you really couldn't sleep. And you really don't sleep even when you got your people. It's one of those sleeps like you never go into a deep slumber. Anything moving, you hear anything, and you are right up. I don't believe I slept a deep sleep for 18 years . . . and I still wake up 2:00 or 3:00 in the morning, looking around."

In some prisons, we learned, everyone has to have a knife—typically self-fashioned from the strut of a bed frame but sometimes imported from the free world. These weapons have to be visible and worn on the hip to ward off the prospect of attack. Guards, issued with stab-proof vests, accept this as a norm. For the most part, there is not much that COs can do, because they are hopelessly outnumbered in Alabama's facilities. The problems of overcrowding are exacerbated by the chronic shortage of COs. When one officer is responsible for 50 or even 100 men, they are no longer in charge, and their personal safety and mental health is far from assured.[59] Their own working conditions are substandard and often perilous. Plumbing and heating in most facilities are dysfunctional, there is no A/C, human waste is often thrown at them, and the risk of being assaulted by buzzed prisoners with homemade weapons is high. As a result, demand for these lowly paid jobs has dwindled. Qualifications have had to be lowered and turnover on the job is sky-high.[60]

Even so, many are willing to sign up in order to run lucrative contraband operations. Smartphones that retail for a few hundred dollars will fetch $1,000 to $1,500 inside. Phone chargers run for $150 and select drugs also have a high market value. At least two interviewees estimated that guards, most of whom are Black these days, could make as much as half a million dollars annually. Involvement is risky but less so when everyone is in on the action. In response to the expanding internal marketplace, we were told that gang members are increasingly recruited as COs to ensure that the flow of goods and revenue stays within the orbit of the dominant street organizations. Incarcerated lifers with gangland affiliations were the most reliable partners in these operations.

All of these activities are much more profitable than the operations run through the state's prison industries. As in other states, Alabama prisons produce goods for public vendors. Formalized under the Prison-Made Goods Act of 1976, Alabama Correctional Industries (ACI) oversees about ten plants that house manufacturing and service operations. Manufactured products include furniture, mattresses, chemicals, printed materials, uniforms, and, as one interviewee put it "bullet-proof judges' benches." According to the 1976 act, part of ACI's mission is to "provide meaningful work and vocational training programs for inmates," but these programs—which were thin to begin with—took a back seat after ACI was restructured in 2007 to emphasize profit-seeking after decades of running at a loss.[61] Even though prisoners who work in these facilities only earn from 25 to 65 cents an hour, ACI still struggles to break even. During the pandemic years, ACI was back in the red. Of course, there are other ways that ADOC helps to extract revenue from prisoners, such as income from price-gouging commissary stores, tablets and phone calls, medical co-pays, ID cards, fines from punitive tickets, and fees for tests.[62] Nor can we discount the firms with tight connections to lawmakers: they benefit from ADOC contracts to undertake construction and provide other services.

It is all too common to hear criticism that America's prisons are now run as profit centers. But we found that evidence for this argument is weaker in Alabama than elsewhere, and that the maintenance of racial and social hierarchy is a stronger reason for keeping up the prison population. ADOC and ACI just don't seem to be very good at making money. And while the daily cost of locking someone up almost doubled from 2013 ($41.94) to 2021 ($82.64), ADOC's budget rose by about the same ratio, largely because the overheated tough-on-crime rhetoric of Alabama's lawmakers and its elected judiciary shows no sign of cooling off.[63] The state has gotten several failing grades from district judges and the DOJ for the conditions inside its prisons, and it doesn't seem any more competent at making them economically productive. In our view, there is no good way to run a prison system, but Alabama is doing a particularly bad job.

CHAPTER 5

Let the Crops Rot in the Fields

Mr. Backlash, Mr. Backlash
Just what do you think I got to lose?
I'm gonna leave you
With the backlash blues
— Nina Simone

On November 8, 2022, Alabama voters passed a measure (by a margin of 74.5 percent to 25.5 percent) to strip racist language out of the state's constitution. It was no small matter. The constitution is by far the longest in the world, and even after the discriminatory provisions were removed, it is still three times longer—at more than 373,000 words—than that of Texas, the nearest contender. The passage in 1901 of the existing constitution had been a highpoint of white supremacy in the South. John Knox, president of that constitutional convention, assured white voters that by "eliminat[ing] the ignorant negro vote," the new document "places the control of our government where God Almighty intended it should be—with the Anglo-Saxon race." In addition to disenfranchising Alabama's Black citizens, the constitution barred interracial marriage, enshrined the segregation of schools and public spaces, and upheld the legality of the convict leasing system.

In 2021, the ASNN organizers Savannah Eldrige and Max Parthas—along with Alabama's longtime prison rights advocate Kenny Glasgow—got wind of an effort to remove the constitution's racist language that was spearheaded by a bipartisan group of legislators. They mobilized discreetly to ensure that the language permitting involuntary servitude as a punishment for crime was included in the omnibus measure. Bundling this reform along with all the others ensured that it would not attract too much attention. "It would never have passed on its own," Eldrige confirmed. Glasgow, who happens to be Al Sharpton's brother, recalled that "we just slid it in, without using any media—we just let the white folks talk to white folks, and they carried the water for us. We never mentioned 'abolish slavery,' we just called it the 'healing process,' and they didn't see the prison labor part coming at all."

The passage of the amendment did not occur in a vacuum. First of all, it was foreshadowed by Glasgow's own strenuous

efforts to restore voting rights to ex-felons. The 1901 Constitution had stipulated that residents who committed a "felony
involving moral turpitude" could be disqualified from voting.
This largely undefined phrase had been used to strike almost all
system-impacted people off the voter rolls—as many as 286,000
in Alabama in 2016.[1] After the state attorney general issued an
opinion in 2005 that the "moral turpitude" language had been
interpreted too broadly, Glasgow reprised civil rights tactics
from the 1960s by registering people to vote while they were in
prison on misdemeanor charges or in county jails awaiting conviction. Having served time himself on a drugs charge, he was
able to win his own "freedom papers" in the process of forcing Alabama to join the small company of states that extended
the right to vote to (some) currently incarcerated people.[2] He
continued the fight in Florida, where he had served a longer
sentence, during which time he formed The Ordinary People Society (TOPS) as a prisoner rights organization. In 2017,
the Alabama legislature finally clarified exactly which crimes
(including murder and rape) were covered by "moral turpitude,"
effectively re-enfranchising those with low-level drug offenses,
liquor law violations, and felony DUIs.[3] Rolling back the discriminatory practice of felony disenfranchisement (15 percent
of Alabama's Black voting age population were affected, compared with fewer than 5 percent of whites[4]) was an important
"turnstile," as Glasgow put it, on the road to eliminating slavery
without exceptions from the constitution.

Another significant backdrop to the constitutional change
was that, for several years, prisoners in the state system had carried out a series of work stoppages that had generated similar,
solidarity efforts in other states. In fact, Alabama had become
the unlikely epicenter of a new prisoner rights movement. As a
result, the effort to remove prison slavery from the constitution
was being driven, in part, from the inside. Yet, as we found,

the aspirations of the strike organizers went far beyond the act of removing racist language from the state constitution.

Free Alabama

The initial strike energy came from the Free Alabama Movement (FAM), founded by Bennu Hannibal Ra-Sun (Melvin Ray) and Kinetik Justice (Robert Earl Council) in 2013 at St. Clair Correctional Facility in Springville, Alabama. Bennu was one of the Gadsden Six—a group of Black youth arrested for a 1988 burglary and theft and unjustly assigned to an adult court for sentencing. These illegal prior convictions, he contends, were then cited as a factor in his subsequent life sentence on a murder charge. Kinetik has also disputed his own conviction, alleging the use of false testimony in the trial.

While they were in Holman Correctional Facility, Bennu and Kinetik both got a legal education from law classes. In accord with Lenin's observation that prisons are universities for revolutionaries, they also received lessons in political education from Richard "Mafundi" Lake, a veteran of the prison movement of the 1960s and 1970s, with whom they had the good fortune of sharing a cell block. Kinetik had already been reading Malcolm X's *Autobiography* and some revolutionary pamphlets by Bob Avakian, and Mafundi had much more of that kind of literature for the men to delve into. When they were both transferred to St. Clair prison—where lots of men had cell phones—they learned about the power of social media, and decided to update the communication tactics of Mafundi's earlier generation of radicals for the twenty-first century.[5]

A work stoppage at Holman in 2007 laid the local seeds for the movement they decided to build. Then a large prisoner strike in Georgia in December 2010 provided an organizing model. In Georgia, the strike organizers had coordinated a work stoppage in six or more facilities using contraband cell phones, drawing attention to their "involuntary servitude," and demanding a living wage for their labor.[6] Bennu and Kinetik adopted the labor strike as a key point of leverage for their own efforts, and learned to use their cell phones not just to communicate among peers but also to circulate images of deplorable prison conditions in "Bloody St. Clair" to the outside world. Noting that the Georgia authorities were able to shape media coverage of the 2010 strike, Bennu described how the FAM organizers took pains to "document all of our grievances and produce proof for the public of why we were protesting" in order to prevent ADOC's efforts to "control the narrative." Overcoming their early "fears of repercussions for going on camera," their peers began "to open up about our conditions in ways that they never had" previously. He noted that "for the first time, we told our stories, in our own words, with our own dialects and phrases." The duo "posted it all over YouTube, Facebook, and anywhere else we could find a space."[7]

After they formed a study group, Bennu produced and circulated estimates of how much revenue they were generating, for the state, from manufacturing products, work release deductions, filing fees, commissary and vending machine markups, incentive packages, co-pays, and other punitive fees and surcharges. "In the chemical plant [at St. Clair] alone," he recalled, "I was able to show the guys that they were producing $25 million worth of chemicals each year." Only so much of that money was being used to fund ADOC, while the surplus looked like sheer profit. Regarding "the $500 billion prison industry" (more sober estimates tend to value nationwide revenues at $74 billion),[8] he pointed out that "nationwide, prison budgets total $86 billion, so where is the remaining $414 billion going? . . . Funny how we 'control' a half trillion dollar market, but we go to bed hungry at night."[9] Bennu also estimated that ADOC employed about a third of the prison population for free. Calculating lost pay at the federal minimum wage, these 10,000 incarcerated workers were providing $600,000 of unpaid labor a day, or $219 million a year.[10]

Even more important to FAM's peers was the fact that it had become increasingly difficult to win parole in the state of Alabama. Typically, the three members of the parole board comprise a former prosecutor, a former probation officer, and a former state trooper. There is no representation from anyone with a criminal defense background. This board, which granted fewer and fewer requests every year, declined to meet in person with most applicants, and neglected to take into account their records of good behavior or completed participation in programs. By 2023, only 7 percent of applications were being approved, in contrast to 54 percent as recently as 2017. The racial disparity in treatment was also clear: white parole applicants were more than twice as likely to be granted parole as Black parole applicants.[11] In effect, Alabama prisons held a captive workforce for which there was no retirement option. As the mortality rate began to rise sharply, coming out in a body bag would soon have better odds than being released at the end of a sentence. To all intents and purposes, the state's penal policy appeared to be a version of "lock them up and throw away the key."

In response, FAM—which espoused non-violent tactics as a rule—called two strikes. The first, in January 2014, spread to three prisons, and the second was planned for April, four months later.[12] Both Bennu and Kinetik were placed in solitary confinement as retribution, and they were denied visitation rights and all other privileges. They continued to organize, even after Kinetik was badly beaten by guards. Dhati Khalid and Swift Justice, two other FAM organizers, were also targeted. They suffered for the lead roles they played. In the wake of the 2014 actions, FAM developed an inside/outside relationship with Glasgow's TOPS, and with the newly formed Incarcerated Workers Organizing Committee, a prisoner-led section of the Industrial Workers of

the World (IWW).[13] Repressive incarceration by the state features prominently in the history of the Wobblies. Indeed, locking
up IWW leaders was a primary weapon employed by President
Woodrow Wilson against the union in the 1910s. His decision to
crush the IWW was allegedly taken after some Wobblies threatened to burn California crops unless some of their local organizers of the 1913 Wheatfields strike were released from prison.[14]

It was appropriate then that FAM's first "manifesto"—issued
in January 2015—was titled *Let the Crops Rot in the Fields*. In this
case, the allusion was to resistance on the plantation.

> LET THE CROPS ROT IN THE FIELD is a proven
> strategy that was passed down to us from our Ances-
> tors from the slave plantations that was used to disrupt
> the economics of the field. The harvest of the planter
> season was reaped when the crops were picked from the
> field and sold on the open market. When the slave master
> had invested all that he owned into his next crop (prison
> factories), the slaves would wait until just before the
> harvest and rebel against the slave system by 'going on
> strike' and causing the crops to rot in the field. This tactic
> would completely ruin the slave master's investment.

The authors of the document reasoned that hunger strikes (like
those at California's Pelican Bay Prison in 2011 and 2013, involving more than 30,000 participants),[15] protest marches, and peti-
tion-based campaigns had not proven effective in winning prison
reforms. A new approach was needed, targeting the economic
base of the modern prison–industrial complex and focusing on
the unpaid labor that kept the prisons operating while also generating profits for states and companies. The FAM manifesto
called for "organize[d] prison shutdowns at prisons with major
economic industries (tag plants, fleet services, food distribution

centers, agriculture, etc.)" Labor strikes, the authors pointed out, hit the prison profiteers where it hurts most by stopping production. But they also pleaded for shutdowns to be accompanied by boycott protests at companies like McDonald's that contract prison labor. And they called for the strikes to be coordinated "with our families, friends, supporters, activists, and others holding protests at the prisons where the people are mass incarcerated and oppressed."[16]

Just as important, *Let the Crops Rot* declared that "when we organize, we have to demand that real 'reforms' take place that will afford everyone an opportunity to earn our freedom, NOT JUST EARN A CHECK FOR OUR LABOR, and that fundamental changes be made throughout the system." To that end, FAM urged organizers in each state to draft their own "FREEDOM BILL." FAM's Alabama version—The Education, Rehabilitation and Re-Entry Preparedness Bill—included provisions for full voting rights, open media access to ADOC facilities, caps on the state's overall incarcerated population, reductions to the design capacity of prisons, robust education, rehabilitation and re-entry preparedness programs, the abolition of involuntary servitude, sentencing reductions for select felonies, upgrading of parole procedures, and a ban on incarcerating mentally ill persons. In addition, the draft bill contained detailed proposals for reorganizing the state's prisons into facilities with specific functions related to the educational and rehabilitative programs. Prisoners should have a clear pathway to "earn" their freedom through participation in these programs.[17] The document was, at once, a compact statement of prisoner rights, a blueprint for moving prisons away from profit and punishment, and a game plan for restructuring the system based on the expertise of those inside— the people who knew it best.

By 2016, the capacity for coordinated "economic direct action" had grown beyond Alabama, in part as a result of the circulation of *Let the Crops Rot.* The Free Mississippi Movement, Free Ohio Movement, and Free Virginia Movement had all formed, along with solidarity clusters in other states. A nationwide strike was called for September 9, 2016, the 45ᵗʰ anniversary of the Attica rebellion. The strike, which began in Alabama's Holman prison, was observed in 23 other states—including Texas, Mississippi, Oregon, Illinois, Virginia, California, Georgia, Washington, South Carolina, Michigan, and Florida. An estimated 57,000 prisoners in at least 46 facilities participated.[18]

FAM decided against a unified list of demands, and so the calls varied from state to state and sometimes from prison to prison in response to specific local grievances. However, another group of organizers—Jailhouse Lawyers Speak—did put forth a list of national demands:

1. Immediate improvements to the conditions of prisons and prison policies that recognize the humanity of imprisoned men and women.
2. An immediate end to prison slavery. All persons imprisoned in any place of detention under United States jurisdiction must be paid the prevailing wage in their state or territory for their labor.
3. Rescission of the Prison Litigation Reform Act, allowing imprisoned humans a proper channel to address grievances and violations of their rights.
4. Rescission of the Truth in Sentencing Act and the Sentencing Reform Act so that imprisoned humans have a possibility of rehabilitation and parole. No human shall be sentenced to death by incarceration or serve any sentence without the possibility of parole.
5. An immediate end to the racial overcharging, over-sentencing and parole denials of Black and brown humans. Black humans shall no longer be denied parole

because the victim of the crime was white, which is a particular problem in Southern states.

6. An immediate end to racist gang enhancement laws targeting Black and Brown humans.

7. No denial of access to rehabilitation programs for imprisoned humans at their place of detention because of their label as a violent offender.

8. State prisons must be funded specifically to offer more rehabilitation services.

9. Reinstatement of Pell grant eligibility to prisoners in all U.S. states and territories.

10. Recognition of voting rights for all confined citizens serving prison sentences, pretrial detainees and so-called "ex-felons." Their votes must be counted. Representation is demanded. All voices count![19]

Formed in 2015 by the incarcerated members of a George Jackson study group to provide legal advice to fellow prisoners, Jailhouse Lawyers Speak followed up by issuing a call for a march in Washington DC. Spotlighting the growing national movement to end prison slavery, the Millions for Prisoners Human Rights March took place in 2017 during Black August (an annual tradition commemorating the political prisoners of the 1960s). Marchers brought the injustice of the Exception Clause to the nation's capital.[20] In a preemptive action, authorities locked down prisons all across Florida and South Carolina, impacting more than 97,000 prisoners. In the wake of the march, the expanding coalition of organizers began to make plans for an even bigger 2019 sequel to the 2016 action. In the meantime, work stoppages and commissary boycotts continued to pop up—most notably in Florida, where prisoners began a four-week strike on MLK Day in 2018, demanding payment for labor, a reduction in canteen prices, and reintroduction of parole incentives.[21]

Four months later, seven prisoners were killed and twenty-two others were seriously injured from stabbings during a riot inside South Carolina's maximum-security Lee Correctional Facility after members of two rival gangs were placed in the same housing unit. Understaffing and overcrowding also contributed to the deadly bloodbath.[22] In response to this incident, the 2019 plan was moved up, and organizers pulled together a second nationwide Shut 'Em Down strike, endorsed this time by more than 150 organizations. It was projected to run for 19 days, from August 21 (the 47th anniversary of George Jackson's death) until the Attica anniversary date of September 9.

After the 2014 and 2016 strikes, the tactic of relying on work stoppages alone had increasingly come into question. Not everyone in prison worked, especially those in solitary confinement, and prisoners who were employed in work release programs were reluctant to endanger their job placements so close to the end of their sentences. In response, FAM circulated a call to "redistribute the pain."[23] Prisoners who wanted to show solidarity could also participate through hunger strikes, sit-ins, and commissary boycotts, while supporters on the outside were encouraged to protest outside the prisons.

The 2018 strike—in all of these forms—was widely observed, stretching in reach from the Deep South states to Nova Scotia in Canada. Harsh reprisals and repression followed, as authorities ordered lockdowns and other collective punishments. The most ruthless treatment, of course, was reserved for individuals fingered as lead organizers. Kinetik Justice, foremost among them, staged his own hunger strike, followed by others in Holman's solitary confinement cells in March 2019.[24] Within a year, however, the COVID pandemic engendered its own comprehensive lockdown, and the movement was put on hold for more than two years. Targeted repression continued, however. Guards tried to murder Kinetik in his segregation cell in January 2021 after he tried to protect a peer from an attack—an incident that occasioned an FBI probe, but lost him an eye.[25]

The movement burst back into life on September 26, 2022, when every prison in Alabama joined a strike aimed at the rapidly worsening conditions and lack of parole consideration. Plans for the strike were months in the making, but the date was also triggered by the viral circulation of images of an extremely emaciated prisoner, Kastellio Vaughan, who had been denied adequate medical attention. The ability to pull off this state-wide organizing feat owed a great deal to Both Sides of the Wall (BSOW), a new group on the outside composed primarily of spouses and partners of incarcerated men. Formed in 2019, BSOW quickly established the capacity to coordinate communications between the more active prisoners in each facility, along with the tactics needed to apply public pressure on lawmakers. Over time, the group created a community of mutual aid among its members. Some had lost loved ones from guard brutality, most of the others were trying to save their partners from further harm and medical neglect by campaigning for their release.

BSOW's founder, Diyawn Caldwell—a former manager with Coca Cola and Walmart—had no prior experience as an organizer. She met her incarcerated husband Cordarius Caldwell (who was serving a 28-year sentence, reduced to 23) through social media. He had been active in the 2016 and 2018 strikes and he was well-connected on the inside. Caldwell, who told us she had a long personal record of building leadership skills, undertook a rapid self-education about the deteriorating prison conditions, including "food that was being served out of boxes, that said, 'not fit for human consumption.'" Then she asked herself; "if I'm in a relationship with this man, how can I be effective in changing things that are going on within the system?" She soon found an equally committed collaborator, Christina Horvat, with whom she could organize an effective pressure group, after Horvat's spouse was stabbed and suffered from the system's acute lack of medical care. Horvat confessed that she had a typical law-and-order mentality before she met her husband in prison: "I was like, if you don't want to do the time, don't do the crime." By the time we interviewed her, this outspoken white woman was on the governor's unofficial public enemy list: after the strike, she told us "anybody who called my phone or Diyawn's phone, got sent to lockup, even if it was just a regular conversation." Four months later in July 2023, she would announce her candidacy for the governorship at one of BSOW's "Break Every Chain" rallies in Bessemer.

The duo formed a Facebook group for spouses and partners, but getting family members and friends involved was not easy at first. "The South," Caldwell reminded us, "is just more conservative" and yet the community-building was necessary in order to "educate them about the conditions . . . because guys on the inside won't tell their families what is going on—they just say that 'everything's OK,' because they don't want to worry their loved ones." Also, she added, "a lot of these guys don't want their families to know they are addicted to drugs because that's the only way they can cope, and so they don't tell them." She had met "a lot of families who didn't know anything about the bloodbath in there, and the only way they know now is through our groups and our meetings."

BSOW officially formed in order to secure a permit for its first "Break Every Chain" rally outside ADOC headquarters in Montgomery. Organizers on the inside had contacted Caldwell and Horvat and decided that they could pull off a labor strike together. Caldwell helped to coordinate strategy meetings in the build-up to ensure unity among different factions and rival gang leaders, a custom established and observed in California during the Pelican Bay Prison strikes of 2011 and 2013.[26] Being the spouse of a former high-ranking gang member helped her appreciate the need for agreements among the street organizations. On September 26, the first day of the strike, BSOW staged its rally and delivered a list of demands to ADOC and the Ivey administration, which included repealing the Habitual Offenders Act, creating conviction integrity units to prevent false convictions, developing consistent standards for mandatory parole, streamlining medical furloughs and elder release procedures, and reducing minimum sentences for young offenders. It also included a repeal of the state's drive-by shooting statute, speaking to a specific concern of the street organizations. As the strike entered its second week, Caldwell and her allies organized an even larger rally on October 14 outside the state capitol.[27] Featuring testimony from activists, formerly incarcerated individuals, and those with loved ones in prison, it received wide media coverage along with the strike itself.[28]

Several days after the strike began, Ivey's office issued a dismissive response, describing the demands as "unreasonable" and claiming that facilities were "well under control."[29] In fact, the strike rolled on for three weeks, during which ADOC resorted to increasingly punitive measures—cancelling weekend visits, canceling access to recreational and educational programs, and, most notoriously, resorting to "bird-feeding," by reducing the number of daily meals from three to two. Prisoners circulated footage on social media of the paltry food on offer—inedible combos of uncooked hot dogs, slices of bread, and dollops of canned fruit.[30] During previous strikes, staff were ordered to prepare the meals. In 2016, administrators and civilians had to do the job when officers refused to show up for work. On *Democracy Now!*, Kinetik Justice reported from Holman: "Right now, the Commissioner is passing out a tray. Warden Peterson is pulling the cart. Deputy Commissioner Culliver passed me my tray . . . No officers came to work. They completely bucked on the administration."[31] By the time of the 2022 strike, which also saw systematic no-shows by correctional officers, most facilities had a significant number of employee vacancies and so staff were even more unavailable. Prisoners on work release and in honor camps were ordered in as scabs—putting them in mortal danger from their peers. Those who refused to cross the picket line were threatened with loss of their release status. Organizers like Kinetik added agitprop statements of their own: "It makes no sense for us to continue to contribute to our own oppression," he declared. "We finance our own incarceration through our free labor and spending every dime we get in the canteens and so forth. It is our money and our family's money that is used to keep us incarcerated and oppressed like this."[32] Once again, he was beaten up by guards and thrown in solitary confinement.

Given how difficult it was to coordinate a total work stoppage under these circumstances, participation across all of ADOC's men's prisons was surprisingly high. We heard from several sources that coercive threats were issued to enforce the strike. This was hardly surprising. Winning and sustaining solidarity required the say-so of powerful figures in each prison. They not only put aside their differences but deployed the necessary muscle to make sure the general population held the line. But it is also notable that we heard no reports of the organizers themselves suffering retaliation from their peers when the food deprivation and other collective punishments kicked in. Solidarity held firm, despite ADOC's clunky efforts to divide the men and retaliate after the fact. Among staff, there were reports of sympathy for the strike. In some of our interviews, we heard that guards had even helped to enforce the stoppage.

Unity was more difficult to achieve in Tutwiler. Some women observed a sit-down—a notice was posted in the kitchen instructing workers to stay off the job—and the authorities stepped up controls over the movement of the general population. However, there was nothing like the critical mass or comprehensive picket achieved in the men's prisons. As one Tutwiler alumna dismissively put it, "women don't know how to stick together like the men do, they are too jealous of each other, and everyone is on drugs anyway, smoking 'paper' or the latest thing." What would it take to get everyone on board? "Maybe a ban on cigarettes," she replied cynically. Another explained that the relationships many women still had with guards worked against horizontal unity, and that there was no peer intimidation applied to join the strike. At Tutwiler, as in other female prisons, the primary form of social structure is through pseudofamilies (strong, intergenerational friendship cohorts that mirror family kinship on the outside) as opposed to the street organizations that are more active in men's facilities.

That said, we also heard from others who had completed longer sentences that Tutwiler had a history of smaller-scale work stoppages, refusals, and boycotts that never made it into the media; one sit-down in 2012, we learned, achieved 25 percent participation. These expressions of dissent about the abusive conditions were regular occurrences. In addition, now that COs were in short supply, a culture of mutual aid had developed among the women that ran counter to the more competitive environment of the men's prisons. As one interviewee put it, "we just took the initiative to take care of ourselves."

The 2022 strike was eventually suspended by organizers out of concern for prisoners with medical issues. ADOC's "bird-feeding" tactics—reducing diets to 1000 calories or less—eventually forced the decision. According to Horvat, "the diabetics were shaking and shivering because they were not getting the caloric intake they needed. There were so many people who did not get any of their medication, and several people were rushed to the hospital because of diabetic and neurologic issues. So the guys said, look, we gotta come up, if this is what it's going to take to save these man's lives and let them get their help." The strikers issued a statement that succinctly summarized their decision: "Unlike the ADOC, we value life."[33]

Recent Ancestors

Alabama is not known for innovations that other states follow, but its prisoner strike movement seemed to catch on. Of course, it didn't come out of nowhere. Working-class Black people in the state have a long history of organizing resistance to their oppression. Alabama's decade in the cockpit of the civil rights movement is the most well-known, from Rosa Parks' arrest in 1955 to the formation of the rural Lowndes County Freedom Party—the first organization to adopt the Black Panther as a logo—after the 1965 Selma to Montgomery march.[34] But the state also hosted a significant chapter in the prisoner rights movement of the late 1960s and 1970s. In fact, "Mafundi" Lake, the mentor of the FAM founders, had a long and prominent career as one of the lead participants in this struggle.

Sentenced to 14 years as a teenager for a $34 robbery, he spent his time in Atmore-Holman prison reading up on Black revolutionary thought. He then formed Inmates for Action (IFA), a militant prisoner organization in 1972.[35] Conditions then were much the same as now, and so he spent many years in solitary for his efforts, which had included leading classes on the Black radical tradition. After his release from prison, he helped to organize the first prisoner support organizations in Alabama: Families for Action, the African People's Survival Committee, the Committee for Prisoner Support in Birmingham, and the Atmore-Holman Brothers Defense Committee. He also became national director of the African National Prison Organization, which he had helped to found in 1978. In May 1983, Mafundi was arrested again, on a trumped-up rape charge, for his role in organizing a National African Liberation Day rally in Birmingham. Under the Habitual Offenders Act, Lake spent the next 35 years behind bars, where he died in 2018.[36]

Mafundi and other IFA members organized their first work stoppages to protest the beating and killing of prisoners on Atmore-Holman's work farms. In 1974, they staged a unified work strike to protest general conditions in the facility, known at the time as "The Slaughterhouse" for its high incidence of guard brutality, prisoner-on-prisoner violence, and rape culture.[37] The protest morphed into a mini-Attica uprising when guards were taken hostage. One officer was killed during the action, unleashing a long season of retributive terror against the IFA. Several of the group's leaders—George Dobbins, Tommy Dotson, Charles Beasley, and Frank X. Moore—were killed while in prison. After his release, Mafundi helped wage a guerilla campaign against the police under the motto "Kill one of ours, we kill two of yours."[38] The IFA's effort at exposing the oppression inside the state's prisons was instrumental in the lawsuits that resulted in the federal takeover of the system in 1976.

The cooperation between the IFA and the support organizations that Mafundi founded in Birmingham looked forward to the inside/outside model that operates in the Alabama movement today, on the eve of another federal takeover of the state's prison system. But IFA, unlike FAM, was not a lead player on the national scene. Lake and others were instead taking their cue from George Jackson and his fellow California militants, inspired by the wave of agitprop-based organizing that pushed prisoner rights onto the center stage of radical politics from the late 1960s to the mid-1970s. Stokely Carmichael's 1966 declaration—"I ain't going to jail no more . . . What we gonna start saying now is Black Power"—is often cited as the turning point away from the patient, reformist tactics of the Civil Rights movement. But one of the ways in which this shift in tactics played out in the years that followed was to replace short-term jail detention for civil protests with the experience of criminalization on long-term prison sentences as the new theater of attention for Black Liberation.

MLK's "Letter from Birmingham Jail" ceded the limelight to more militant chronicles of imprisonment, like Malcolm X's *Autobiography*, Eldridge Cleaver's *Soul on Ice*, and, above all, Jackson's *Soledad Brother*. Each, in turn, broadcast the belief that Black people in the U.S. were imprisoned at birth and lived out a captive existence. As Malcolm X put it to Black audiences, "don't be shocked when I say I was in prison. You're still in prison." For Jackson, the actual experience of incarceration "required only minor psychic adjustments" from his prior life.[39] Being put in a cell or in shackles only dramatized an already existing condition. Being forced to perform unpaid labor rammed home the association with the servitude of slavery days. According to this way of thinking, the pathway from plantation to prison had been a straight and largely uninterrupted line, and so the freedom movement had to be focused around the penitentiary. It would be replenished through conscious revolt, uncompromising demands, wall-to-wall litigation, the spectacle of public propaganda, and by any other means necessary. As historians like Dan Berger and Robert Chase have pointed out, the equation of prison with slavery was a constant in the Black Liberation discourse of these years.[40] African American prisoners in particular were seen as natural recruits in this new frontline struggle, in which the foe was the white supremacist state. The logical conclusion to this line of thinking was that imprisonment was an immoral act of bondage and therefore an illegal expression of state violence.

Even though many of the movement leaders did not actually perform much work—they were mostly confined to isolation cells—the issue of forced prison labor was central to the demands that accompanied a series of actions beginning in 1968, when work stoppages shook up San Quentin. Some of the more militant participants were transferred to Folsom in November

1970, where they organized a mass strike that was observed by almost 2,500 prisoners and lasted for 19 days. Their evolving grievances were fully laid out in the "Folsom Prisoners Manifesto of Demands," which listed thirty-one demands. Because prisoners essentially had few rights that were respected at that time (were even viewed in some quarters as "civilly dead"), a Bill of Rights was appended to this list. First and foremost was "the right to organize prisoner unions." News of the Folsom Manifesto and the California strikes circulated nationally, providing the model for theory and action at numerous prisons in other states. The assassination of George Jackson—the most prominent Soledad Brother—in San Quentin in August 1971 fueled the prairie fire which reached Attica the following month.

During the Attica revolt (the largest, most influential, and best-documented of the uprisings), the injustice of unpaid prison labor was an abiding and central issue, as we discussed in chapter two. The insurgency, along with public outrage at its bloody repression, helped to fuel a wave of prison reforms that rolled through state after state. In courts of law, the "rights revolution" took hold. As a result of *Robinson v. California* (1962), state governments could be sued in federal courts under the Eighth Amendment's prohibition against cruel and unusual punishment and through Section 1983 of the 1871 Civil Rights Act. *Cooper vs. Pate* (1964) gave prisoners actionable legal rights for the first time. After the *Wolff v. McDonnell* (1974) ruling that "there is no iron curtain drawn between the Constitution and the prisons of this country," jailhouse lawyers pursued these rights vigorously in the courts. The changes were felt even in the South, and especially after *Ruíz vs. Estelle*, a far-reaching 1980 case in which a Texas inmate named David Resendez Ruíz successfully sued the state for allowing conditions of confinement that violated his constitutional rights. The issue of prisoner rights most clearly established itself as a legitimate cause in the public mind after the international clamor to "Free Angela Davis" culminated in her high-profile trial in 1972.

The right to union representation prominently featured in the Folsom Prisoners Manifesto of Demands was taken up all across the country. Under the umbrella of the United Prisoners Union on the West Coast and under the Prisoners Labor Union (PLU) on the East Coast, prisoners' unions began to form in several states, including Delaware, Maine, Massachusetts, Michigan, Minnesota, Ohio, Pennsylvania, New York, Washington, DC, and Wisconsin. The Prisoners' Union Committee was also formed as a bargaining agent for Canadian prisoners. In North Carolina, which hosted the most sustained membership drive, the PLU collected cards from 5,000 prisoners, almost half of the state's incarcerated population.[41]

None of these unions won formal certification or signed a collective bargaining agreement. The revanchist backlash to Attica and the subsequent rollback of rights under the Rockefeller Drug Laws proved to be more powerful than the forward momentum. The death penalty was reinstated by the Supreme Court in 1976. The following year, the Supreme Court (in *Jones v. North Carolina Prisoners' Labor Union*) decided that prisoners do not have the right under the First Amendment to form labor unions. After 1980, Ronald Reagan picked up where Richard Nixon left off, deploying the racist dog whistle of law-and-order rhetoric to preside over a rapid expansion of the carceral system. But it was under Bill Clinton that the national population of criminalized people grew most rapidly. His administration's 1994 Law Enforcement Act accelerated the flow of poor and racialized people into cages, while the Prison Litigation Reform Act of 1996 closed off many of the doors opened by *Ruíz vs. Estelle* for prisoners to litigate against cruel and unusual punishment. These harsh measures dampened many of the efforts of prison organizers, though they did not stop strikes entirely. Prisoners have always resisted the routines of forced labor, whether through stoppages, sabotage, or soldiering, and they continued to do so. But these actions were no longer part of a discernible movement on the march, at least until FAM re-lit a fire that seemed to want to burn beyond Alabama.

The prisoner rights movement of the 1960s and 1970s was often polarized by the face-off between advocates of reform and revolution. How did this debate play out around the issue of prison labor? Given the priority afforded to prisoner unions in the Folsom and Attica manifestos, the subsequent organizing drives followed the logic that prison workplaces had to be brought into line with the free world—through the introduction of minimum wages, protections, safety standards, and collective bargaining. Yet Dan Berger argues that this ideal tended to appeal more to white prisoners. For radical Black nationalists, the overcrowded modern penitentiary was a direct descendant of the slave ship. They had less interest in cleaning up an institution they saw as fundamentally illegitimate and punitive in nature. The nationalists' revolt against forced labor was not aimed at turning the prison into a tidy, law-abiding workplace, with prevailing wages, workers comp, and OSHA standards. Even if it conformed to regulations in the free world, prison labor would still be an instrument of racial control, and so they assumed the reforms would change nothing about the state's continuing use of incarceration for that purpose. Improving the labor conditions might even help to legitimize the racist designs of law-and-order politics.

Was wage labor, associated since the early days of the Industrial Revolution with coercive, capitalist discipline, really worth fighting for? In the antebellum North, free labor abolitionists often assailed the new industrial order as a form of "wage slavery," a condition that stripped artisans of their independent control over time and production, and delivered them into the thralldom of factory bosses. As David Roediger has shown, the widespread use of this slogan, in the U.S. and Europe, was implicitly anti-slavery, since it equated the new wage labor of the "free market" with plantation labor.[42] Even Frederick Douglass, who more than anyone vocalized the fundamental and meaningful difference between being enslaved and being free to sell one's labor, was quick to acknowledge the evils of wage slavery. In 1883, he declared: "Experience demonstrates that there may be a wages of slavery only a little less galling and crushing in its effects than chattel slavery, and that this slavery of wages must go down with the other."[43]

The difference between the two was central to the debate about reform vs. revolution in the 1970s. It is still a point of contention among prison activists. Today's incarcerated organizers and their outside allies have not moved beyond the race-centered arguments of the Black nationalist heyday. References to the words of the leaders from that era are scattered throughout FAM's early communiques. But there is no consistent nationalist line about Black people being a "captive nation." Black voices and Black experience are appropriately front and center in Alabama, where African Americans account for 54 percent of those in prison but only 28 percent of the general population. Nationally, the numbers are 38 percent and 12 percent respectively.[44] So, too, the lead actors on the inside and the outside tend to be Black. Noting the relative absence of Latinx prisoners in the movement, Jorge Renaud—the national criminal justice director of Latino Justice—explained: "many Latinos, who make up 33 percent of the prison population, are very much 'do your time, you brought this on yourself,'" and so, as a result, Latinx prisoners "have very little family support because of the attitude of 'you brought shame on us.'" He noted that "there is a good percentage of African Americans who realize that there is a 'system' and they welcome the people coming out of prison, and are trying to create prison reform abolitionist movements and are saying, yes, go forward and fight the system. But we don't do that."

Although the dominance of Black voices within the movement is unquestioned, radical Black politics have mutated over the decades, and nationalism no longer plays a leading-edge role, while the expanded economy of mass incarceration and the pluralism of today's abolitionist scene has changed the political landscape. To cite one example, André Gorz's concept of non-reformist reforms (robust changes that can significantly alter the balance of power) has become popular among abolitionists for its capacity to move beyond the old conflict over reform vs. revolution. Would the removal of involuntary servitude from constitutions and the subsequent provision of adequately paid prison labor meet the bar for non-reformist reform? On the evidence of the testimony we collected for this book, we believe that it would. The formal outlawing of the threat of force in prison workplaces backed up by the tactical refusal of labor is a credible strategy for achieving such changes. They can open a door that would lead to other transformative milestones on the road to abolition. But only if the door remains ajar for long enough.

Three Rallies

In a competition to select the building most evocative of white supremacy, Alabama's hilltop state capitol in Montgomery would be a top contender. It served as the first capital of the Confederacy at a time when its pillared, Greek Revival façade formed the terminus of the road leading to the city's slave auction market, one of the largest in the South. It was on the steps of this building in 1963 that George Wallace made his notorious inaugural speech promising "segregation now, segregation tomorrow, segregation forever." Later that year, he raised the Stars and Bars above the gleaming white building, and this flag flew there until 1991. It wasn't until 2015 that the last Confederate flags were removed from the memorial to the rebel soldiers that still occupies a prominent place on the grounds. A statue of J. Marion Sims, the "father of gynecology" who experimented on enslaved women, still stands there. Tourists flock daily to Jefferson Davis's first White House of the Confederacy across the road.[45]

It was against this loaded backdrop that BSOW held their third "Break Every Chain" rally on March 5, 2023. Caldwell, the master of ceremonies, had been up for 24 hours, printing T-shirts and lining up the participants. She introduced speaker after speaker, enduring more than four hours under an unseasonably hot Montgomery sun. The messaging was tight and well-coordinated. Hardline calls for action were offset by the harrowing testimony of women whose loved ones had suffered or died behind bars or who were being denied parole. Caldwell's 10-year-old grandson was with her from Atlanta. "He will learn more here than he would have done at school today," she pointed out. "I refuse to lose my grandchildren to this system," she vowed, "they are next if we don't do enough now. They are young Malcolms and Martins, we need to teach them to fight early, or they will be inside twenty years from now." In a system bent on profiteering from every filled prison bunk, "our children," she declared, "literally have a price on their heads." Another speaker talked about her own son, who was only 15 years old and innocent of all charges when he was given a 25-year sentence. "This state does not use its juvenile system," she declared, "so our boys go directly to prison. They have to kill to defend themselves in there, and so it's the prison that makes them into murderers." Addressing the mothers around her, she advised: "we can't teach our boys how to be men, but we can teach them not to be so hard."

Caldwell closed out the rally by picking up a length of chain links in each hand. Behind her loomed a statue of Jefferson Davis. Swaying back and forth as Tasha Cobbs' hit version of the gospel song "Break Every Chain" filled the air, she slowly let the links fall to the ground. This was the spot where MLK and his allies reached the end of their historic march from Selma to issue the declaration: "We have come not only five days and fifty miles but we have come from three centuries of suffering and hardship. We have come to you, the governor of Alabama, to declare that we must have our freedom now." George Wallace had little to say in response at the time, though on the 30th anniversary of the march, he offered words of repentance: "My message to you today is, welcome to Montgomery. May your message be heard. May your lessons never be forgotten."

BSOW's rally was timed for the eve of the governor's State of the State speech. But the current incumbent was even less likely to be paying attention than Wallace had been. There was a small crowd gathered on the capitol steps, though the more important audience for the speeches was inside the prisons listening to the livestreamed event. The rally had also been planned to coincide with another prison strike, an action labelled as the Alabama Spring. But the shutdown had not materialized. Many of the speakers addressed themselves to the aborted stoppage, lifting up supportive allies and scolding those who had not responded to the strike call. What had happened to the unity of September?

Two months before, in one of the first acts of her new term, Governor Ivey—labelled Poison Ivey by the activists—issued an executive order threatening to withdraw correctional incentive time (better known as "Good Time") as a punishment for anyone "refusing to work" or "encouraging or causing" a work stoppage.[46] This threat of retaliation was directly at odds with the removal of the language about involuntary servitude from the state constitution. Activists were used to seeing Ivey and other Alabama lawmakers circumvent the rule of law through loopholes, diversions, or subterfuge, but this move was rightly interpreted as a direct and transparent hit on the prison strike movement. Caldwell described it as "illegal" and "a direct abuse of power," while Gemma, a BSOW member, addressed the material impact of Ivey's threat to withdraw Good Time credit. "That's not even a thing," she scoffed, "since less than 15 percent of our incarcerated citizens have access to Good Time anyway, and even that's not guaranteed. Besides, if you can't get parole, Good Time is not all that good."

Nevertheless, the governor's threatening order seemed to have inhibited some of the men and women on the inside, especially those on work-release, who could see the end of their sentence coming. These were the prisoners who could be conscripted as scabs, as had happened before, to keep the prison running. Additionally, the well-timed circulation of a meeting's minutes by an ADOC official floating the possibility of a large release of ten thousand prisoners (Caldwell called this out as a "straight blatant lie") encouraged others to hold back in hopes of an early exit. The shutdown was planned, in part, to prompt Ivey to violate the constitution by following through on her threat to discipline strikers. But the hope for this outcome dissipated. In the end, she was not caught in the trap that was laid for her.[47]

One of the reasons for the lack of response was that ADOC had taken preemptive measures to dissuade those with less appetite for the strike this time around. Visitation and mail delivery were curtailed, and wardens shut down the commissaries in many facilities in advance. As a result, there was no opportunity to stockpile food in order to counteract the bird-feeding tactics expected of the administration. Too many already relied on store supplies for daily survival, and so the prospect of being cut off for a lengthy period was a real risk, especially for those with diet-sensitive health issues. Even so, the faint-hearted were pilloried by Caldwell for their unwillingness to make sacrifices, while she and other mothers and wives were "out here fighting this fight for you":

Are you saying that a Honey Bun Cake is more valuable than coming out here to see your mother and father who might not make it until you come home? What is a soup worth, or a summer sausage, or a turkey sandwich with all that sodium in it? Is a zoo zoo or wam wam more valuable than you standing up for yourself? Grow a pair and stand up! Rise up and be a man! You might miss the snack line, but sacrificing is what it takes to get results, or you're only waiting in line to die.

A lack of backbone among the soldiers on the inside was not the only obstacle to reprising the unity of the last strike. In another more worrying development, a divide had opened up on the outside between BSOW and TOPS. The strike had been called without the initial involvement of BSOW, and Caldwell and Horvat had been called in too late to save it. The day before the BSOW rally, we attended a march and rally organized by TOPS at Selma's Edmund Pettus Bridge (named for a former KKK leader), which was the hallowed site of "Bloody Sunday" in 1964. Kenny Glasgow was the presiding figure in Selma, and this was clearly his crowd. The speakers had much the same message as those at the BSOW rally, but there were only a few people who attended both events. In the course of the interviews we conducted, both camps took care not to speak ill of their counterparts. Many others on the periphery of the leadership circles politely refused to be drawn into the imbroglio when we questioned them. But the rift was obvious, and we learned that it had eroded some of the unity networks on the inside, which were already struggling to recover from a split between the leading FAM organizers.

Several weeks after the September 2022 strike, Glasgow was indicted on tax evasion, mail fraud, and drug conspiracy charges. Changing his plea several times, he finally stuck with guilty, though parts of the Selma rally were devoted to speakers railing against the DOJ's frame-up of Glasgow, who had been a tireless champion of Alabamans' civil rights and the most prominent early champion of FAM on the outside. But the taint of the charges and the long sentence they carried (in July 2023, he was sentenced to 30 months in federal detention) were hazardous for the movement, and so some leading figures made discreet efforts to distance themselves from TOPS. The rapid ascendancy of BSOW had rubbed some TOPS loyalists the wrong way. After all, they had been in the fight for longer. The gender dynamic also drove the division. BSOW's overwhelmingly female constituency made a claim, not just to be heard, but to be on an equal footing when it came to decision-making. Their sacrifices and their support should no longer be taken for granted. They needed to be at the table. Inevitably, this was a move that shook up the all-male network behind the planning of earlier phases of the movement.

According to Kinetik Justice, calls for the shutdown had been made without adequate consultation of the organizers on the inside. Unity requires an established "communication tree" and accords between "the street organizations and the heads of spiritual communities." He explained to us that "the way we operate here is that the heads of the Crips, the Bloods, and the Disciples get together with the heads of the Nation of Islam, the Five Percent Nation, and various White groups, and once we have an agreement, then we go back to our groups, and then we commit guys to be the security on the block." This process had not been properly followed and "confusion and chaos" had resulted. "We'll get back to the drawing board," vowed Kinetik, "but right now there is animosity and division."

The result was undeniably a blow to momentum. We asked Caldwell whether ADOC might now conclude that the movement was broken and powerless. "Let them think that, I wish they would," she retorted defiantly, "because when it hits them again, they will think they can perform the same tactics, but they won't work, because we'll be properly prepared for them." Caldwell was sure of BSOW's ability to pull off another strike: "It just takes time and patience to get the buy-in, mentally and spiritually, but, if you have the heavy hitters who control the facilities and the dorms, and, if you can counteract the lies and get the men to pay attention to the facts, then it will all make sense again to them." That said, something else would be needed to trigger another shutdown. "It might take something bigger," she mused, "than the bodies coming out of the prison every day, which they are numb to by now." In the meantime, she had decided that BSOW would go into impacted communities to do some town halls and legislative action trainings. They would be doing public education about the prison crisis and building more grassroots support. In this next phase, "we will be teaching people how to draft and push laws to get their loved ones home." Envisaging a road tour, she warned: "we'll be coming to them, so people won't have an excuse for not showing up for us."

The following day saw another, much bigger, event in front of the Capitol. A mass "Vigil for the Victims" of ADOC was held to honor and remember those who had died within the walls. About ninety family members stood on the steps, holding up images of their loved ones on placards. "These are battlefield numbers," someone near us pointed out, even though they amounted to less than a third of the previous year's body count. In response to growing criticism that the state's prisons had become death camps, the governor had stopped issuing monthly death reports.[48]

A short march proceeded to the revered ground of Dexter King Memorial Baptist Church where MLK had been a pastor and where the plans for the Montgomery Bus Boycott were hatched. In front of that historic landmark, the placard bearers testified to the circumstances of the deaths of their fathers, brothers, sons, and uncles. Some fatalities had been at the hands of abusive guards or peers. Others were from a drug overdose, suicide, or lack of medical care. Still others were the result of an execution order. Many of the deceased should never have been locked up—they were too young, or too mentally ill—while others had been falsely accused or over-sentenced. Several speakers said they were not notified of the deaths directly. They had only learned though Facebook or from peers or after the burial. That were also not given an accurate cause of death. The ADOC is not in the business of issuing information, let alone, apologies to family members. Those who pressed for an accurate explanation or cause of death described how they were disrespected and felt further victimized as a result.

Most importantly, the testimonials told us was that all of these deaths could and should have been prevented. Regardless of the technical cause of death, these people were all victims of *state violence*, a direct consequence of the deplorable conditions, criminal neglect of human rights, and illegal acts on the part of ADOC administrators and employees. Alongside the hurt and the trauma of the survivor families—which were on full display, as one after another of them took the mic—we heard fulsome denunciations of the lawmakers in session up on the hill. To close out the vigil, Chaplain Browder, a legendary pastor throughout the state's prisons, was introduced to say a prayer. Instead, he promptly handed the mike to Eric Buchanan, a younger Black man to his right who delivered a full-throated invocation:

God, we call on your name to open up these corrupt doors, and blow your mighty wind into these buildings, through the parole board, and through the Capitol. Remove those whose hearts are bent toward evil and raise up men and women of valor who will make the right choice concerning your people. In this wicked state of Alabama, remove the wicked people who have been in these positions for generations. We are the people who have endured so much affliction, who have always been despised and looked down on, been spat upon, and shackled in prison. Raise us up and reverse the roles, not just in politics, but all the way down through the neighborhoods and the churches. Let this prayer go into the lockup cells, the dungeons, let it reap through the warden's office and the classification and the infirmary and the canteen and the town hall. Lord, I call on you to loose your angels to go into the Department of Corruptions and turn this situation around.

Released five years previously after serving 20 years, Buchanan is now a religious volunteer inside the system. He also runs a painting and pressure-washing business that employs formerly incarcerated men. During his youthful, pre-carceral life on the street, he learned to constantly look over his shoulder to anticipate oncoming assaults. "I always had to carry guns and be on the alert knowing this could be the day someone would take my life." During his time inside, this habit got taken to "a whole other level" and he had still not shaken off the trauma. His wife has to repeatedly remind him, "you are not in prison anymore." A self-described "soldier" in the movement since he joined FAM in St. Clair prison, he recalled breaking bread together with a Muslim friend during the 2018 strike in order to promote unity among the faith groups. On the outside, he has become a stalwart of BSOW and had just signed up for Caldwell's next phase, the road tour.

At his Birmingham home the day after his powerful speech in front of the church, we asked him how God would deliver justice in Alabama. "Faith in God without the action is a cemetery," he replied, "because faith without works is dead . . . If I want God to move on behalf of the state of Alabama to redirect and uproot, then there's a part that you and I have to play." While serving his term, Buchanan repeatedly called on God to give him "an exodus, a way out of prison," but he had come to understand that "God will also give you the ability to walk into other peoples' lives and make a difference. He brought me out for a reason, not to sit idle, but to walk into protest and liberation. And he also brought me out to walk back into prison, as an advocate."

The Rain This Time

Lauren Faraino, the organizer of the Dexter King church vigil, came from a more secular part of the movement landscape. Prior to her prisoner advocacy, she had been a corporate lawyer at the white-shoe Wall Street firm of Wachtell, Lipton, Rosen, and Katz. But she ditched her high-profile professional career after taking a pro bono case on behalf of Nathaniel Woods, a twenty-three-year-old Black man convicted of capital murder in the shooting of three police officers even though he had not pulled the trigger.[49] Stunned by the injustice of his death sentence and his subsequent execution, she threw herself into prison work as director of the new Woods Foundation. Deeply skeptical about the prospect of getting justice in Alabama—"the law doesn't matter here," she assured us—she committed to pursuing it anyway. Trusted on the inside for her work with Woods, this white Harvard-educated woman had emerged as an unlikely voice within the movement. Yet, due to the high respect she commanded, the vigil she organized had achieved the rare feat of bringing together everyone in the Alabama prison movement together, in addition to winning some new recruits.

After Woods' execution, Faraino continued to focus on those who had been wrongfully convicted for non-capital and capital offenses. In this work, she was adding to the more well-known efforts of Bryan Stevenson, author of *Just Mercy*, the founder of Montgomery's Equal Justice Initiative (EJI) and the successful defender of many death penalty cases. The EJI drew widespread attention and praise for its installation of the National Memorial for Peace and Justice on a six-acre hilltop site overlooking Montgomery. The names of thousands of Black lynching victims are engraved on weathered steel columns hanging down from a roof, and the soil from the locations of their murders is collected in jugs. There are many sobering messages imparted by the memorial. Among them is the proposition that lynching was not just an instrument of racial terror, but also an unofficial form of capital punishment for Black people. When lynching as an institution was threatened, the tradition was continued by state-sanctioned execution through the death sentence. In order to stop Washington from sending in federal troops, Alabama and other Southern states just "moved the lynchings indoors, in the form of executions," according to Stevenson, a move that "guaranteed swift, sure, certain death after the trial, rather than before the trial."[50]

The same day we visited the memorial, a BSOW member with a husband on Death Row reminded us over dinner that a death sentence—even more than other prison sentences—is a collective punishment that envelops the lives of whole families. "I'm in prison too, I'm in bondage every day I wake up," explained this twenty-nine-year-old woman, "because I am not allowed to have a family, and I don't have the opportunity to live a normal life, my life is on hold, and that is unfair. Sometimes, I even feel guilty when I eat good food, because I know my husband would like it, but all they have in there is sodium and processed food." That diet is also part of the death sentence, she reminds us, because it inevitably leads to "high blood pressure, hypertension, congestive heart failure. Either way, you are going to die, of a needle or nitrogen, or by a stroke."

There are many good reasons why Stevenson, Faraino, and others—such as the Federal Defenders—focus so much of their attention and energies on Alabama's death row. The state's capital sentencing process is the final and most fiendish device in

ADOC's torture chamber. Alabama imposes death sentences at the highest rate in the nation. It is the only state that allows people to be sentenced to death by a non-unanimous jury (as happened in the Woods case) and also the only one which allows a judge to send someone to Death Row by overruling a jury verdict of life without parole. In any other state, 146 of the 164 currently on Death Row would not be there.

The state has also acquired a macabre reputation for its repeatedly botched efforts to carry out executions using lethal injections.[51] After companies refused to supply the chemicals, the state decided to adopt nitrogen hypoxia as their new, untested execution method. Death would be caused by forcing the condemned to breathe only nitrogen, thereby depriving them of the oxygen needed to maintain bodily functions. The gas has never been used for the purpose of executing a prisoner. As the state began to build its gas chamber, a leading gas supplier in Alabama announced that it would not fill any order from ADOC.[52]

The state resumed its executions by injection in July 2023, and in September the attorney general asked the state supreme court to use the nitrogen hypoxia method to execute Kenneth Smith, the survivor of an aborted lethal injection ten months previously.[53] Visibly writhing and convulsing, he reportedly took up to 20 minutes to die when he was executed in January 2024.[54] But the loudest message of the March vigil had been that any kind of sentence in Alabama's prisons could easily turn into a death sentence. With less and less prospect of parole, and with the mortality rate in prison skyrocketing, men were "more likely to come out in a body bag," as Caldwell put it, than at the end of their sentence. With each year served of sentences of Life Without Parole—even for nonviolent offences under the Habitual Offenders Act—the chances of becoming another mortality statistic increased. As if to reinforce that point, on the same day as the vigil the parole board turned down all the requests on its docket.

Weighed against these high odds of premature and often violent death, abolishing the requirement to perform prison labor might seem like small change. Yet the labor strikes had proven to be the most effective way of challenging the power of ADOC to operate illegally and without respect for human rights. The publicity generated by the stoppages had once again brought unwelcome national scrutiny to the state's barbaric practices. Faraino was in no two minds about the threat they posed:

> I have seen how close ADOC is to cracking realistically. They are two good strike weeks away from totally crumbling. You have 1500 to 1800 individuals and less than 10 officers overseeing them, and so the men basically run the prison, they just don't realize it sometimes . . . When you have a death every other day, that gets all the attention, and yet it's labor that's the tool that could dismantle the system . . . if you stop going to work, the prison doesn't function, the organizers very clearly understand that is their power.

She was also certain about the consequences of introducing paid labor: "If you were to pay minimum wage," she insisted, "that would change the equation entirely, and it would make mass incarceration unsustainable." [55]

In the meantime, Fairano was central to the effort of pulling together a crack legal team drawn from across the country to take on Alabama's prison establishment. Their lawsuit, filed in December 2023 on behalf of incarcerated and formerly incarcerated plaintiffs, targeted the governor, the attorney-general, ADOC, and a range of municipalities and corporations for using forced labor in prisons, especially in Alabama's work release programs. [56] Several labor unions also joined the suit, which was an unusual and promising development. The lawsuit

invoked the parole board's racial discrimination, the constitutional amendment, and the governor's executive order, and it
appealed to anti-trafficking laws to challenge the state's under-
payment of prison wages.[57] If the lawsuit is successful, Alabama
could follow the influential example of its prison strike movement by delivering another consequential blow against prison
slavery in the courts of justice.

It was fitting that one of the plaintiffs was Kinetik Justice,
who had suffered so much for his organizing efforts. Several
months before the suit was filed, Kinetik—isolated in his segregation cell—called and gave us a lesson in the economics of
the prison. "Most people see the leaves on the tree, but few see
the roots," he mused, "and the machine of free labor is the root
to all the problems we see here." In his view, it was the lack of
income and the threat of starvation—"just like in the ghetto"—
that forces people into what he called "the worst manifestations
of human behavior":

> You don't have to be a criminal to be in an Alabama
> prison, but, by the time you leave, you have been well
> groomed in criminality, because the only way to avoid
> being the prey is to learn the ropes and prey on others
> through the black market. So when you steal sugar or
> chicken from the kitchen, you are stealing from the gen-
> eral population. When you steal the sugar, who loses the
> cake? It's not the warden's cake. It's not police cake. It's
> our cake. You are stealing from us to sell it back to us.
> When you are forced to steal from your own brother and
> sell it to them to survive, that's not a legitimate hustle, it's
> a system that is designed to keep us in competition with
> each other and make us resort to the darkest behavior.
> The system produces criminals on the inside. And free
> labor is at the root.

The same explanation applied to the widespread sale of sexual favors. Viagra and condoms, we had been told, were two of the most popular contraband items available on the black market behind the walls. But the trade in sex had nothing to do with the free indulgence of pleasure. For Kinetik, it was a pure offshoot of poverty, "because we work for nothing and we are broke."

For ten years now, he and FAM had pursued a non-violent line in the face of "a long drawn-out debate on the inside about whether to pursue peaceful methods or resort to sabotage." Guards had been attacked in the past and had refused to come to work. In response, Kinetik had argued "that we lose our support from society if we resort to any means necessary. We have humanized ourselves, shown that we are not animals, and that we are doing this intelligently and peacefully and doing it the right way, and a lot of our support is based on that." He tried hard to "avoid a conversation that will lead to an Attica situation" even though he said he "had lost some status" in the process, and even though he did not believe that the authorities "would see the error of their ways" simply as a result of FAM's tactics. Although Kinetik had been directing DOJ officials to talk to others in the system, he was frustrated, like everyone else, that the Feds had not yet intervened. How high does a body count need to be to qualify as an emergency? "I don't want to see anyone get hurt," he vowed, but at the same time, he was "hoping and praying that someone will intervene to stop this before it turns into a blood-bath." At first he said, "I can smell rain, I ain't gotta see the clouds in the sky, I smell it coming." Then he changed his metaphor: "I can smell blood in the air."

CHAPTER 6

Hopping off the Wheel

Aiyuba Thomas, interviewed by
Andrew Ross and Tommaso Bardelli

AR/TB: Let's start by talking about your own work experiences, during the five years you spent in New York State prisons.

AT: In New York, most people start off as porters, but my first job assignment at Adirondack was at commissary, restocking, packing up the bags, taking the orders, and making sure everybody got the stuff that they ordered. I had to choose between that or the kitchen. And it also happened to be my first experience with prison violence. During their introductory spiel, one of the officers told a joke, and I didn't find it so funny. "You didn't laugh at my joke," he said, "you think you're tough? We leave niggers like you up here." He was warning me that I might not make it home from Adirondack, which is about six hours from New York City, and half an hour from Canada.

AR/TB: How did you respond to him?

AT: I told him "I'm not tough, or anything like that, but I can assure you I am going to go home." And then the fact that I had mail already waiting for me at the prison meant that I didn't really have too many issues with him after that. When they know that people care about you and are checking for you, they're less likely to carry through on their threats. But the next day I had an incident with another officer from what they called the "beat-up squad." It involved smoking in the bathrooms, which was not allowed. So, they wrote me a ticket for smoking, and I got loss of commissary and movement for a while.

AR/TB: Can you recall other incidents of force, or threat of force, involving others around their jobs?

AT: My leg swelled after an accident, but they still had me walk up and down the walkway to the job. I saw plenty of guys get sick, and they forced them to work, or people literally getting dragged out of their bed to go to work. Some kid, his grandmother died, and they didn't let him go to the funeral. He refused to work, so they handcuffed him and threw him down several flights of stairs, before giving him a ticket and ultimately taking him to the box [solitary confinement].

AR/TB: Control or sadism?

AT: It's a little bit of both. There's often a lack of control in their own personal lives and the CO position gives them access to the sadism so that they can take all the anguish about their own life and turn their anger on people who are presumed guilty. Then there's also the psychological warfare. Most COs think that you're there to be punished, not rehabilitated, and so you must do what we say, when we say it, and not get paid much for it.

AR/TB: Can you remember what you first thought about the ultra-low pay?

AT: I just laughed. Working at commissary, I could see the price list of items and realized pretty quickly that our pay was not a means to survive in prison. You can't get much more than two or three items with it, unless it's a 25-cent soup. Anything else is going to be $1 or more and that's almost what you're getting paid every two weeks. But as soon as I arrived, I had letters from my family coming to me with money, so I wasn't really counting on the state pay.

AR/TB: What did you do after the commissary job?

AT: Prior to incarceration, I had a few years of college education—117 credits from York College, a few credits shy of my bachelor's. So, after commissary, I was given the job of a teaching assistant or facilitator, facilitating Anger Management, for about a year and change. And then I went to Wallkill, which was a completely different space because a lot of people were on their way out and had already completed their programs, so there was more idleness there. I wanted to work in Corcraft's optics shop, because, if you can get the American Board of Optometry certification, you could get six months off your sentence, though I only ended up getting four months off. I facilitated Anger Management again and served a few months on the Inmate Liaison Committee before I could get into the optics training class. In that shop, the pay was a little better, and you got double if you reach your production quotas. The best pay was for making "special" high-power lenses. You're responsible for doing the math to cut them, then you surface and fit them. Those glasses are like $1,600 or $1,700 for the lenses alone. I did the whole process, from start to finish, and also did quality control inspections. On the outside, for making the regular lenses, you might get paid $20 an hour, and then more like $30 an hour for someone in my position, who had certification, and experience in making specials. On the inside, I made it to 57c an hour, or a little less than $1.20 an hour with the quota bonus. And I could be making 500 pairs of $1000 glasses in one three-hour period and getting paid pennies on the dollar. So do the math.

AR/TB: That's a whole lot of revenue and profit. At the same time as you worked in optics, you were also enrolled in our Prison Education Program, taking classes for a degree?

AT: I've always been an advocate of education. I taught in an after-school program and used to run a mentoring program back in 2009. But the NYU degree program was a way for me to get involved in situations that would elevate me outside of my circumstances. If I come to the NYU Prison Research Lab now, then I'm not hanging out with people in the hood and, over time, that kind of took precedence over the "salary" that I could have out there. You know, I got some As to get rid of this F [laughter].

AR/TB: I like that. We interviewed many people who felt forced to find a hustle in order to afford bare essentials while behind bars. They really had no alternative, so we think of it as a force of circumstance that is non-optional.

AT: The prison replicates the street, and for some people, the same social ills that cause their incarceration in the first place circle over into prison where they will do the illicit thing to come up. But the informal economy isn't just purely drug abuse, or illegal trades. People are just trying to fulfill their daily needs as human beings. There is only so much that you can get from the prison system. Take laundry as an example: in prison you take your clothes to the laundry once a week; they throw your clothes in with everyone else's clothes, no matter how dirty their stuff is, no matter how contaminated, whatever they put in, they put in. There's really no care taken. But there are people who do want to take care about how they present themselves, and about their cleanliness, so they hire someone to do their laundry for them, someone to wash their whites. So that's like a need that the facility really isn't fulfilling. And then there's food. We heard so many times in our interviews that food is really bad, it's not nutritious, that it's actually unhealthy. It makes you angry to have to eat what they serve you, and creating that anger is part of the psychological warfare that they play with people they have incarcerated. They strip you of your pride, strip you of your dignity, and rile you up. Eating well is not just self-care, it is necessary for survival in prison, and so it means everything. The underground economy is flooded with food. There are stores that provide snacks to people who just don't have the money right now. Sometimes it's exploitative, but it's a service that people are stepping up to provide. And naturally, people will also hire you to cook.

There are also those who specialize in helping others maintain a connection to their family. For a while, I made Christmas cards, birthday cards, Mother's Day cards and things of that nature. Some people don't have the skills, or they don't know how to communicate the things that they want to say to their family. So, I used to make cards, with original artwork on the cover. Others made and sold decorative handkerchiefs, picture frames—there are all kinds of craft work for purchase to express that they cared about their families and loved them. The more things people can send to their families on the outside, the more they feel like they are still connected. In many of our interviews people mentioned they were cognizant of the debts that family members had to take on to support them. The cards, the artwork, crafts, are gestures that they are not just taking from their families, but that they want to give what little they can. These are all part of the underground economy because anything that is not provided by the state is considered to be contraband, and it is illegal to exchange.

AR/TB: Would you say that these practices are also a form of work?

AT: Yes, and I think a lot of what goes on in the informal economy can also be described as care work. Maintaining the cleanliness of your space, for example, which is a physical and mental health issue. The cleaner the space you're in, the better you might feel about yourself, the higher the chance you might be active or productive. If you're living in filth, you will feel unclean, and you're not going to feel motivated. Also, the things that people do to help others stay connected to their family can be seen as care work. They are the very essence of it: building and maintaining relationships and connections during this terrible time of incarceration is a hard thing to do. Another thing that is hard to do or requires a certain dedication/skill not possessed by everyone, is working out—aka bodybuilding. Because of the need to stay in shape, some people work for hire as personal trainers, and that service is another part of the informal economy. It takes a lot of work, and discipline, to maintain your body and health under those conditions, especially without access to nutritious food.

AR/TB: It's interesting to consider how all of this informal work, even though it is outlawed, actually keeps facilities running, and keeps people inside them alive. Do you think COs are aware of this, that if people stopped bartering and trading, things would just collapse?

AT: I think so, that's why they don't do much to stop it. Any kind of exchange is illegal, and yet they happen all day. Even gambling happens in the day room, where the TV and other amenities are located, in plain sight, and so the COs know it is going on. That's not to say that there aren't COs who see their role as really punishing people for whatever crime they have committed, so they try to make your life harder, to disrupt things. But the average officer, the average person working in a facility, they want to go home, so they don't want things to be in a lockdown situation, and they certainly don't want it to be where they're in fear of their life. So, they are going to let most things slide. They understand that if they disrupt the system that ensures that people are being taken care of and provides some kind of comfort, then it's going to be an uncomfortable situation for them as well. There's going to be unrest and protests, there's going to be rebellion—that's all too problematic for someone who really just wants to go home after their shift. Most of our interviewees reported that officers and staff were not only aware of what goes on, but many of them also played a role in fostering and profiting from the underground economy.

AR/TB: Let's talk about trauma. You mentioned that you discovered the impact of your carceral trauma, including pre-carceral, long after the fact. Tell us about that experience, and how you didn't recognize it at the time.

AT: A lot of things that I thought were normal—the violence and the lifestyle involved in the streets—were really outrageous, but it was all accepted as a facet of my everyday life. I thought I would be abstracted from it while I was in prison, to actually see the type of trauma for what it was, and to recognize that it wasn't just me as an individual, that it involved the whole community. But, of course, the violence continues inside prison, where people are getting abused by COs or cutting themselves or cutting you. It's an environment where you just have to keep going, and it's not easy to reflect on how you are being damaged, emotionally and spiritually. So, it really took me up until the time I got to be a researcher at NYU, and began to interview others, to realize that I had some kind of PTSD from being incarcerated myself. Not as bad as some other people, because suffering is always relative, but I still have it. Hearing a janitor's keys jingling gets to me because it sounds like the COs. That stuff leaves its mark on you.

AR: How did this recognition emerge in the course of the interviews you did?

AT: When I began to interview formerly incarcerated peers for our earlier projects, I tried to omit my own personal experience. That made it easier for me to feel empathy or sympathy for their situation, without bringing mine into the mix. I wanted them to tell me how they felt, and not to think, "oh, you already know how

I feel about prison." But for this book, which focuses on forced labor, it was more difficult to separate my emotions, because so much of the material reminded me of the violence I myself had experienced. Still, many of the people I interviewed didn't know that I too am formerly incarcerated, they just saw me as an NYU researcher. Otherwise, they might have glossed over things, or just told it to me in a bit less detail. Some people did figure it out during the conversation, but I didn't lead with it.

There were exceptions to this, depending on who I was interviewing. For instance, for someone supporting a currently incarcerated loved one, knowing that I was formerly incarcerated provided them with a sense of comfort, and helped them open up more. Some of our female interviewees who were supporting their husbands inside, talked a lot about the lack of compassion in the prison system. And I wanted them to know that I understood what they were talking about because I had put my loved ones in the same situation they are in, and that created a special connection, I believe. That's what a peer researcher does.

I have always known the importance of being able to speak to different types of people. This skill, coupled with my carceral experience and also what I learned in academia, allowed me to adjust my angle of approach to what the situation called for. Being a peer researcher means that you have different hats to wear depending on who you are interviewing.

AR/TB: You've worked on other projects with the Lab, what did you learn from them that helped with this one?

AT: Through these other projects, I learned about theories of mass incarceration, including the "warehousing theory," which suggests that prisons primarily store surplus labor. After our research, I have a more nuanced picture, where incarcerated individuals are also exploited for profit by a variety of systems and both private and public actors. Including things like rural towns replacing lost factory jobs with prison industry jobs, banks financing prison construction, and corporations providing services to prisons which incarcerated individuals and their families are forced to pay for.

AR/TB: What's an example of that nuanced picture inside a facility where you did time?

AT: Rikers Island in NYC for example. Even though it's a jail, people can spend up to a year there. From the outside, it would appear to reinforce the warehousing theory, but, from what I observed through the time I spent there and what we were told in interviews, the conditions at Rikers speak as much to commercial exploitation and mass imprisonment of a specific people. Hardly anyone works and the idleness is more than an issue of storing bodies. For years, there have been well-documented patterns of physical and mental abuse, on top of the lack of work opportunities or constructive things to do. Rikers has also been a site of alarmingly high suicide rates, showing the mental and emotional toll of such conditions. One of the few jobs is in suicide prevention. The high prices of services and goods within the jail play a significant role in the economic exploitation of the inmates. These are not isolated issues, but they don't add up to a single-minded analysis of what's going on there.

AR/TB: What did you know about the Exception Clause coming into this research on labor?

AT: I admit that I did not know about the Exception Clause when I was in prison. To be honest, I might have heard but it was beyond me to grasp its significance at the time, and so many other people still don't know about it.

AR/TB: So, let's think about that for a minute. People know that they're being forced to work for this shitty wage and accept that as normative. But they aren't saying, "Legally how is that possible, and how is it not slavery?"

AT: It's just like living in the hood or what might be referred to as the ghetto. Most people who live in that environment don't do the calculation as to why it's like this. They don't look closely at the laws, they don't question the policing that pulls you in simply for riding a bike on the sidewalk. As a Black male, you are told: "Look, this is what's going to happen to you." One in three Black boys are going to be incarcerated. This is part of your life. When you're living through it, that's like driving in a car doing 85 miles per hour, where everything is pretty much a blur; your observation of a tree is way different when you are standing still in front of the tree, watching the birds move, watching the ants. If the wheel is always moving, and you're stuck on that wheel, you don't know you can hop off because it's moving so fast, and you don't know what's keeping the wheel going and more than likely don't realize the part you play in keeping it going. I think it's the same thing inside prison.

AR/TB: You weren't aware at the time, but can you describe what it's been like coming to terms with this bizarre, but very American, constitutional amendment that abolished chattel slavery at the very same time that it enabled involuntary servitude to be imposed on a population among which people of color were disproportionately represented?

AT: My family was very politically active, they were heavily into the community, during the Civil Rights era and after, so I was brought up with the understanding that the system will screw us. It wasn't made to be against us, but it wasn't made for us. So, when I found out about the Exception Clause, it was a shock, but it wasn't like, "Oh, how could they?" Because I know what the other side is capable of.

AR/TB: A shock, but not a surprise.

AT: Yes, and also upsetting because I found out about it late in my life.

AR/TB: Let's talk about your response to some of our interviewees. You did time in New York State, so it's a system you're familiar with. But were there new things you actually learned from some of the interviews? Because everyone's experience is a little bit different, right?

AT: The system is pretty much the same for everyone in New York, though a lot of experiences are facility-specific, and can even differ from floor to floor or section to section, depending on who's in authority there. One thing that I did note was how few of the respondents, especially in New York, didn't think that their particular job assignment was dangerous, though they acknowledged that being in prison was dangerous in general. Also, some people steered clear of certain jobs because it brought them into interaction with certain people, like COs, or lieutenants, whom they had reasons for avoiding. Otherwise, I was a little surprised by just how many people reported threats of violence, or box time, or loss of privileges for refusing to take on work details.

AR/TB: So the violence was endemic. Were there any particular interviews or differences of opinion that stood out for you?

AT: I interviewed someone who served 8 years in multiple federal penitentiaries throughout the country, and what he had to say was interesting to me for several reasons. Contrary to what I expected, what he told me (and what I also heard in several off-the-record conversations) about the experience of those in federal custody was very similar to that of people who endured incarceration within state and county prison systems. Like the majority of our interviewees, he also spoke about how the lack of a fair wage for work perpetuates this "illicit" economy. On that topic, he had views that are similar to mine on what would be a fair wage. Just as a living wage depends on where you live on the outside, he said that a fair wage in prison would depend largely on "the overall economy in each facility." In the New York system, for example, I saw the disparities in pricing and cost of commissary goods between different facilities, which should be a factor to consider when determining wages. We were more or less in agreement on the need to push for a minimum wage, but, because of our common experience of being incarcerated, we are also inclined to think about what a feasible wage would be. We know all too well that many people on the outside would take it as a slap in the face, or just unfair, to pay prisoners the same exact wage as free world workers. Though we agreed on the 13th Forward tactic of bargaining for $15, we also know what a difference even $5 or $6 an hour would make for folks to make more store purchases, and not be such an encumbrance on their family from the outside. A little goes a long way when you are just trying to survive.

AR/TB: That's a question we have wrestled with. What you're saying reflects what we've found and noted, that there is a gap between what the legal advocates are for, and what people who have done time believe is possible. So do you push for what's just, or do you go for what seems feasible in law and policy?

AT: I would go for what's just. But we need to talk about how to get more people on board, like the general public and the politicians. To persuade them, we'd have to allow the authorities to take some of that money and allocate it toward the bills, like rent, that people on the outside have to pay.

AR/TB: Yes, as they do with private (PIE) labor contracts in other states, where federal law requires you to pay the prevailing wage, but then these systems garnish room and board from that, typically, and they take a cut for themselves, and of course people have to pay taxes. So PIE workers are doing the same work as outside workers, and they are getting the minimum wage, but also paying taxes, social security, room and board—in other words, the same bills as on the outside.

AT: Yes, though I think, in states that do that, there is more corruption, and some of that money flows into pockets of the corrupt, whereas in New York, there are more checks and balances. What would be the outcome of higher wages? One concern we heard a lot is that with this influx of new money, there would be more spending on drugs, and all of the illicit things that people do in prison would multiply. Another concern is that this money might simply flow back into the prison systems and its private benefactors through the increase in commissary purchases and prices, phones services, stamp sales, catalog sales and other things that incarcerated people have to spend money on to survive. The interviewee that I mentioned reflected on this influx of money and equated it to the stimulus money that came in during the pandemic. "When everyone got their stimulus checks," he said "everything went up" because the prison raised their prices for goods and services, as did the people who hustled. The price gouging caused people to be in the same dilemma they were in when they didn't have the extra money.

AR/TB: All the more reason why the numbers need to be crunched, and the benefits and the costs have to be weighed against one another. But can you draw out, from a particular interview, say, the specific reasons why formerly incarcerated people don't set their sights as high as some of the legal advocates who haven't done time?

AT: Generally, I asked people towards the end of the interview, what they would say to the advocates and legislators who are needed to make this happen. Most people wouldn't even ask for full minimum wage. I remember one man from Georgia, where prisoners are not paid for their work, pleading for "just a little bit more," saying that "it would just help people live a little bit better."

AR/TB: Why do you think many incarcerated or formerly incarcerated folks wouldn't ask for more?

AT: I think people in prisons have many reasons to be skeptical of any positive change happening there. Based on their experience, they know that whenever something beneficial to incarcerated people happens, prison administrations are going to drag their feet. And the situation is so desperate for many of them that think they would rather have "a little bit more" sooner, rather than waiting longer for more radical change. People in prison, but also poor people who use social services, they know that if the system gives you something, it's only a matter of time before they want their money back, somehow. When there is a give, there is always a take. So they are skeptical. They think that if they get paid more, the prison will take more from them, through garnishments, commissary chargers, or whatnot. And so the outcome—an illusory fair wage—can be even more discouraging than not being paid at all.

AR/TB: We can come back to that, but we wonder if there was a prisoner rights movement, as there was in the '60s and '70s, whether the disparity might be on the other side. In other words, the people behind bars would be demanding the maximum, while the legal advocates on the outside, would be trailing behind. Whereas today, incarcerated people have been so beaten down within the system, and the movement inside is so weak, they feel they are not in a position to make more radical demands.

AT: That makes sense, but when people say "we just want a little bit more," I don't think it's so much a case of, "we're not in a position to demand." It's more about their immediate needs. "Pay me enough so that I can survive, because I'm not trying to get rich in jail, I just want to be able to do my time, and to go home healthy, not feeling downtrodden and less of a man because I'm coming home empty handed." So people on the outside who want to lead should be checking to see what the people on the inside really need, rather than deciding on their own what's just or not.

AR/TB: Agreed. So, you have referred to your experience in the New York system. When we went on our field trips to Alabama, we encountered a different kind of world. Can you summon up some of your memories?

AT: I was really surprised, and not just because of the race dynamics in Alabama, although it's clear that there are people in power who are not at all opposed to slave labor in prison because of the history in that state. A lot of people that we spoke to in Alabama, even in just general conversation, would openly talk about the corruption and the chaos in the criminal justice system, so this is common knowledge. Coming from New York, I somehow expected that the prison system, given the history of the South, would be more stringent and harder on the inmates. Behind bars, I thought the COs would be on top of stuff. But we found the opposite. Many facilities are pretty much run by prisoners. And I collected similar reports about Georgia too. The COs are pretty much just there to facilitate the movement of the general population. Because of all the budget cuts, there aren't anywhere near enough guards, and then that's where the corruption comes in too. Most of them know that a CO's job with minimal pay is going to put themselves in a dangerous position, so there's a good chance they might not even come home intact. They don't take that kind of job just to collect a paycheck, they're there to capitalize off of that position.

AR/TB: What about the racial dynamics inside these prisons? What did you feel that we were discovering there that was maybe different from New York?

AT: As far as racial favoritism in job assignments, it was pretty much the same—what you would expect in other words. The big difference is that a large percentage of the prison guards are African American. In New York, most prisons are upstate in predominantly white counties, so the prison workforce is white. In a state like Alabama, there are a lot more Black officers injecting themselves into that caustic job situation. What does that say about what's happening on the outside that they feel that they need to expose themselves to those levels of danger and coercion?

AR/TB: We talked to a lot of advocates who were involved in the prison strike movement. And, for a while at least, it looked as if Alabama might the epicenter of some revival of the prisoner rights movement. What did you take away from that, the strength and the influence and the commitment that we saw?

AT: First of all, when you actually see it in its context, it wasn't all that surprising, because of the need for it. As I said, the corruption, the deaths, the murders, these are so clearly oppressive someone eventually would have to stand up. And at the rallies we attended, there were people from Florida and Texas, and other parts of the country who had come there because of what had been happening in Alabama, and not just recently, of course. Alabama is a strong symbol of the historic fight for liberties and civil rights for so many people. Why? Because every so often, it gets so explosive down there that something has to be done. And I also spoke to people in Georgia who were involved in the strike in 2016. Georgia and Alabama have a lot of shared history when it comes to both prison labor and civil rights struggle, whether it was in the business of convict leasing, or SNCC's challenges to segregation laws in the 1960s. People of all races think of these states as places to fight back, not just against the oppression, but also against the myth of the genteel South, with the big houses, the weeping willows, and the polite talk that hides the Jim Crow part underlying it all.

AR/TB: Alabama is pretty consistent—it continues to live up to its worst reputation. But Atlanta does have this "Black mecca" reputation. How did that manifest in the Georgia prison system, which was really your field because you did all the work there, on your own?

AT: There were less advocates to talk to there, and the people I interviewed were not particularly politically involved, so the movement for change was not something at the forefront of their minds. But there were many of the same kind of stories about the shortage of guards and the overcrowding. And they were in a similar labor regime to the degree to which they're not paid at all, except for some private industry contract jobs. Otherwise, they're supposed to be allotted Good Time credit upon receiving a sentence. There is also the possibility to "earn" additional time credits.

According to state law in Georgia, time is earned for "up to 1 day per 1 day of participation in educational or other counseling program, satisfactorily completing work tasks, and good behavior." Therefore, working for zero wages is a contingency of good time.

AR/AT: But do they get it? In Texas, we were told that Good Time can get you a quicker parole hearing but it doesn't guarantee anything more.

AT: From what I was told about the credit in Georgia, it is just another part of their system and they will use it as a tool to inflict abuse when they feel like it. They honor the time for the most part, but they have also been known to hold people ransom after the parole board grants them release. The warden is very much in charge and wardens can use and manipulate these incentives to recruit informants, so it's not a straightforward process. There is a liaison, or grievance, committee to act as intermediary between prisoners and administration, but it's not a real check or balance. Mostly people take those committee jobs for the perks, and to be in with the warden. Alabama is another story all together when it comes to good time and serving time in general. In January 2023, Gov. Kay Ivey issued her executive order EO-725, which threatened anyone refusing to work with loss of Good Time. In April, she followed up in Alabama's war on prisoners by signing a bill into law that reduced the amount of Good Time credit received for serving time by close to half, even for exemplary prisoners. A class I prisoner who would have previously gotten 75 good time days for every 30 days served, now only gets 30 days for every 30 days served. Which is a huge slap, especially because Alabama has become infamous for not letting people out on parole. This Good Time, of course, is contingent on mandatory work, the same way that earned time in Georgia and other states is predicated on good behavior, which includes not refusing work.

AR/TB: Of the interviews you did, were there particular characters or particular interviews that stood out? "Billy" the barber, for instance, who seemed to be very much on top of what he was doing. He had no prior experience cutting hair, but he learned on the job and established control over his environment and then he parlayed that into a professional post-carceral career as a barber.

AT: Yes, he was a standout. He had been to prison previously, and had been on the bad guy side, and decided he wanted instead to use his skills to gain more skills. There's a lot of perks that come with that barber job—the freedom of movement, the tips from people he was in a position to do favors for, and the opportunity to circulate contraband. He also could be a mentor for some of the new guys coming in who would not know what they are facing, or how to operate.

AR/TB: What about the cutting of the hair itself?

AT: When he was initially brought in to get his own head shaved, he experienced it as degrading. "Balding the inmates," as he put it, was a way to "take away your dignity, to strip that pride that's on you as a man." This stripping away of your individuality is supposed to conform any kind of aspect of who you are as a person. Like in the army, that's the beginning of your institutionalization—you're nobody, you're starting fresh, you're naked, you're now a new person. Because I have locks, he mentioned that with certain religions—Rastafarians, Native Americans, Jews—you're allowed to keep your hair, and a short beard if you are Muslim. And that's part of their strength, and it sets them apart. But for the system to shave the others, it's a direct attack on their pride and dignity. The first cut is the deepest, and then you can maintain more of a regular haircut. And so he realized that he was complicit with that stripping process, in having his labor used as a tool to dehumanize others. That's partly why he took more interest in mentoring the guys coming in. When I was incarcerated, I asked why they did that. And they said it's medical, to make sure that lice are not spreading to the general population. To some degree, that makes sense. But at the same time, I experienced it as the first strike in a process of psychological warfare.

AR/TB: The shaved head was probably introduced in Auburn in the 1820s, along with the striped uniforms, the chains and the lockstep—these were all part of a look, central to the process of dehumanization. You described the head shave as the first strike. What was the second strike?

AT: Another Georgia interviewee told me that the first detail in his facility was to be sent out on a road crew, working with the Department of Transportation, to pick up garbage. He told me it was eight miles to walk out there, and eight to come back, often in extreme heat conditions. He said it quite simply made him "feel like a slave." You're on a side of the road, in chains, where anyone, possibly your own family members, can see you in the prison uniform. And so they are already building up the stigma, to distinguish you from the rest of humanity. What is psychologically happening to the people on the side of the road? A lot of people end up in jail because they're very prideful, maybe too prideful, and so they have a strong ego. That is why they go to the lengths that they go to, and do the things that are outside of what's right in society. If it's not a drug or mental health issues, it's the proud mentality of "I have to be a provider," and so stripping away that pride from a person is part of the mental warfare. It can happen with the hair, or through the labor, or through the food. There are unlimited things they do on a daily basis to cut you down. As I said, I didn't realize my trauma until I left prison. Take something as simple as serving you spaghetti with a spoon. You know how that fucks with your head?

AR/TB: That's intentional?

AT: Yes, this happens in New York State prisons. They have forks, but they serve spaghetti with a spoon. Most people have no choice but try and manage, but the pasta is spilling off, and the sauce is splashing around. I refused to eat spaghetti because I realized they're just messing with you. Even today—and I am a foodie—I'll eat linguini, fettuccine, but I'm not going to ever order spaghetti. [laughter]

AR/TB: That is even more insidious than the many stories we collected about substandard or inedible food. Obviously, the serving up of food that is unfit for human consumption is meant to convey that you are less than human. For some, being forced to work without pay sends a similar message, which is why it's often referred to as slavery. But some jobs, like Billy's for example, demand complicity with the system, and that can be even more tricky. He told you: "Whether it's 10:30 at night, 4 in the morning, or 11:30 later in the morning, the officer can make you get up and cut hair, because it's your detail. That's how they push the anger button." Not only was he called upon at any time to cut the hair of an officer, or the warden's hair, but he also had physical contact with their bodies, which is more unique in the prison environment.

AT: Mmm-hmm, it's very unique. I look at it like letting a slave shave you. Even though he's working with clippers, that's still a dangerous tool, very sharp.

AR/TB: Slavery days are relevant in that regard, since the enslaved people who had the most access and contact with the masters were the ones that are distrusted and disparaged by the field labor population, if you like. So much of the prison system depends on distancing, and isolating the incarcerated from everyone else, and yet there are still work assignments that require some close cooperation, if not intimacy.

AT: Yeah, but the house slave generally was not part of the resistance at all. They were there because they were very subservient. They felt that they needed the master, and that they were chosen as someone who was special for that position. Someone like Billy played both sides of the coin; he knew the responsibility of his position, but he didn't really set himself above his peers, especially because the job didn't carry too many privileges.

AR/TB: We have found that many people believe there's a lot of continuity between the chattel slavery of the plantation and the prison system. What are your thoughts when you hear people making that argument about the straight line of descent from the plantation to the prison?

AT: Well to state the obvious, prisoners get beaten up, there's a lot of institutional violence, but everyone isn't being whipped. You could also say there are people who are picked out as examples. The Georgia road crews, for instance, where workers are publicly exposed, can be compared to putting the runaway slave on display.

But the impact of physical violence sometimes heals over. It's the psychological trauma from being caged under these conditions that has a longer lasting effect. And so I look to Jim Crow for a better point of comparison. As brutal and horrific as chattel slavery was, the experience of being freed, and then not really being free is a terrible thing to have to live with. That's why the Exception Clause sticks out. The 13th Amendment was supposed to free us, but the exception introduced another unfreedom, a different kind of violence.

Notes

Introduction

1   Martha Mendoza, "Obama Bans US Imports of Slave-Produced Goods," Associated Press, February 26, 2016, https://www.ap.org/explore/seafood-from-slaves/Obama-bans-US-imports-of-slave-produced-goods.html.

2   "Mass Incarceration," ACLU, https://www.aclu.org/issues/smart-justice/mass-incarceration; ACLU and University of Chicago Law Center, *Captive Labor: Exploitation of Incarcerated Workers*, June 2022, 17. This cites $2 billion in goods, from a 2021 survey, and $9 billion in services, from a 2004 report. The real amounts are much higher today.

3   As a result of this exception, the 1930 prohibition on these imports had only been invoked 39 times in 86 years. According to the Congressional Research Service, "Beginning in 1890, the United States prohibited imports of goods manufactured with convict labor. In 1930, Congress expanded this prohibition in Section 307 of the Tariff Act to include any (not just manufactured) products of forced labor. Although a few Members brought up humanitarian concerns during debate, the central legislative concern was protecting domestic producers from competing with products made with forced labor." "Section 307 and Imports Produced by Forced Labor," July 26, 2022, https://crsreports.congress.gov/product/pdf/IF/IF11360.

4   According to the Vera Institute of Justice, at the end of 2021, there were 1,199,600 individuals incarcerated in state and federal prisons. "Incarceration Statistics," Vera Institute of Justice, https://www.vera.org/incarceration-statistics.

5   E. Tammy Kim, "A National Strike Against 'Prison Slavery,'" *The New Yorker*, October 3, 2016, https://www.newyorker.com/news/news-desk/a-national-strike-against-prison-slavery; Beth Schwartzapfel, "A Primer on the Nationwide

Prison Strike," The Marshall Project (September 27, 2016), https://www.themarshallproject.org/2016/09/27/a-primer-on-the-nationwide-prisoners-strike.

6   "Strike Tracking and Retaliation Support," SupportPrisonersResistance.net, 2016. Firehawk and Ben Turk, "Freedom First!," Incarcerated Workers Organizing Committee, https://incarceratedworkers.org/freedom-first.

7   Meg Anderson, "Colorado Banned Forced Prison Labor 5 Years Ago. Prisoners Say It's Still Happening," NPR, November 13, 2023, https://www.npr.org/2023/11/13/1210564359/slavery-prison-forced-labor-movement.

8   Stephen Wilson, Minali Aggarwal, Jacqueline Groccia, and Lydia Villaronga, "Better Work Won't Fix Prisons," Law and Political Economy Project, May 18, 2023, https://lpeproject.org/blog/better-work-wont-fix-prisons/.

9   Ivan Kilgore, "Not Worker, But Chattel," *Inquest*, May 11, 2023, https://inquest.org/against-work/.

10   See the testimony presented by imprisoned authors in Joy James, *The New Abolitionists: (Neo)slave Narratives and Contemporary Prison Writings* (New York: SUNY Press, 2005).

11   At the height of the prison reform movement in the 1910s, there was much public discussion about the benefits of placing a fair prison labor wage at the center of the rehabilitation process. In May 1993, the federal General Accounting Office issued a report, "Prisoner Labor: Perspectives on Paying the Federal Minimum Wage," that narrowly focused on the high cost of paying a minimum wage, balanced against the likely boost in industrial productivity and access to training. See https://www.gao.gov/assets/ggd-93-98.pdf.

12   Ruth Wilson Gilmore's *Golden Gulag: Prisons, Surplus, Crisis, and Opposition in Globalizing California* (Berkeley, CA: University of California Press, 2007) is an influential account of the boom in California. See also her collected essays in *Abolition Geography: Essays Toward Liberation* (New York: Verso, 2022). For an analysis of profiteering, see Tara Herivel and Paul Wright, eds., *Prison Profiteers: Who Makes Money from Mass Incarceration* (New York: New Press, 2007), and for a detailed breakdown of corporate beneficiaries, see Worth Rises, "The Prison Industry Corporate Database," https://data.worthrises.org/?_gl=1*12qwvyj*_gcl_au*MTU1ODg2NDM1OC4xNjg0ODYwMjQx.

13   Gilmore, *Abolition Geography*, 474.

14 Bruce Western and Katherine Beckett, "How Unregulated Is the US Labor Market? The Penal System as a Labor Market Institution," *American Journal of Sociology* 104, 4 (1999), 1052; Bruce Western, "The Impact of Incarceration on Wage Mobility and Inequality," *American Sociological Review* 67, 4 (2002) 526–46; Bruce Western, *Punishment and Inequality in America* (New York: Russell Sage Foundation, 2006).

15 Erin Hatton ed., *Labor and Punishment: Work in and out of Prison* (Berkeley: University of California Press, 2021); Noah Zatz, "Working at the Boundaries of Markets: Prison Labor and the Economic Dimension of Employment Relationships," 61 *Vanderbilt Law Review* 857 (2008), and "The Carceral Labor Continuum: Beyond the Prison Labor/Free Labor Divide," in *Labor and Punishment* (Berkley, CA: University of California Press, 2021); and "Labor Governance in the Shadow of Racialized Mass Incarceration," *Law and Political Economy Project* (March 16, 2021) https://lpeproject.org/blog/labor-governance-in-the-shadow-of-racialized-mass-incarceration/.

16 Tasseli McKay, *Stolen Wealth, Hidden Power: The Case for Reparations for Mass Incarceration* (Berkeley, CA: University of California Press, 2022).

17 Tommaso Bardelli, Zach Gillespie, and Thuy Linh Tu, "'You Need Money to Live in Prison': Everyday Strategies of Survival in the American Neoliberal Prison," *South Atlantic Quarterly* 121, 4 (2022), 838–845. Lynne Haney, *Prisons of Debt: The Afterlives of Incarcerated Fathers* (Berkeley, CA: University of California Press, 2022).

18 Loïc Wacquant, *Prisons of Poverty* (Minneapolis: University of Minnesota Press, 2009). Also see Tara Herivel and Paul Wright, eds., *Prison Nation: The Warehousing of America's Poor* (New York: Routledge, 2002) and Marie Gottschalk, *Caught: The Prison State and the Lockdown of American Politics* (Princeton: Princeton University Press, 2015).

19 Even the most "organic," survey, initiated by incarcerated researchers, restricts its purview to formal work assignments. See "The Work and Us," a valuable "abolitionist participatory research project" undertaken by Stevie Wilson and Minali Aggarwali. https://theworkandus.wordpress.com/publications/.

20 John Schmitt and Jori Kandra, "The Carceral State and the Labor Market," Economic Policy Institute, April 29, 2021, https://www.epi.org/blog/the-carceral-state-and-the-labor market/.

21 "Prison Industry: How it Started, How it Works, How It Harms," Worth Rises, https://worthrises.org/wk5-programslabor.

22 Marxist sociologists Georg Rusche and Otto Kirchheimer were the first to argue that rates of incarceration are tied to the state of the capitalist labor market. When jobs were scarce, and the "idle poor" were likely to engage in civil strife, judges and lawmakers were more punitive in locking people up. According to the principle of "less eligibility," the conditions of imprisonment must also be worse than those of the most precarious segments of the working class. Otherwise, that class fraction would not work. Georg Rusche and Otto Kirchheimer, *Punishment and Social Structure* (New York: Columbia University Press, 1939, 2003).

23 The report also listed many of the benefits that could not be easily quantified:

☐ The increased physical and mental health of incarcerated people, and associated costs, from a recognition of their humanity and dignity with the granting of the basic human right to be protected from slavery and the ability to meet one's own basic needs.

☐ The increased physical and mental health of incarcerated people and corrections officers, and associated costs, from the reduced reliance on informal "hustles" and increased connection with loved ones that together lower related violence and victimization in prisons.

☐ The increased physical and mental health of incarcerated workers and their families and children, and associated costs, from reduced financial stress, reduced poverty, and increased connection, during and after incarceration.

☐ The financial relief for families and children of communication costs beyond just phone calls, namely video calls and electronic messages.

☐ The increased economic mobility, and related physical and mental health, of incarcerated workers and their families and children stemming from increases in earnings during and after release that can have generational impacts.

☐ The increased payment of fines and fees to governments.

☐ The increased payment of local taxes during and after incarceration.

☐ The reduced financial burden of formerly incarcerated workers on government welfare programs in retirement."

See Steve Bronars, Coleman Bazelon, Bianca Tylek and Tommaso Bardelli, "A Cost-Benefit Analysis: The Impact of Ending Slavery and Involuntary Servitude as Criminal Punishment and Paying Incarcerated Workers Fair Wages," Edgeworth Economics (January 31, 2024), https://static1.squarespace.com/static/5f47b3641ee69c69c7889cc6/t/65b9750c440294445b60056f/1706652940634/2024+-+CBA+of+Ending+Prison+Slavery+Report.pdf.

24 Devah Pager, *Marked: Race, Crime, and Finding Work in an Era of Mass Incarceration* (Chicago, IL: University Of Chicago Press, 2007); James B Jacobs, *The Eternal Criminal Record* (Cambridge, MA: Harvard University Press, 2015).

25 Jamiles Lartey, "How Criminal Records Hold Back Millions of People," The Marshall Project (April 1, 2023), https://www.themarshallproject.org/2023/04/01/criminal-record-job-housing-barriers-discrimination.

26 *Captive Labor*, 5.

27 According to the ACLU survey, 13 cents is the "average minimum hourly wage paid to workers for non-industry jobs," and 52 cents is the average maximum hourly wage. *Captive Labor*, 10.

28 The Conversation, "States Are Putting Prisoners to Work Manufacturing Coronavirus Supplies," *U.S. News and World Report* (April 21, 2020), https://www.usnews.com/news/best-states/articles/2020-04-21/states-are-putting-prisoners-to-work-manufacturing-coronavirus-supplies; Kim Kelly, "New York Prison Labor Makes Hand Sanitizer, Prepares to Dig Graves if Coronavirus Worsens," *Daily Beast* (March 25, 2020), https://www.thedailybeast.com/rikers-inmates-will-dig-graves-if-coronavirus-batters-new-york.

29 Michel Foucault, *Discipline and Punish: The Birth of the Prison* (New York: Vintage Books, 1995), 11.

30 See Jeffrey Reiman and Paul Leighton, *The Rich Get Richer and the Poor Get Prison: Ideology, Class and Criminal Justice* (Boston: Allyn and Bacon, 1998).

31 *Captive Labor*, 10.

32 Jolie McCullough, "Prisoners' Relatives and Former Inmates Plead for Help as Deaths Mount in Sweltering Texas Prisons," *Texas Tribune*, July 18, 2023, https://www.texastribune.org/2023/07/18/texas-prisons-heat-deaths. See Kwaneta Harris, "Facing the Climate Crisis from a Texas Prison Cell," July 28, 2023, https://theappeal.org/texas-prisons-heat-climate-crisis/. Louisiana and other Southern states recorded similar, inhumane conditions: see Jamiles Lartey, "'Concrete Coffins': Surviving Extreme Heat Behind

Bars," The Marshall Project (July, 22, 2023), https://www.themarshallproject. org/2023/07/22/texas-heat-prison-louisiana?utm_campaign=opening-statement&utm_medium=email&utm_source=newsletter&utm_ term=3307-when-police-are-called-to-a-mental-health-crisis-violence-often-ensues&utm_source=TMP-Newsletter&utm_campaign=69d74766e9-EMAIL_CAMPAIGN_2023_07_24_11_42&utm_medium=email&utm_ term=0_5e02cdad9d-69d74766e9-%5BLIST_EMAIL_ID%5D.

33 Michael Gibson-Light offers the most comprehensive ethnographic description of labor hierarchy inside a prison in *Orange-Collar Labor: Work and Inequality in Prison* (New York: Oxford University Press, 2023).

34 *Captive Labor*, 17–31.

35 *Captive Labor*, 8. Among other statistics presented by the report, 76 percent of those surveyed were forced to work or would face additional punishment, 70 percent were unable to afford basic necessities on their wages, 70% received no formal job training, while 64 percent felt concerned about their safety while working.

36 Nicole Fleetwood's remarkable book on "carceral aesthetics" contains many observations on how "penal time" is served and maximized in creative ways. *Marking Time: Art in the Age of Mass Incarceration* (Cambridge, MA: Harvard University Press, 2020).

37 Richard Davies, "From Pecan Pralines to 'Dots' as Currency: How the Prison Economy Works," *The Guardian*, August 30, 2019, https://www.theguardian. com/us-news/2019/aug/30/prison-economy-informal-markets-alternative-currencies.

38 Vivian Giang, "Prisoner Shares with Us a Glimpse of the Hustle Behind Bars," *Business Insider*, July 2, 2012, https://www.businessinsider.com/prisoner-shares-with-us-a-glimpse-of-the-hustle-behind-bars-2012-6.

39 Tommie Shelby, *Dark Ghettos: Injustice, Dissent, and Reform* (Cambridge, MA: Harvard University Press, 2016),194-5.

40 See Elizabeth Hinton, *From the War on Poverty to the War on Crime: The Making of Mass Incarceration in America* (Cambridge, MA: Harvard University Press, 2016).

41 Free Alabama Movement, "Let the Crops Rot in the Field," Incarcerated Workers Organizing Committee, January 17, 2017, https://incarceratedworkers.org/ resources/free-alabama-movement-let-crops-rot-field.

Chapter 1: Ending the Exception

1   "New Jersey Racial and Ethnic Disparities in Prisons Are Worst in Nation,"
    ACLU, October 19, 2021, https://www.aclu-nj.org/en/press-releases/report-
    new-jersey-racial-and-ethnic-disparities-prisons-are-worst-nation.

2   See the Abolish Slavery National Network Anniversary Celebration, August
    28, 2022, https://www.cctv.org/watch-tv/programs/abolish-slavery-national-
    network-anniversary-celebration.

3   A recent poll commissioned by Worth Rises revealed that 68 percent of
    Americans don't know that there's an exception in the Thirteenth Amendment
    to the U.S. Constitution—the amendment celebrated for abolishing slavery.
    Another 20 percent think there's an exception if the sitting president decides,
    as part of wartime efforts, or in the interest of public safety. Bianca Tylek, "Is
    Slavery Still Legal in the U.S.? Yes, Under the 13th Amendment Exception"
    Teen Vogue, February 3, 2022, https://www.teenvogue.com/story/slavery-legal-
    us-13th-amendment.

4   "600K to Damage Our Kids Forever: A Youth Incarceration Disaster," New
    Jersey Institute for Social Justice, June 2022, https://www.njisj.org/youth-
    incarceration-disaster; Comptroller Scott Stringer "Cost of Incarceration
    per Person in New York City Skyrockets to All-Time High," (December 6,
    2021), https://comptroller.nyc.gov/newsroom/comptroller-stringer-cost-of-
    incarceration-per-person-in-new-york-city-skyrockets-to-all-time-high-2.

5   Michael Hirsh, "Charles Koch, Liberal Crusader?" *Politico*, March/April
    2015, https://www.politico.com/magazine/story/2015/03/charles-koch-
    overcriminalization-115512/; Michelle Chen, "Beware of Big Philanthropy's
    New Enthusiasm for Criminal Justice Reform," *The Nation*, March 16, 2018,
    https://www.thenation.com/article/archive/beware-of-big-philanthropys-new-
    enthusiasm-for-criminal-justice-reform/.

6   Angela Davis, *Abolition Democracy: Beyond Prison, Torture and Empire* (New York:
    Seven Stories Press, 2005); W.E.B. Du Bois, *Black Reconstruction in America 1860-
    1880* (New York: Harcourt, Brace and Company, 1935).

7   Allegra McLeod, "Prison Abolition and Grounded Justice," *UCLA Law Review*
    62, 5 (June 2015) 1156–1239.

8   James Gray Pope, "Mass Incarceration, Convict Leasing, and the Thirteenth
    Amendment: A Revisionist Account," *94 N.Y.U.L. REV. 1465, 1470* (2019),
    notes 400 and 401.

9   James Gray Pope, "Section 1 of the Thirteenth Amendment and the Badges and Incidents of Slavery," 65 *UCLA L. Rev.* 426 (2018), 485.

10 In *The Civil Rights Cases* (1883) the Supreme Court interpreted the 13th Amendment as empowering Congress "to pass all laws necessary and proper for abolishing all badges and incidents of slavery in the United States."

11 Pope, "Mass Incarceration, Convict Leasing, and the Thirteenth Amendment," 1468.

12 Pope, "Mass Incarceration, Convict Leasing, and the Thirteenth Amendment," 1554.

13 "Thirteentherism" is a term that Daryl Michael Scott coined to refer to the thinkers and activists who see the Exception Clause as an intentional tactic to restore slavery in another form. Daryl Michael Scott, "The Scandal of Thirteentherism," *Liberties* 1, 2 (2021).

14 Northwest Ordinance of 1787, art. VI, 1 Stat. 50, 53 n.(a) (1789).

15 James Davie Butler, "British Convicts Shipped to American Colonies, *"American Historical Review*, 2, 1, (October 1896), 12–33.

16 Vermont was the first to abolish slavery with exceptions, in its 1777 Constitution, but its language did not have the same influence as the federal act of Northwest Ordinance: it decreed that that no person serve any other "as a servant, slave or apprentice, after he arrives to the age of twenty-one years, nor female, in like manner, after she arrives to the age of eighteen years, unless they are bound by their own consent, after they arrive to such age, or bound by law, for the payment of debts, damages, fines, costs or the like."

17 See Sean Wilentz, "The Emancipators' Vision," *New York Review of Books*, December 22, 2022, https://www.nybooks.com/articles/2022/12/22/the-emancipators-vision-black-ghost-of-empire-kris-manjapra/.

18 See Derrick Bell's foundational writings on this history, in *And We Are Not Saved: The Elusive Quest for Racial Justice* (New York: Basic Books, 1987), and *Faces at the Bottom of the Well: The Permanence of Racism* (New York: Basic Books, 1992).

19 Patrick Rael, "Demystifying the 13th Amendment and Its Impact on Mass Incarceration," *Black Perspectives*, December 9, 2016, https://www.aaihs.org/demystifying-the-13th-amendment-and-its-impact-on-mass-incarceration/; See Dennis Childs' response to Rael, "Slavery, the 13th Amendment and Mass Incarceration, " *Black Perspectives*, December 12, 2016,

https://www.aaihs.org/slavery-the-13th-amendment-and-mass-incarceration-a-response-to-patrick-rael/.

20 Rebecca McLennan, "The Buried Roots of Carceral Labor," *Inquest*, May 16, 2023, https://inquest.org/the-buried-roots-of-carceral-labor/.

21 Pope, "Mass Incarceration, Convict Leasing, and the Thirteenth Amendment," 1492.

22 Pope, "Mass Incarceration, Convict Leasing, and the Thirteenth Amendment," 1492.

23 "Drafting of the Thirteenth Amendment," Legal Information Institute, Cornell Law School, https://www.law.cornell.edu/constitution-conan/amendment-13/drafting-of-the-thirteenth-amendment#:~:text=145%20(1864).-,Senator%20Charles%20Sumner%20unsuccessfully%20proposed%20a%20different%20formulation%20of%20the,effect%20everywhere%20in%20the%20United.

24 There are only two states—Louisiana and Arkansas—whose penal laws still include explicit sentences of hard labor.

25 See Raja Raghunath, "A Promise the Nation Cannot Keep: What Prevents the Application of the Thirteenth Amendment in Prison?" *18 Wm. & Mary Bill Rts. J. 395* (2009).

26 *Ruffin v. Commonwealth*, 62, Va. 790 (1871).

27 *Wolff v. McDonnell*, 418 U.S. 539 (1974).

28 *Cooper v. Pate*, 378 U.S. 546 (1964); James B. Jacobs, "The Prisoners' Rights Movement and Its Impacts, 1960-80," *Crime and Justice 2* (1980), 435.

29 James B. Jacobs offers an account of two decades of litigation in "The Prisoners' Rights Movement and Its Impacts, 1960-80."

30 Angela Davis et al., *If They Come in the Morning: Voices of Resistance* (New York: The Third Press, 1971). There is no doubt that the state used prisons to incapacitate the leaders of the Black liberation movement in the 1960s and 1970s, and kept them behind bars for decades afterwards. Dan Berger puts this story in perspective alongside the incarceration of advocates for "Puerto Rican independence, Native American sovereignty, Chicano radicalism, white antiracist and working-class mobilizations, pacifist and antinuclear campaigns, and earth liberation and animal rights" in *The Struggle Within: Prisons, Political Prisoners, and Mass Movements in the United States* (Oakland, CA: PM Press, 2014).

31 Jones v. North Carolina Prisoners' Union, 433 U.S. 119 (1977); Bell v. Wolfish, 441 U.S. 520 (1979).

32 Ruth Wilson Gilmore and James Kilgore, "The Case for Abolition," Marshall Project, June 19, 2019, https://www.themarshallproject.org/2019/06/19/the-case-for-abolition.

33 See Kristin Henning, *The Rage of Innocence: How America Criminalizes Black Youth* (New York: Pantheon, 2021); Khalil Gibran Muhammad, *The Condemnation of Blackness: Race, Crime, and the Making of Modern Urban America* (Cambridge, MA: Harvard University Press, 2019); Peter Elikan, *Superpredators: The Demonization of Our Children by the Law* (New York: Da Capo Press, 1999).

34 Here is just one statistic of many: "In Washington state, 33 percent of prisoners serving a sentence longer than 15 years for an offense committed before their 25th birthday are Black. Blacks make up 4.3 percent of the state's population." Antoine Davis and Darrell Jackson, "What to the Incarcerated is Juneteenth?" *History News Network*, June 18, 2023, https://historynewsnetwork. org/article/185834#:~:text=Here's%20just%20one%20statistic%20 of,percent%20of%20the%20state's%20population.

35 Saeed Shabazz, "Colorado Voters Keep Slavery Clause in State Constitution by Mistake," *New York Amsterdam News* (December 1, 2016), https:// amsterdamnews.com/news/2016/12/01/colorado-voters-keep-slavery-clause-state-constitu/.

36 Kamau Waset Allen, "How We Got Colorado to Become the First State to Abolish Slavery," *Waging Nonviolence* (June 7, 2019), https://wagingnonviolence. org/forusa/2019/06/colorado-first-state-abolish-slavery-constitution/.

37 Ethan Pickering, "Forever Prohibited": How an Amendment to Abolish Slavery Appeared on Tennessee's Midterm Ballot," *Sideline*, November 3, 2022, httpp://mtsusidelines.com/2022/11/03/forever-prohibited-how-and-amendment-to-abolish-slavery-appeared-on-tennessees-midterm-ballot/.

38 Kaelan Deese, "Utah, Nebraska Voters Approve Measures Stripping Slavery Language from State Constitutions," *The Hill*, November 4, 2020, https:// thehill.com/homenews/state-watch/524469-utah-nebraska-voters-approve-measure-stripping-slavery-language-in/.

39 *Abolition Today*, https://www.blogtalkradio.com/abolitiontoday. Before *Abolition Today*, there was *New Abolitionists Radio*, broadcast since 2012. See http:// blacktalkradionetwork.com/.

40 "California Senate Rejects Involuntary Servitude Amendment," Associated Press, June 23, 2022, https://www.usnews.com/news/politics/articles/2022-06-23/california-senate-rejects-involuntary-servitude-amendment.

41   Ruth Wilson Gilmore, *Golden Gulag*.

42   Claire Brown, "'Essential' and Exploitable," *The Counter*, May 27, 2021, https://thecounter.org/essential-and-exploitable-prison-factories-stayed-open-during-pandemic/.

43   CBM Newswire, "California Assembly Approves Constitutional Amendment Abolishing 'Involuntary Servitude,'" *Sacramento Observer*, March 29, 2022, https://sacobserver.com/2022/03/california-assembly-approves-constitutional-amendment-abolishing-involuntary-servitude/.

44   Abby Cunniff, "California Is Dependent on Prison Labor for Fighting Fires. This Must End," *Truthout*, September 23, 2022, https://truthout.org/articles/california-is-dependent-on-prison-labor-for-fighting-fires-this-must-end/.

45   "California Reparations Task Force Releases Interim Report Detailing Harms of Slavery and Systemic Discrimination on African Americans, "June 1, 2022, https://oag.ca.gov/news/press-releases/california-reparations-task-force-releases-interim-report-detailing-harms.

46   "Final Report of the Task Force to Study and Develop Reparation Proposals for African Americans," June 29, 2023, https://oag.ca.gov/ab3121/report.

47   Kurtis Lee, "California Panel Calls for Billions in Reparations for Black Residents," *The New York Times*, May 6, 2023, https://www.nytimes.com/2023/05/06/business/economy/california-reparations.html.

48   Lorena O'Neil, "The Story Behind Why Louisiana Voted Against a Ban on Slavery," *Louisiana Illuminator*, November 17, 2022, https://lailluminator.com/2022/11/17/the-story-behind-why-louisiana-voted-against-a-ban-on-slavery/.

49   Curtis Bunn, "Black Voters in Louisiana 'Embarrassed' by State's Failure to Pass Anti-Slavery Amendment," NBC News, November 23, 2022, https://www.nbcnews.com/news/nbcblk/black-voters-louisiana-embarrassed-states-failure-pass-anti-slavery-am-rcna57162.

50   O'Neil, "The Story Behind Why Louisiana Voted Against a Ban on Slavery."

51   Remarks by Curtis Davis in "Louisifornia—the 2023 Remix," *Abolition Today*, April 30, 2023, https://www.blogtalkradio.com/abolitiontoday/2023/04/30/s4-e15-louisifornia-the-2023-remix. Davis was released from Angola in 2016 and authored a book about the Louisiana criminal justice system, *Slave State: Evidence of Apartheid in America* (Mindfield Publishing, 2019).

52   For a fuller commentary from the sponsor of the bill, Edmond Jordan, see "Louisiana Remains a Slave State AGAIN," *Abolition Today*, June 18, 2023,

https://www.blogtalkradio.com/abolitiontoday/2023/06/18/s4-e20-la-louisiana-remains-a-slave-state-again-wguest-la-rep-edmond-jordan.

53 Greg Hilburn, "Louisiana Senate Kills Bill to Symbolically Ban Slavery in State Constitution," *Shreveport Times*, June 5, 2023, https://www.shreveporttimes.com/story/news/2023/06/05/louisiana-senate-kills-bill-to-symbolically-ban-slavery-in-state-constitution/70289801007/.

54 Lester Duhé, "NAACP Proposes Travel Advisory for Louisiana after Recent 'Legislative Policies and Actions'" *WAFB*, June 7, 2023, https://www.wafb.com/2023/06/07/naacp-proposes-travel-advisory-louisiana-after-recent-legislative-policies-actions/.

55 John Glenn, "Alabama Voters Approve New Constitution, 10 Amendments on Ballot," *Alabama Political Reporter*, November 9, 2022, https://www.alreporter.com/2022/11/09/alabama-voters-approve-new-constitution-10-amendments-on-ballot/.

56 However, after the Nebraska amendment passed, some jails started paying prisoners where they had worked for free before. Riley Johnson, "Lancaster County Jail Inmates Now Paid for Work After Nebraska Voters Pass Slavery Ban," *Lincoln Star Journal*, December 12, 2020, https://journalstar.com/news/local/crime-and-courts/lancaster-county-jail-inmates-now-paid-for-work-after-nebraska-voters-passed-slavery-ban/article_ced74ec6-7255-5955-a16c-106922ba10bc.html.

57 "Colorado Inmates Sue Over 'Slave Labor,' Demand Minimum Wage, Paid Vacations, Paid Sick Leave," *CBS News Colorado*, July 27, 2020, https://www.cbsnews.com/colorado/news/slave-labor-prison-lawsuit-minimum-wage/.

58 "Lawsuit Filed Challenging Alleged Violations of CO State Constitutional Amendment Prohibiting Involuntary Servitude," Towards Justice, February 15, 2022, https://towardsjustice.org/litigation/amendment-a/; Allison Sherry, "Prisoners Allege Forced Labor Violates Colorado's Anti-Slavery Law," Colorado Public Radio, February 15, 2022, https://www.cpr.org/2022/02/15/prisoners-allege-forced-labor-violates-states-anti-slavery-law/#:~:text=Prisoners%20in%202020%20alleged%20they,and%20they%20didn't%20appeal.

59 Michael Karlik, "Appeals Court Says Prohibition on Involuntary Servitude Not Applicable to Prison Labor," *Colorado Politics*, August 22, 2022, https://www.coloradopolitics.com/courts/appeals-court-says-prohibition-on-involuntary-

servitude-not-applicable-to-prison-labor/article_f18a725c-2267-11ed-b33c-
6f1fbd3a1b84.html#:~:text=Colorado%20voters%20who%20made%20
slavery,constitutional%20challenge%20of%20inmate%20A.

60 The Supreme Court ruling in *United States v. Kozminski*, 487 U.S. 931 (1988)
generated a narrow definition of involuntary servitude as involving "physical or
legal coercion." According to Valerie Collins, this ruling unfortunately excluded
other interpretations, including "psychological coercion."

61 By November 2023, an NPR investigation of data from the Colorado
Department of Corrections found "that more than 14,000 prisoners have been
written up for failing to work since 2019, the year after the amendment passed.
Hundreds of them were reprimanded, including being assigned more work
or losing other privileges." Meg Anderson, "Colorado Banned Forced Prison
Labor 5 Years Ago. Prisoners Say It's Still Happening," NPR (November 13,
2023), https://www.npr.org/2023/11/13/1210564359/slavery-prison-forced-
labor-movement.

62 "Merkley, Clay, Propose Constitutional Amendment to Close Slavery Loophole
in the 13th Amendment," December 2, 2020, https://www.merkley.senate.gov/
news/press-releases/merkley-clay-propose-constitutional-amendment-to-close-
slavery-loophole-in-13th-amendment-2020.

63 Worth Rises, "End The Exception," https://endtheexception.com/.

64 Worth Rises, "Prison Industry Corporate Database," https://data.worthrises.
org/.

65 American Correctional Association, "Supporting Repeal of the 'Exclusion
Clause' in Section 1 of the 13th Amendment of the U.S. Constitution," August
9, 2016, https://www.house.mn.gov/comm/docs/469186d6-bf9d-4a9d-9211-
fdfedb48bcee.pdf.

66 Tylek, "Is Slavery Still Legal?"

67 The reference is to Jens Soering's book, *An Expensive Way to Make Bad People
Worse: An Essay on Prison Reform from an Insider's Perspective* (New York: Lantern
Books, 2004).

68 In a speech on October 10, 2014, AFL-CIO president Rich Trumka argued,
"It's a labor issue because mass incarceration means literally millions of people
work jobs in prisons for pennies an hour—a hidden world of coerced labor
here in the United States. And when some people are forced to work for close
to nothing, all workers' living standards are pushed down. It's a labor issue

because those same people who work for pennies in prison, once they have served their time, find themselves locked out of the job market by employers who screen applicants for felony convictions. It's a labor issue because families and entire communities crumble when able-bodied men and women come home and aren't allowed to work." See https://aflcio.org/speeches/trumka-criminal-justice-reform-labor-issue.

69 "Booker Introduces Package of Bills to End Unfair and Abusive Labor Practices in U.S. Correctional Facilities," February 17, 2023, https://www.booker.senate.gov/news/press/booker-introduces-package-of-bills-to-end-unfair-and-abusive-labor-practices-in-us-correctional-facilities.

70 Bronars et al., "A Cost-Benefit Analysis."

71 13th Forward, https://13thforward.com/.

72 Justice Road Map is a coalition of New York advocates pushing for interconnected legislation affecting the criminalization of immigrants and Black and brown communities; see https://justiceroadmapny.org/.

73 No Slavery in New York Act (S225B), https://www.nysenate.gov/legislation/bills/2023/S225/amendment/B#:~:text=2023%2DS225A%20%2D%20Bill%20Text%20download%20pdf&text=follows%3A%20%C2%A7%2020.-,ABOLITION%20OF%20SLAVERY%20FOR%20PERSONS%20CONVICTED%20OF%20CRIMES.,FOR%20PERSONS%20CONVICTED%20OF%20CRIMES; The Fairness and Opportunity for Incarcerated Workers Act (S416A), https://www.nysenate.gov/legislation/bills/2021/S416.

74 Worth Rises estimated that a national total of $14 billion was being stolen annually from incarcerated men and women by denying them a federal minimum wage. "Prison Industry: How it Started, How it Works, How It Harms," https://worthrises.org/wk5-programslabor.

75 See Terry-Ann Craigie et al, *Conviction, Imprisonment, and Lost Earnings: How Involvement with the Criminal Justice System Deepens Inequality*, Brennan Center for Justice, September 15, 2020, https://www.brennancenter.org/our-work/research-reports/conviction-imprisonment-and-lost-earnings-how-involvement-criminal. According to the report, time in prison reduces a person's annual earnings by an average of 52 percent, and their lifetime earning potential by nearly half a million dollars on average. Even persons convicted of a misdemeanor see their annual earnings reduced by an average of 16 percent.

The ACLU's *Captive Labor* estimates that the mass unemployment of formerly incarcerated people costs as much as $55.2 billion annually (p. 77).

76　"According to data from Corcraft obtained thorough a Freedom of Information Law (FOIL) request, incarcerated people work in high-skilled trades as carpenters, electricians, plumbers, and welders. They possess jobs that contribute to the ecosystem of feeding a community like baker, cook, and farmworker. They even provide professional skills through jobs like interpreter and nurse aide. However, there is no guarantee of a job that provides transferrable skills or even a guarantee of safety while working in these facilities. Some incarcerated workers have job responsibilities that consist of a great amount of physical danger including chainsaw operator, chipper, construction worker, and fireman helper. Once released, the mere fact of a conviction allows employers to further discriminate against formerly incarcerated people. For this work, the pay is pennies on the dollar." Testimony of Legal Aid Society before the 2022 Joint Legislative Budget Hearing Committee on Workforce Development on "Ending Forced Prison Labor in New York State, January 31, 2022, https://nyassembly.gov/write/upload/publichearing/001269/003581.pdf.

77　Samantha Michaels, "New York State Has Prisoners Making Hand Sanitizer. It's Unclear If Prisoners Can Use It," *Mother Jones*, March 9, 2020, https://www.motherjones.com/crime-justice/2020/03/new-york-state-has-prisoners-making-hand-sanitizer-its-unclear-if-prisoners-can-use-it/.

78　Teri Weaver, "Coronavirus in NY: Prisoners Ramp Up Coffin Production to 1,400 Pine Boxes a Week," *Syracuse.com*, April 24, 2020, https://www.syracuse.com/coronavirus/2020/04/coronavirus-in-ny-prisoners-ramp-up-coffin-production-to-1400-pine-boxes-a-week.html.

79　"The Criminal Justice Reform Act: One Year Later," New York City Council, 2017, https://council.nyc.gov/the-criminal-justice-reform-act-one-year-later/#:~:text=Since%20its%20passage%20on%20June,clearly%20affected%20communities%20of%20color.

80　"The Facts on Bail Reform," NYCLU, https://www.nyclu.org/en/campaigns/facts-bail-reform.

81　New York State Senate Bill S211A (2023-24), https://www.nysenate.gov/legislation/bills/2021/S2836.

82 New York State Senate Bill S211A (2023-24), https://www.nysenate.gov/legislation/bills/2023/S211/amendment/A.

83 "The 13th Amendment, 'New Slavery,' Political Unity, and Abolition: A Conversation between Stephen Wilson and Molly Porzig," *The Abolitionist*, 38 (Fall 2022), https://criticalresistance.org/abolitionist/issue-38-labor-struggles-pic-abolition/.

Chapter 2: The Yankee Invention

1 Rebecca McLennan, "The Convict's Two Lives: Civil and Natural Death in the American Prison," in David Garland, Randall McGowen, and Michael Meranze, eds., *America's Death Penalty: Between Past and Present* (New York: New York University Press, 2011), 201.

2 David M. Shapiro, "Solitary Confinement in the Young Republic," *Harvard Law Review* 133, no. 2 (December 2019), 546.

3 David Lewis, *From Newgate to Dannemora: The Rise of the Penitentiary in New York, 1796–1848* (Ithaca, NY: Cornell University Press, 1965), 43.

4 William Coffey, *Inside Out, Or, An Interior View of the New-York State Prison* (New York: J. Costigan, 1823), 141.

5 David Lewis, *From Newgate to Dannemora*, 52.

6 "At least one northern state (Illinois) leased the entire prison population (not just their labor power), body and soul, to a single contractor (Samuel A. Buckmaster) for a period of twenty years." Rebecca McLennan, "The Buried Roots of Carceral Labor," *Inquest*, May 16, 2023, https://inquest.org/the-buried-roots-of-carceral-labor/.

7 Rebecca McLennan, *The Crisis of Imprisonment: Protest, Politics, and the Making of the American Penal State, 1776-1941* (Cambridge: Cambridge University Press, 2008), 8.

8 McLennan, "The Buried Roots of Carceral Labor."

9 Denis Brian, *The Inside Story of a Notorious Prison, Sing Sing* (New York: Prometheus, 2005); Lewis, *From Newgate to Dannemora*, 136–56.

10 E. T. Hiller, "Labor Unionism and Convict Labor," *Journal of the American Institute of Criminal Law and Criminology* 5, no. 6 (1915), 871.

11 William Leete Stone, *History of New York City from the Discovery to the Present Day* (New York: Virtue and Yorston, 1872), 466.

12 William Leete Stone, *History of New York City from the Discovery to the Present Day*, 456.

13 The involvement of the guard inspired city officials to form a standing police force, to replace the night watch, and so these events are an important point of origin for the growth of the New York Police Department.

14 See Daniel Walkowitz, "The Artisans and Builders of Nineteenth-Century New York; The Case of the Stonecutters Riot," in Rick Beard and Leslie Berlowitz eds., *Greenwich Village: Culture and Counterculture* (New Brunswick, NJ: Rutgers University Press, 1993), 199-211.

15 Benson John Lossing, *History of New York City*, Volume 2 (New York, 1884) 341.

16 The location decision turned out to be flawed, or fraudulent. The initial survey suggested that the mines were "inexhaustible," but they ran out by the 1860s. Prison labor at Clinton was subsequently converted into state-use, and later, for the purpose of road-building. See Clarence Jefferson Hall, *A Prison in the Woods: Environment and Incarceration in New York's North Country* (Amherst: University of Massachusetts Press, 2020).

17 Preamble to the *Constitution of the Knights of Labor* (1878), http://www.historymuse.net/readings/preambleknights.html.

18 Alexander Pisciotta, *Benevolent Repression: Social Control and the American Reformatory-Prison Movement* (New York: New York University Press, 1994), 23.

19 Pisciotta, *Benevolent Repression*, 33–59.

20 David J. Rothman, *Conscience and Convenience: The Asylum and Its Alternatives in Progressive America* (Boston, MA: Little, Brown and Co, 1980); Estelle B. Freedman, *Their Sisters' Keepers: Women's Prison Reform in America, 1830–1930* (Ann Arbor: University of Michigan Press, 1981); Larry E. Sullivan, *The Prison Reform Movement: Forlorn Hope* (Boston, MA: Twayne Publishers, 1990).

21 The Convention was held in Albany from May 8 through September 29, 1894. *Fourth Constitution of the State of New York* (The New York State Archives. New York, 1894) A1807-78.

22 Cited by McLennan, *The Crisis of Imprisonment*, 214.

23 Stagg Whitin, *Penal Servitude* (New York: National Committee on Prison Labor, 1912).

24 McLennan, *The Crisis of Imprisonment*, 326.

25 Thomas Mott Osborne, *Within Prison Walls: Being a Narrative of Personal Experience During a Week of Voluntary Confinement in the State Prison of Auburn, New York* (New York and London: D. Appleton and Co, 1914).

26 McLennan, *The Crisis of Imprisonment*, 371.

27 Frank Tannenbaum, *Osborne of Sing Sing* (Chapel Hill: University of North Carolina Press, 1933), 105–7.

28 Frank Tannenbaum, *Osborne of Sing Sing*, 122–134.

29 Tannenbaum, *Osborne of Sing Sing*, 130.

30 Ibid. p. 133. However, McLennan cites the pay as only six dollars a week; see *The Crisis of Imprisonment*, 395. So, too, the reformers on National Committee on Prisons and Prison Labor joined forces with the AFL to lobby President Woodrow Wilson to pass a wartime executive order authorizing the federal government to purchase goods directly from state prisons "so long as it paid market prices for the goods and the prisoners' wages and hours were the same as those of free workers in the vicinity of the prison in question." Wilson's order meant that "the federal government had formally recognized the principle that prisoners ought to be paid a wage" (McLennan, 423).

31 McLennan, *The Crisis of Imprisonment*, 389.

32 Tannenbaum, *Osborne of Sing Sing*, 187.

33 Elton Mayo and Fritz Roethlisberger established the foundations of the management theory known as "human relations," in a series of behavioral experiments conducted on the workforce at the Hawthorne plant of the Western Electric Company in Cicero, Illinois. See Elton Mayo, *The Human Problems of an Industrial Civilization* (New York: Macmillan, 1933); Fritz J. Roethlisberger, William J. Dickson, and Harold A. Wright, *Management and the Worker* (Cambridge, MA: Harvard University Press, 1939).

34 Rothman, *Conscience and Convenience*, 4.

35 Cited by Ted Conover, *Newjack: Guarding Sing Sing* (New York: Random House, 2000), 200.

36 In *Conscience and Convenience*, Rothman provides the most comprehensive analysis of why prison reform, while it was driven by the laudable belief that every individual deserved a customized solution to their problems, was doomed to failure from the outset.

37 Tannebaum, *Osborne of Sing Sing*, 288–90.

38 Cited in Joseph Spillane, *Coxsackie: The Life and Death of Prison Reform* (Baltimore, MD: Johns Hopkins University Press, 2014), 21.

39 Austin MacCormick, *The Education of Adult Prisoners: A Survey and a Program* (New York: The National Society of Penal Information, 1931). Also see Edward Thorndike et al., *Adult Learning* (New York: MacMillan, 1928), which was particularly influential for establishing that adults could be taught just as effectively at youth.

40 See Estelle B. Freedman, *Their Sisters' Keepers*.

41 Cited in Rothman, *Conscience and Convenience*, 138.

42 Spillane, *Coxsackie*, 22–6.

43 "Wallkill," New York Correction History Society, http://www.correctionhistory. org/html/chronicl/docs2day/wallkill.html.

44 "From 'Guard' School to Training School: New York's Evolution," *DOCS Today*, August 2000, https://www.thefreelibrary.com/From+%22guard%22+school +to+training+school%3A+New+York%27s+evolution.-a0140220407.

45 "Wallkill," New York Correction History Society.

46 For reflections on prison education, see Rebecca Ginsburg, ed., *Critical Perspectives on Teaching in Prison: Students and Instructors on Pedagogy Behind the Wall* (New York: Routledge, 2019); Howard Davidson, ed., *Schooling in a "Total Institution": Critical Perspectives on Prison Education* (London: Bergin & Garvey, 1995); Daniel Karpowitz, *College in Prison: Reading in an Age of Mass Incarceration* (New Brunswick, NJ: Rutgers University Press, 2017); Ellen Condliffe Lagemann, *Liberating Minds: The Case for College in Prison* (New York: The New Press, 2017).

47 Michael Balfour, Brydie-Leigh Bartleet, Linda Davey, John Rynne and Huib Schippers, eds., *Performing Arts in Prisons: Creative Perspectives* (Chicago: University of Chicago Press, 2019); Buzz Alexander, *Is William Martinez Not Our Brother?: Twenty Years of the Prison Creative Arts Project* (Ann Arbor: University of Michigan Press, 2010).

48 See Nicole Fleetwood, *Marking Time: Art in the Age of Mass Incarceration* (Cambridge, MA: Harvard University Press, 2020), 150–189.

49 Joseph Spillane, *Coxsackie*, 149.

50 Spillane, *Coxsackie*, 127–8, 148.

51 "Derick McCarthy and Aiyuba Thomas Talk to Akeel Adil," PEP Research Lab, https://soundcloud.com/nyu-pep-researchlab/point of view-of-change-episode-1?utm_source=www.pepresearchlab.com&utm_

campaign=wtshare&utm_medium=widget&utm_content=
https%253A%252F%252Fsoundcloud.com%252Fnyu-pep-
researchlab%252Fpoint-of-view-of-change-episode-1.

52 Robert Martinson, "What Works? Questions and Answers about Prison
Reform," *The Public Interest* 42 (August 1974), 22–54.

53 Eric Schlosser, "The Prison-Industrial Complex," *The Atlantic*, December,
1998, https://www.theatlantic.com/magazine/archive/1998/12/the-prison-
industrial-complex/304669/.

54 The many books on this topic include Loïc Wacquant, *Punishing the Poor:
The Neoliberal Government of Social Insecurity* (Durham, NC: Duke University
Press, 2009); Angela Y. Davis, *Are Prisons Obsolete?* (New York: Seven Stories
Press, 2003); Ruth Wilson Gilmore, *Golden Gulag: Prisons, Surplus, Crisis, and
Opposition in Globalizing California* (Los Angeles: University of California Press,
2007); Elizabeth Hinton, *From the War on Poverty to the War on Crime: The Making
of Mass Incarceration in America* (Cambridge, MA: Harvard University Press,
2016); James Forman Jr., *Locking Up Our Own: Crime and Punishment in Black
America* (New York : Farrar, Straus and Giroux, 2017); Naomi Murakawa, *The
First Civil Right: How Liberals Built Prison America* (Oxford University Press,
2014); Marie Gottschalk, *Caught: The Prison State and the Lockdown of American
Politics* (Princeton, NJ: Princeton University Press, 2015); and James Kilgore,
*Understanding Mass Incarceration: A People's Guide to the Key Civil Rights Struggle of
Our Time* (New York: The New Press, 2015).

55 Michael Meranze, *Laboratories of Virtue: Punishment, Revolution, and Authority in
Philadelphia, 1760–1835* (Chapel Hill: The University of North Carolina Press,
1996).

56 McLennan, *The Crisis of Imprisonment*, 44.

57 The British history of Saint Monday is analyzed in Douglas A. Reid, "The
Decline of Saint Monday 1766–1876," *Past & Present*, no. 71 (1976), 76–101.
For the broader context of resistance in American workplace culture, see
Herbert G. Gutman, "Work, Culture, and Society in Industrializing America,
1815–1919," *American Historical Review* 78, no. 3 (June 1973), 531–588.

58 Clifford Stott and John Drury "Striking the Right Balance: Toward
a Better Understanding of Prison Strikes" *Harvard Law Review* 132
(March 2019), 1490–1519, https://harvardlawreview.org/wp-content/
uploads/2019/03/1490-1519_Online-1.pdf.

59 McLennan, *The Crisis of Imprisonment*, 147.

60 Eric Cummins, *The Rise and Fall of California's Radical Prison Movement* (Palo Alto, CA: Stanford University Press, 1994), 201.

61 Heather Ann Thompson, *Blood in the Water: The Attica Prison Uprising of 1971 and Its Legacy* (New York: Pantheon, 2016); Thompson, "Rethinking Working-Class Struggle through the Lens of the Carceral State: Toward a Labor History of Inmates and Guards," *Labor* 8, no. 3 (2011), 28-29.

62 "50 Years Ago: Attica Prison Riot," *Buffalo News*, September 9, 2021, https://buffalonews.com/50-years-ago-attica-prison-riot/collection_7d533f6c-10df-11ec-9973-f3640658f94a.html#1.

63 Joshua Melville, *American Time Bomb: Attica, Sam Melville, and a Son's Search for Answers* (Chicago: Chicago Review Press, 2021), 151–152.

64 Thompson, *Blood in the Water*, 23.

65 "Attica Prisoners Manifesto of Demands" (1971), https://abolitionnotes.org/attica-prisoners-manifesto-of-demands.

66 Thompson, *Blood in the Water*, 70.

67 Michelle Alexander, *The New Jim Crow: Mass Incarceration in the Age of Colorblindness* (New York: The New Press, 2012).

68 "Incarceration Trends in New York," Vera Institute (2018), https://www.vera.org/downloads/pdfdownloads/state-incarceration-trends-new-york.pdf.

69 Heather Ann Thompson covers much of this history in "Rethinking Working-Class Struggle through the Lens of the Carceral State," 15–45. She argues that COs, unlike foremen, are not part of management, and that they belong to the working class (25). For an account of working as a guard, see Ted Conover's *Newjack*.

70 Michael Winerip, et al, "The State That is Taking on the Prison Guards Union," The Marshall Project, April 11, 2016, https://www.themarshallproject.org/2016/04/11/the-state-that-is-taking-on-the-prison-guards-union.

71 Benjamin Weiser and Jonah Bromwich, "Federal Prosecutor Urges Takeover of Rikers Island," *The New York Times*, July 17, 2023, https://www.nytimes.com/2023/07/17/nyregion/rikers-island-federal-takeover.html.

72 The concept of "carceral society" is associated with Michel Foucault. For a range of different approaches to carcerality, see Joe Sim, ed., *Punishment and Prisons: Power and the Carceral State* (London: Sage, 2009); Mariame Kaba, *We Do This 'Til We Free Us: Abolitionist Organizing and Transforming Justice* (Chicago:

Haymarket Books, 2021); Jackie Wang, *Carceral Capitalism* (New York: Semiotexte, 2018); Abolition Collective, *Abolishing Carceral Society* (Philadelphia: Common Notions, 2018).

73 Brian Mann Brian Mann, "The Drug Laws That Changed How We Punish," NPR, February 14, 2013, https://www.npr.org/2013/02/14/171822608/the-drug-laws-that-changed-how-we-punish#:~:text=Due%20in%20%20part%20to%20Rockefeller,were%20working%20as%20prison%20guards.

74 See Orisanmi Burton, *Tip of the Spear: Black Radicalism, Prison Repression*, and the *Long Attica Revolt* (Berkeley, CA: University of California Press, 2023).

75 Dani Anguiano, "US Prison Workers Produce $11bn Worth of Goods and Services A Year for Pittance," *The Guardian*, June 15, 2022, https://www.theguardian.com/us-news/2022/jun/15/us-prison-workers-low-wages-exploited#:~:text=Incarcerated%20workers%20in%20prison%20industries,Association%2C%20a%20prison%20industry%20group.

76 "2022 Joint Legislative Budget Hearing Committee on Workforce Development," Legal Aid Society, January 31, 2022, https://nyassembly.gov/write/upload/publichearing/001269/003581.pdf.

77 "Program Details," UNICOR, https://www.bop.gov/inmates/custody_and_care/unicor_about.jsp.

78 "PIECP Final Guideline," National Correctional Industries Association, April 7, 1999, https://www.nationalcia.org/piecp-final-guideline.

79 Donna Selman and Paul Leighton, *Punishment for Sale: Private Prisons, Big Business, and the Incarceration Binge* (Rowman and Littlefield Publishers, 2010); Tara Herivel and Paul Wright eds., *Prison Profiteers: Who Makes Money from Mass Incarceration* (New York: New Press, 2009).

80 Anita Sarah Jackson, Aaron Shuman, Gopal Dayaneni, *Toxic Sweatshops: How UNICOR Prison Recycling Harms Workers, Communities, the Environment, and the Recycling Industry*, Center for Environmental Health, Prison Activist Resource Center, Silicon Valley Toxics Coalition, Computer TakeBack Campaign (October 2006), https://static.prisonpolicy.org/scans/ToxicSweatshops.pdf; Jonathon Booth, "How Private Prisons Profit from Forced Labor," *Current Affairs*, October 26, 2020, https://www.currentaffairs.org/2020/10/how-private-prisons-profit-from-forced-labor.

81 Steve Fraser and Joshua B. Freeman, "21st Century Chain Gangs," *Salon*, April 19, 2012, https://www.salon.com/2012/04/19/21st_century_chain_gangs/.

82 Wendy Sawyer and Peter Wagner, "Mass Incarceration: The Whole Pie 2023," *Prison Policy Initiative*, https://www.prisonpolicy.org/reports/pie2023.html; and James Kilgore, "Confronting Prison Slave Labor Camps and Other Myths," *Social Justice*, August 28, 2013, http://www.socialjusticejournal.org/confronting-prison-slave-labor-camps-and-other-myths/.

83 Laura Maruschak and Emily D. Buehler, "Census of State and Federal Adult Correctional Facilities, 2019—Statistical Tables," U.S. Department of Justice (November 2021), 2, https://bjs.ojp.gov/content/pub/pdf/csfacf19st.pdf.

84 The reverse is true in the realm of immigrant detention, where, in 2021, 79 percent of detainees were held in private facilities. Eunice Cho, "More of the Same: Private Prison Corporations and Immigration Detention Under the Biden Administration," ACLU, October 5, 2021, 2021https://www.aclu.org/sites/default/files/field_document/2021.10.07_private_prisons_and_ice_detention_blog_factsheet_003.pdf.

85 Department of Correctional Services, "Staff Study: Alternatives to Enhance New York State's Prison Industries Program," State of New York Office of the State Comptroller Division of Management Audit and State Financial Services, March 9, 1998, https://web.osc.state.ny.us/audits/audits/9798/96d28.pdf.

86 AFL-CIO, Executive Council Statement, "The Exploitation of Prison Labor," May 8, 1997, https://aflcio.org/about/leadership/statements/exploitation-prison-labor. Also see James Kilgore, "Mass Incarceration and Working Class Interests: Which Side are the Unions On?" *Labor Studies Journal* 37, no. 4 (2012), 356–372.

87 "Governor Hochul Announces 'Jail to Jobs,'" State of the State 2022, New York State, https://www.governor.ny.gov/news/governor-hochul-announces-jails-jobs-new-initiative-improve-re-entry-workforce-and-reduce; FY 2023 New York State Executive Budget Public Protection and General Government Article VII Legislation, https://www.budget.ny.gov/pubs/archive/fy23/ex/artvii/ppgg-bill.pdf.

Chapter 3: From State to State

1   Bernard E. Harcourt, *The Illusion of Free Markets: Punishment and the Myth of Natural Order* (Cambridge: Harvard University Press, 2012); Worth Rises, "The Prison Industry: How It Started. How It Works. How It Harms," December

2020, https://static1.squarespace.com/static/58e127cb1b10e31ed45b20f4/t/621682209bb0457a2d6d5cfa/1645642294912/The+Prison+Industry+How+It+Started+How+It+Works+and+ How+It+Harms+December+2020.pdf.

2   Hadar Aviram, *Cheap on Crime: Recession-Era Politics and the Transformation of American Punishment* (Berkeley, CA: University of California Press, 2015).

3   Marie Gottschalk, *Caught: The Prison State and the Lockdown of American Politics.*

4   Matthew Hamilton, "State Feeds Inmates for $2.84 a Day," *Times Union*, September 21, 2017, https://www.timesunion.com/news/article/State-feeds-inmates-for-2-84-a-day-8761618.php. On food in US prisons see also: Soble, L., Stroud, K., & Weinstein, M., *Eating Behind Bars: Ending the Hidden Punishment of Food in Prison.* Impact Justice, 2020, https://impactjustice.org/wp-content/uploads/IJ-Eating-Behind-Bars.pdf.

5   Wendy Sawyer, "How Much Do Incarcerated People Earn In Each State?," Prison Policy Initiative, April 10, 2017, https://www.prisonpolicy.org/blog/2017/04/10/wages/.

6   Lea Wang, "The State Prison Experience: Too Much Drudgery, Not Enough Opportunity," *Prison Policy Initiative*, September 2, 2022, https://www.prisonpolicy.org/blog/2022/09/02/prison_opportunities/.

7   Juan's reasoning was sound: on the association between postsecondary education in prison and success post-release see: Oakford et al., "Investing In Futures: Economic And Fiscal Benefits Of Postsecondary Education In Prison," Vera Institute Of Justice, January 2019, https://www.vera.org/downloads/publications/investing-in-futures.pdf.

8   Breuer et al., "The Needs and Experiences of Mothers While in Prison and Post-Release: A Rapid Review and Thematic Synthesis," *Health & Justice*, Vol. 9 (31), (2021).

9   NEW YORK STATE DIVISION OF THE BUDGET, Public Safety Briefing Book (2021); OFFICE OF THE NEW YORK STATE COMPTROLLER, Comptroller's Annual Report to the Legislature on State Funds Cash Basis of Accounting 64 (2021), https://www.osc.state.ny.us/files/reports/finance/cash-basis/pdf/cash-basisannual-2021.pdf (last visited Jan 28, 2022).

10   OFFICE OF THE NEW YORK STATE COMPTROLLER, Comptroller's Annual Reports to the Legislature on State Funds Cash Basis of Accounting (2020-22), 64, 65, and 68, https://www.osc.state.ny.us/files/reports/finance/cash-basis/pdf/cash-basisannual-2020.pdf.

11 ACLU, *Captive Labor: Exploitation of Incarcerated Workers.*

12 "United States: Prolonged Solitary Confinement Amounts to Psychological Torture, Says UN Expert," United Nations Human Rights, February 28, 2020, https://www.ohchr.org/en/press-releases/2020/02/united-states-prolonged-solitary-confinement-amounts-psychological-torture.

13 See Robert Perkinson, *Texas Tough: The Rise of America's Prison Empire* (New York: Metropolitan Books, 2010).

14 Marie Gottschalk, "Tougher Than The Rest: No Criminal Justice Reform Miracle In Texas", *Prison Legal News*, January 1, 2021, https://www.prisonlegalnews.org/news/2021/jan/1/tougher-rest-no-criminal-justice-reform-miracle-texas/.

15 Marie Gottschalk, "The Prisoner Dilemma: Texas Fails to Confront Mass Incarceration," *The Baffler*, 46 (July 2019), https://thebaffler.com/salvos/the-prisoner-dilemma-gottschalk.

16 Manny Fernandez, "In Bid To Cut Costs At Some Texas Prisons, Lunch Will Not Be Served On Weekends," *The New York Times*, October 20, 2011, https://www.nytimes.com/2011/10/21/us/texas-reduces-weekend-meals-for-prisoners.html?_r=1&pagewanted=all.

17 Matt Clarke, "Texas Slashes Prison Education Budget," *Prison Legal News*, December 15, 2012, https://www.prisonlegalnews.org/news/2012/dec/15/texas-slashes-prison-education-budget/https://www.prisonlegalnews.org/news/2012/dec/15/texas-slashes-prison-education-budget/.

18 *Trends In Prison Population And Spending: 2010–2015*, Vera Institute of Justice, https://www.vera.org/publications/price-of-prisons-2015-state-spending-trends/price-of-prisons-2015-state-spending-trends/price-of-prisons-2015-state-spending-trends-population-and-spending.

19 Harold Garfinkel, "Conditions of Successful Degradation Ceremonies," *American Journal of Sociology*, Vol. 61, No. 5 (March 1956), 420–424.

20 Vicky Camarillo, "The Penal System Today Is Slavery: Lawmakers Finally Start To Talk About Unpaid Labor In Texas Prisons," *Texas Observer*, May 10, 2019, https://www.texasobserver.org/penal-system-slavery-unpaid-labor-texas/.

21 Data from the National Correctional Industries Association (NCIA) shows that over 58 percent of the wages paid to incarcerated workers in PIE jobs since the program's inception have been garnished. See NCIA, *Q2 2023 Cumulative*

Data Report, https://569cf7d0-220c-4d22-b7ec-bd95c2d4f97b.usrfiles.com/
ugd/569cf7_9b1e7363a7ba4de69c3510413a545d23.pdf.

22   Alabama Appleseed Center for Law and Justice, *Mass Incarceration and
Unconstitutional Prisons* (Montgomery, AL, 2022), https://alabamaappleseed.org/
mass-incarceration/.

23   Jo Ellen Not, "Federal Judge Finds Alabama DOC Mental Health Care
Horrendous, Orders: Start Hiring," *Prison Legal News,* March 1, 2022, https://
www.prisonlegalnews.org/news/2022/mar/1/federal-judge-finds-alabama-
doc-mental-health-care-horrendous-orders-start-hiring/.

24   US Department of Justice, Civil Rights Division, *Investigation of The Mississippi
State Penitentiary (Parchman),* April 20, 2022.

25   Beth Shelburne, "Report: Alabama's Habitual Offender Law, Driving Mass
Incarceration Since 1977," *ACLU Smart Justice: Alabama,* May 1, 2020, https://
www.alabamasmartjustice.org/reports/hfoa.

26   Brian Lyman and Melissa Brown, "Decades In Making, Alabama's Prison
Crisis Is Bigger Than Declining Buildings, Critics Say," *Montgomery Advertiser,*
September 23, 2021, https://www.montgomeryadvertiser.com/story/
news/2021/09/24/new-construction-help-alabama-bring-order-violence-
prison-system/5821097001/.

27   Connor Sheets, "Etowah Sheriff Pockets $750k in Jail Food Funds, Buys $740k
Beach House," *Birmingham Real-Time News,* March 13, 2018, https://www.
al.com/news/birmingham/2018/03/etowah_sheriff_pocketed_over_7.html.

28   Walt Bogdanich and Grace Ashford, "An Alabama Sheriff, a Mystery Check,
and a Blogger Who Cried Foul," *The New York Times,* December 14, 2017,
https://www.nytimes.com/2017/12/14/us/ana-franklin-alabama-sheriff.html.

29   Loïc Wacquant, *Punishing The Poor: The Neo-Liberal Government of Social Insecurity*
(Durham: Duke University Press, 2009).

Chapter 4: No Shame in Alabama

1   "Alabama Ranks Among Nation's Lowest in Child Well-Being, Life
Expectancy," Equal Justice Initiative, April 14, 2022, https://eji.org/news/
alabama-ranks-among-nations-lowest-in-child-well-being-life-expectancy/.

2   "Alabama Profile," Prison Policy Initiative, https://www.prisonpolicy.org/
profiles/AL.html#:~:text=Alabama%20has%20an%20incarceration%20
rate,than%20any%20democracy%20on%20earth.

3   "Third Alabama Prison Homicide in a Month," Equal Justice Initiative, March
     9, 2023, https://eji.org/news/felix-ortega-third-alabama-prison-homicide-in-
     a-month/#:~:text=In%202022%2C%20270%20people%20died,most%20
     recently%20reported%20national%20average.

4   Patrick Darrington, "325 People Died in Custody of ADOC in 2023,"
     Alabama Political Reporter, February 2, 2024, https://www.alreporter.
     com/2024/02/02/__trashed-8/.

5   Melissa Brown and Brian Lyman "DOJ Lawsuit 'Deliberately Indifferent':
     Federal Government Sues Alabama Over Prison Conditions," *Montgomery
     Advertiser*, December 9, 2020, https://www.montgomeryadvertiser.com/story/
     news/2020/12/09/alabama-prisons-sued-federal-government-over-inhumane-
     conditions/3872241001/.

6   Aaron Morrison, "Slavery, Involuntary Servitude Rejected by 4 States' Voters,"
     Associated Press, November 9, 2022, https://apnews.com/article/2022-midterm-
     elections-slavery-on-ballot-561268e344f17d8562939cde301d2cbf.

7   Many of the state's elderly prisoners are held for life without parole as a
     result of Alabama's Habitual Offender sentencing laws. They are the most
     expensive to house and the least likely to re-offend. Justin McCleskey et
     al., "Unsustainable: Alabama's Increasing Trend of Keeping the Elderly
     Behind Bars," Alabama Appleseed Center for Law and Justice, November
     2022, https://www.alabamaappleseed.org/wp-content/uploads/2022/11/
     Unsustainable_Alabama-Appleseed.pdf. While the number of young
     incarcerated people had fallen dramatically since the 2005 peak, the elderly
     population had doubled. In another report, "Condemned" (2023), Appleseed
     researchers Carla Crowder et al., explain how sentences of life without parole
     have turned Alabama's "honor dorms" into just "another Death Row," with
     most of the occupants incarcerated on cases that involved no physical injury,
     http://alabamaappleseed.org/wp-content/uploads/2023/03/Alabama-
     Appleseed-Condemned-Report-2023.pdf.

8   "Deliberate indifference" is a legal term for the conscious or reckless disregard
     of the consequences of one's acts or omissions, and it is cited frequently in
     the DOJ reports on Alabama prisons. It is also the title of a revealing podcast
     series about the state's prison system by journalist Mary Scott Hodgins,
     https://www.deliberateindifference.org/.

9   "History of the ADOC," Alabama Department of Corrections, https://doc.
     alabama.gov/history.

10 Mary Ellen Curtin, *Black Prisoners and Their World, Alabama, 1865–1900*
    (Charlottesville and London: University of Virginia Press, 2000). For other
    important books about the convict leasing system in the South, see David M.
    Oshinsky, *Worse Than Slavery: Parchman Farm and the Ordeal of Jim Crow Justice*
    (New York: Free Press, 1996); Alex Lichtenstein, *Twice the Work of Free Labor:
    The Political Economy of Convict Labor in the New South* (London: Verso, 1996); C.
    Vann Woodward, *Origins of the New South, 1877–1913* (Baton Rouge: Louisiana
    State University Press, 1951); Talitha LeFlouria, *Chained in Silence: Black Women
    and Convict Labor in the New South* (Chapel Hill, NC: University of North
    Carolina Press, 2015); Edward Ayers, *Vengeance and Justice: Crime and Punishment
    in the Nineteenth Century American South* (New York: Oxford University Press,
    1984); Matthew Mancini, *One Dies, Get Another: Convict Leasing in the American
    South, 1866–1928* (Columbia: University of South Carolina Press, 1996); Dennis
    Childs, *Slaves of the State: Black Incarceration From the Chain Gang to the Penitentiary*
    (Minneapolis: University of Minnesota Press, 2015) and Douglas Blackmon,
    *Slavery by Another Name: The Re-Enslavement of Black Americans from the Civil War
    to World War II* (New York: Anchor Books, 2008).

11 Alabama's law was "notorious for being the first post-Civil War code to contain
    an anti-miscegenation law. Though it was enforced with less vigilance over
    time, this law remained in force until November 2000." "The Penal Code of
    Alabama; Prepared by G. W. Stone and J. W. Shepherd," *The Lawbook Exchange*,
    https://www.lawbookexchange.com/pages/books/70053/alabama-geo-w-
    stone-j-w-shepherd/the-penal-code-of-alabama-prepared-by-g-w-stone-and-j-
    w-shepherd#:~:text=The%201866%20Penal%20Code%20is,in%20force%20
    until%20November%202000.

12 Oshinsky, *Worse Than Slavery*, 23.

13 Robert Perkinson, *Texas Tough*, 105.

14 According to Oshinsky, "not a single leased convict ever lived long enough to
    serve a sentence of ten years or more," *Worse Than Slavery*, 46.

15 See Angela Davis, "From the Prison of Slavery to the Slavery of Prison:
    Frederick Douglass and the Convict Lease System" in Joy James, ed., *The Angela
    Davis Reader* (Cambridge, MA: Blackwell, 1998).

16 Mary Ellen Curtin, "Convict-Lease System," *Encyclopedia of Alabama*
    (September 12, 2007), https://encyclopediaofalabama.org/article/convict-
    lease-system/#:~:text=In%20exchange%2C%20TCI%20agreed%20
    to,coal%2Drich%20areas%20surrounding%20Birmingham.

17 Oshinsky, *Worse Than Slavery*, 73.

18 Oshinsky, *Worse Than Slavery*, and Blackmon, *Slavery by Another Name*.

19 Mancini, One *Dies, Get Another*.

20 Blackmon, *Slavery by Another Name*, 155–269.

21 Douglas Blackmon, "From Alabama's Past, Capitalism Teamed With Racism to Create Cruel Partnership," *Wall Street Journal*, July 16, 2001, https://www.wsj.com/articles/SB995228253461746936.

22 Blackmon, *Slavery by Another Name*, p. 21.

23 Robin D. G. *Kelley, Hammer and Hoe: Alabama Communists During the Great Depression* (Chapel Hill: University of North Carolina Press, 1990); Sarah Haley, *No Mercy Here: Gender, Punishment, and the Making of Jim Crow Modernity* (Chapel Hill, NC: University of North Carolina Press, 2016); and Steven Hahn, *A Nation Under Our Feet: Black Political Struggles in the Rural South from Slavery to the Great Migration* (Cambridge, MA: Harvard University Press, 2003).

24 See Khalil Gibran Muhammad, *The Condemnation of Blackness: Race, Crime, and the Making of Modern Urban America* (Cambridge: Harvard University Press, 2019).

25 Amanda Bell Hughett, "From Extraction to Repression: Prison Labor, Prison Finance, and the Prisoners' Rights Movement in North Carolina," in Erin Hatton, ed., *Labor and Punishment: Work in and out of Prison* (Berkeley, CA: University of California Press, 2021).

26 Mark Colvin, *Penitentiaries, Reformatories and Chain Gangs: Social Theory and the History of Punishment in Nineteenth-Century America* (New York: St. Martin's Press, 1997).

27 Rick Bragg, "Chain Gangs to Return to Roads of Alabama," *The New York Times*, March 26, 1995, https://www.nytimes.com/1995/03/26/us/chain-gangs-to-return-to-roads-of-alabama.html.

28 "Austin v. James," Southern Poverty Law Center, https://www.splcenter.org/seeking-justice/case-docket/austin-v-james.

29 Lynn M. Burley, "History Repeats Itself in the Resurrection of Prisoner Chain Gangs: Alabama's Experience Raises Eighth Amendment Concerns," *Minnesota Journal of Law and Inequality* 15, no.1 (1997), https://scholarship.law.umn.edu/lawineq/vol15/iss1/6.

30 Adam Nossiter, "Judge Rules Against Alabama's Prison 'Hitching Posts'," *The New York Times*, January 31, 1997, https://www.nytimes.com/1997/01/31/us/judge-rules-against-alabama-s-prison-hitching-posts.html.

31 Larry W. Yackle, *Reform and Regret: The Story of Federal Judicial Involvement in the Alabama Prison System* (Oxford and New York: Oxford University Press, 1989).

32 "U.S. Relinquishes Alabama Prisons," *The New York Times*, January 15, 1989, https://www.nytimes.com/1989/01/15/us/us-relinquishes-alabama-prisons. html#:~:text=In%201972%2C%20Federal%20District%20Judge,of%20 sick%20and%20injured%20prisoners.

33 Johnson's ruling in *Pugh v. Locke*, 406 F. Supp. 318 (M.D. Ala. 1976), U.S. District Court for the Middle District of Alabama, https://law.justia.com/ cases/federal/district-courts/FSupp/406/318/2143390/.

34 The Office of Alabama Governor, "Alabama Responds to US Department of Justice Findings Letter Regarding Alabama Prisons" (April 3, 2019), https://governor.alabama.gov/newsroom/2019/04/alabama-responds-to-us-department-of-justice-findings-letter-regarding-alabama-prisons/.

35 Elizabeth Alexander, "Book Review of *Reform and Regret: The Story of Federal Judicial Involvement in the Alabama Prison System* by Larry W. Yackle," *Constitutional Commentary* 7 (1990), https://scholarship.law.umn.edu/concomm/308.

36 Kelley, *Hammer and Hoe*, 16.

37 Andrew Manis, *A Fire You Can't Put Out: The Civil Rights Life of Birmingham's Reverend Fred Shuttlesworth* (Tuscaloosa: University of Alabama Press, 1999).

38 Diane McWhorter, *Carry Me Home: Birmingham, Alabama: The Climactic Battle of the Civil Rights Revolution* (New York: Simon and Schuster, 2001) 346.

39 McWhorter, p. 393.

40 Zoe Colley, *Ain't Scared of Your Jail: Arrest, Imprisonment, and the Civil Rights Movement* (Gainesville: University Press of Florida, 2013).

41 Perkinson, *Texas Tough*, 13.

42 Robert Chase refers to this package of paramilitary practices, privatized facilities, massive prison building programs, and twenty-three-hour cell isolation as the "Sunbelt" model of a carceral state. *We Are Not Slaves: State Violence, Coerced Labor, and Prisoners' Rights in Postwar America* (Chapel Hill, NC: University of North Carolina Press, 2020).

43 The Right On Crime initiative (https://rightoncrime.com/) was created in Texas in 2007 by the Texas Public Policy Foundation in partnership with the American Conservative Union Foundation and Prison Fellowship. It pioneered a fiscally conservative alternative to the "tough on crime" policies that drove mass incarceration.

44 Elizabeth Chuck, "'Frequent and Severe' Sexual Violence Alleged at Women's Prison in Alabama," NBC News (May 23, 2012), https://www.nbcnews.com/news/world/frequent-severe-sexual-violence-alleged-womens-prison-alabama-flna790281#:~:text=In%202007%2C%20a%20Justice%20Department,to%20be%20lax%2C%20Stevenson%20alleged.

45 "Findings: Equal Justice Initiative Investigation into Sexual Violence at Tutwiler Prison for Women," May 2012, Equal Justice Initiative, https://eji.org/files/eji-findings-tutwiler-prison-investigation.pdf.

46 U.S. Department of Justice, Civil Rights Division, "Investigation of the Julia Tutwiler Prison for Women and Notice of Expanded Investigation," January 17, 2014, https://www.justice.gov/sites/default/files/crt/legacy/2014/01/23/tutwiler_findings_1-17-14.pdf.

47 U.S. Department of Justice, Civil Rights Division, "Investigation of Alabama's State Prisons for Men," April 2, 2019, https://www.justice.gov/crt/case-document/file/1149971/download.

48 U.S. Department of Justice, Civil Rights Division, "Investigation of Alabama's State Prisons for Men," July 23, 2020, https://www.justice.gov/crt/case-document/file/1297031/download.

49 "Braggs, et al. v Jefferson Dunn, et al.," Southern Poverty Law Center, https://www.splcenter.org/seeking-justice/case-docket/braggs-et-al-v-jefferson-dunn-et-al.

50 Ayumi Davis, "Judge Sends Out 600-Page Opinion Again Blasting Inadequacies of Alabama Prison System," Newsweek, December 27, 2021, https://www.newsweek.com/judge-sends-out-600-page-opinion-again-blasting-inadequacies-alabama-prison-system-1663536.

51 Pat Duggins, "Federal Judge Has Bad News for Alabama's Prison System," Alabama Public Radio, February 11, 2023, https://www.apr.org/news/2023-02-11/federal-judge-has-bad-news-for-alabamas-prison-system.

52 Olivia Paschal and Elisha Brown, "How Alabama Organizers Blocked Gov. Ivey's Prison Lease Plan," Facing South, June 17, 2021, https://www.facingsouth.org/2021/06/how-alabama-organizers-blocked-gov-iveys-prison-lease-plan.

53 Danielle Moran and Amanda Albright, "Alabama Sells Munis for Prisons After Deal Cut by $216 Million," Bloomberg, June 29, 2022, https://www.bloomberg.com/news/articles/2022-06-29/alabama-prison-bond-deal-slashed-by-200-million-on-poor-demand?leadSource=uverify%20wall.

54   Caleb Taylor, "New Elmore County Prison Will Cost Taxpayers Over $1 Billion," *1819 News*, September 27, 2023, https://1819news.com/news/item/new-elmore-county-prison-will-cost-taxpayers-over-1-billion#:~:text=The%20State%20of%20Alabama%20will,%24270%2C500%20per%20bed. Josh Moon, "Alabama Wants to Build a Billion Dollar Prison. You Should Pay Attention," *Alabama Political Reporter*, March 17, 2023, https://www.alreporter.com/2023/03/17/opinion-alabama-wants-to-build-a-billion-dollar-prison-you-should-pay-attention/.

55   Ivana Hrynkiw and Ramsay Archibald, "Alabama's Billion-Dollar Prison Plan Does Not End the Overcrowding," *Alabama.com* (April 7, 2023), https://www.al.com/news/2023/04/alabamas-billion-dollar-prison-plan-does-not-end-the-overcrowding.html.

56   *Pugh v. Locke*, 406 F. Supp. 318 (M.D. Ala. 1976), U.S. District Court for the Middle District of Alabama, https://law.justia.com/cases/federal/district-courts/FSupp/406/318/2143390/.

57   Alabama Department of Corrections, "Monthly Statistical Report," December 2022, http://www.doc.state.al.us/docs/MonthlyRpts/December%202022.pdf.

58   Minnah Arshad, "Lawsuit Says Prison Labor System in Alabama Amounts to 'Modern-Day Form of Slavery,'" *USA Today*, December 14, 2023, https://www.usatoday.com/story/news/nation/2023/12/14/alabama-prison-labor-modern-slavery/71898583007/.

59   "Former Officer: Alabama 'Not in Control' of State Prisons," Associated Press, November 5, 2022, https://apnews.com/article/prisons-alabama-treatment-of-prisoners-50e1832966f34b0a5a2f65520a4cdc83#:~:text=November%205%2C%202022-,MONTGOMERY%2C%20Ala.,should%20intervene%20in%20the%20system.

60   Mary Scott Hodgin, "Episode 6: The Officers," in *Deliberate Indifference* (podcast), 40:49, https://www.deliberateindifference.org/episodes/the-officers/. In September 2023, ADOC Commissioner John Hamm reported that the system was short 700 correctional officers. "When we can get someone to come in for an interview," he said, "they decline because they don't want to work for corrections because of what they've read or seen in the news." Erin Davis, "ADOC Gives Update on Construction of New Prison," WSFA 12 News, September 20, 2023, https://www.wsfa.com/2023/09/20/adoc-gives-update-construction-new-prison/.

61 Desiree Hunter, "Alabama Correctional Industries Scaling Back," Associated
    Press (August 17, 2007), https://www.manufacturing.net/operations/
    news/13062462/alabama-correctional-industries-scaling-back.

62 Prisoners used to be charged $200 to petition a court, the only way to file a
    complaint, since Alabama's prisons had no grievance procedure until recently:
    https://solitarywatch.org/2016/05/05/prison-labor-strike-in-alabama-
    we-will-no-longer-contribute-to-our-own-oppression/. A grievance process
    was only established in August 2023; see https://doc.alabama.gov/docs/
    AdminRegs/AR406.pdf.

63 Alabama Department of Corrections, "Annual Report for the Fiscal Year
    2021," https://doc.alabama.gov/docs/AnnualRpts/2021%20Annual%20
    Report.pdf. prison-labor-strike-in-alabama-we-will-no-longer-contribute-to-our-
    own-oppression/. Alabama Department of Corrections, "Annual Report for
    the Fiscal Year 2021," https://doc.alabama.gov/docs/AnnualRpts/2021%20
    Annual%.

Chapter 5: Let the Crops Rot in the Fields

1   Andrew Yawn, "Felony Voting Rights Restored for Some in Alabama, But
    Many More 'Do Not Know They Can Vote,'" *Montgomery Advertiser*, March 27,
    2019, https://www.montgomeryadvertiser.com/story/news/2019/03/27/
    felony-voting-rights-restored-some-alabama-but-many-more-do-not-know-
    they-can-vote/3289050002/.

2   Nina Martin, "Murder Charge Can't Deter Sharpton's Brother from Voting
    Rights Crusade," *ProPublica*, November 4, 2018, https://www.propublica.
    org/article/kenneth-glasgow-murder-charge-sharpton-brother-voting-rights-
    crusade.

3   Editorial Board, "A Meaningful Move on Voting Rights in Alabama," *The New
    York Times*, May 31, 2017, https://www.nytimes.com/2017/05/31/opinion/
    alabama-governor-felons-voting.html.

4   "Alabama Law Preventing Formerly Incarcerated from Voting Challenged as
    Racially Discriminatory," Equal Justice Initiative, October 3, 2016, https://eji.org/
    news/lawsuit-challenges-alabama-felony-disenfranchisement-law/ #:~:text=In%20
    Alabama%2C%20the%20law%20disenfranchises,of%20felony%20
    offenses%2C%20CLC%20said.

5   In his account of the California prison movement of the 1960s, Dan Berger described the effort to adopt "a strategy of visibility" to the outside world in order to counteract the enforced isolation of prison life. *Captive Nation: Black Prison Organizing in the Civil Rights Era* (Chapel Hill, NC: University of North Carolina Press, 2015).

6   Sarah Wheaton, "Prisoners Strike in Georgia," *The New York Times*, December 12, 2010, https://www.nytimes.com/2010/12/12/us/12prison.html.

7   Annabelle Parker, "'Let's Just Shut Down': An Interview with Spokesperson Ray of the Free Alabama Movement," *San Francisco Bay View National Black Newspaper*, December 2, 2014, https://sfbayview.com/2014/12/lets-just-shut-down-an-interview-with-spokesperson-ray-of-the-free-alabama-movement/.

8   Vaishali Bansal, "Prison Profiteers," *Business Review at Berkeley*, April 23, 2022, https://businessreview.berkeley.edu/prison-profiteers/.

9   Annabelle Parker, "'Let's Just Shut Down.'"

10 Melvin Ray, *Free Alabama Movement: A Book*, February 22, 2014, 5, https://freealabamamovement.files.wordpress.com/2019/08/fam-book.pdf. That same year, he estimated that ADOC could save more than $250 million if it reduced the prison population to the actual design capacity of its facilities (23).

11 "Parole Watch Board," ACLA Alabama, September 23, 2023, https://www.aclualabama.org/en/news/new-report-exposes-parole-board-behavior-and-outcomes.

12 The second strike was less successful in mobilizing support. George Lavender, "Alabama Prison Work Strike 'Stalls' but Wins Support from Wobblies," *In These Times*, April 25, 2014, https://inthesetimes.com/article/alabama-prisoners.

13 "About," Incarcerated Workers Organizing Committee, https://incarceratedworkers.org/about.

14 Eric Thomas Chester, *The Wobblies in Their Heyday: The Rise and Destruction of the Industrial Workers of the World During the World War I Era* (Santa Barbara, CA: Praeger, 2014).

15 Firehawk and Ben Turk, "Freedom First!," Incarcerated Workers Organizing Committee, https://incarceratedworkers.org/freedom-first.

16 "Let the Crops Rot in the Fields," Free Alabama Movement, February 26, 2015, https://freealabamamovement.wordpress.com/2015/02/26/let-the-crops-rot-in-the-fields/.

17 "Alabama Freedom Bill," Free Alabama Movement, https://
    freealabamamovement.wordpress.com/free-alabama-movement-f-a-m-s-
    freedom-bill-video/, and https://incarceratedworkers.org/sites/default/files/
    resource_file/fam-free-alabama-bill.pdf.

18 Cited by Firehawk and Ben Turk, "Freedom First!," note 1.

19 An updated (February 2021) list can be found at Jailhouse Lawyers Speak, "10
    Demands," https://www.jailhouselawyersspeak.com/10-demands.

20 Brian Sonenstein and Jared Ware, "America is Still a Slave Nation: Massive
    Abolitionist Gathering Held in Washington, D.C.," *Shadowproof*, September 5,
    2017, https://shadowproof.com/2017/09/05/millions-for-prisoners-human-
    rights-march/.

21 "Operation PUSH: Florida Prison Strike," Incarcerated Workers Organizing
    Committee, February 5, 2018, https://incarceratedworkers.org/campaigns/
    operation-push-florida-prison-strike.

22 Jared Ware, "South Carolina Prisoners Challenge the Narrative Around
    Violence at Lee Correctional Institution," *Shadowproof*, May 3, 2018, https://
    shadowproof.com/2018/05/03/interview-south-carolina-prisoners-challenge-
    narrative-around-violence-lee-correctional-institution/.

23 Bennu Hannibal Ra-Sun, "Seeing the Problem, Being the Solution, Making
    the Practice—Part VII: Campaign to Redistribute the Pain 2018," *San Francisco
    Bay View National Black Newspaper*, February 2, 2018, https://sfbayview.
    com/2018/02/seeing-the-problem-being-the-solution-making-the-sacrifice/.

24 Andrew Yawn, "8 Holman Inmates on Hunger Strike After 'Preventative'
    Placement in Solitary Confinement," *Montgomery Advertiser*, March 18, 2019,
    https://www.montgomeryadvertiser.com/story/news/2019/03/18/8-
    holman-inmates-hunger-strike-protest-preventative-placement-solitary-
    confinement/3202736002/.

25 Howard Koplowitz, "Activists Protest Alleged Beating of Alabama Prisoner
    Kinetik Justice by Bessemer Guards," *Alabama.com*, February 15, 2021, https://
    www.al.com/news/2021/02/activists-protest-alleged-stabbing-of-alabama-
    prisoner-kinetic-justice-by-bessemer-guards.html.

26 "Agreement to End Hostilities," Prisoner Hunger Strike Solidarity, August 12,
    2012, https://prisonerhungerstrikesolidarity.wordpress.com/agreement-to-end-
    hostilities/.

27 According to Caldwell, BSOW in-state allies included Alabama Appleseed, ACLU and the Southern Poverty Law Center. Out-of-state allies included Opportunities Peoples Justice Leaders, Out of Ohio, the Anti-Violence, Safety, and Accountability Project, from California, and Forward Together in New Mexico.

28 Kim Chandler, "Families Protest Prison Conditions at Alabama Capitol Rally," AP News, October, 14 2022, https://apnews.com/article/prisons-alabama-treatment-of-prisoners-government-and-politics-d6f86e6f1891f560c55de532692feffe.

29 Howard Koplowitz, "Striking Alabama Inmate Workers' Demands 'Unreasonable,' Ivey Says," *Alabama.com*, September 30, 2022, https://www.al.com/news/2022/09/striking-alabama-inmate-workers-demands-unreasonable-ivey-says.html.

30 Keri Blakinger, "Alabama Said Prison Strike Was 'Under Control.' Footage Shows System in Deadly Disarray," The Marshall Project, October 6, 2022, https://www.themarshallproject.org/2022/10/06/alabama-said-prison-strike-was-under-control-footage-shows-system-in-deadly-disarray.

31 "Alabama Guards Stage Work Strike Months After Prisoner Uprising at Overcrowded Holman Facility," *Democracy Now!*, September 28, 2016, https://www.democracynow.org/2016/9/28/alabama_guards_stage_work_strike_months.

32 Haley Czarnek, "'Society Has Shut Down On Us:' Prison Strikers Across Alabama Demand Change Despite Severe Retaliation," *Labor Notes*, October 6, 2022, https://www.labornotes.org/blogs/2022/10/society-has-shut-down-us-prison-strikers-across-alabama-demand-change-despite-severe.

33 Ryan Fatica, "Alabama Prison Strike on Hold After 3 Weeks," *Unicorn Riot*, October 23, 2022, https://unicornriot.ninja/2022/alabama-prison-strike-on-hold-after-3-weeks/.

34 See the documentary film *Lowndes County and the Road to Black Power*, directed by Geeta Gandbhir and Sam Pollard (2022).

35 "African Freedom Fighter and Political Prisoner Richard Mafundi Lake Dies in Prison Captivity!," *The Burning Spear*, February 11, 2018, https://theburningspear.com/2291/.

36   Lake's thoughts on prison organizing can be sampled, in a FAM interview, at https://www.youtube.com/watch?v=tAvpc3g-bUE and https://www.youtube.com/watch?v=Od5_ZPXJjTQ.

37   Michael Kimble "Black August Resistance 2018: Remembering The Inmates for Action," *It's Going Down* (September 25, 2018), https://itsgoingdown.org/black-august-remembering-inmates-for-action/.

38   Michael Kimble, "Black August Resistance 2018."

39   George Jackson, *Soledad Brother: The Prison Letters of George Jackson*, (Chicago: Lawrence Hill Books, 1970) 10.

40   Dan Berger, *Captive Nation*; Robert Chase, *We Are Not Slaves*.

41   Jonathan Michels, "'Prisoners' Organizations Were Thought to be Dangerous.': Conversations with Organizers of the North Carolina Prisoners' Labor Union," *Scalawag*, June 26, 2018, https://scalawagmagazine.org/2018/06/prisoners-organizations-were-thought-to-be-dangerous-conversations-with-organizers-of-the-north-carolina-prisoners-labor-union/.

42   Over time, however, many in America's fledgling labor movement adopted the term "white slavery" to describe the factory system, a phrase that was pro-slavery, because it implied that this new industrial condition was unfitting for white workers only. David Roediger, *The Wages of Whiteness: Race and the Making of the American Working Class* (London: Verso, 1991), 65–94.

43   Address of Hon. Frederick Douglass [delivered before the National Convention of Colored Men, at Louisville, Ky., September 24, 1883], https://udspace.udel.edu/server/api/core/bitstreams/1f0cdc11-84cb-4f19-9b8c-007dcfa0a75e/content.

44   "Incarceration Trends in Alabama," Vera Institute of Justice, December 2019, https://www.vera.org/downloads/pdfdownloads/state-incarceration-trends-alabama.pdf; Wendy Sawyer and Peter Wagner, "Mass Incarceration: The Whole Pie 2023," *Prison Policy Initiative*, March 14, 2023, https://www.prisonpolicy.org/reports/pie2023.html.

45   Alabama still observes Confederate Memorial Day (the last Monday in April) and Jefferson Davis's birthday (celebrated on the first Monday in June). In lieu of a separate Martin Luther King, Jr., Day, the state celebrates a joint Martin Luther King, Jr.–Robert E. Lee holiday.

46   Office of the Governor, "Executive Order No. 725 Promoting Public Safety by Establishing Standards and Accountability for Correctional Incentive

Time," January 9, 2023, https://governor.alabama.gov/newsroom/2023/01/executive-order-725/.

47 Nonetheless, the executive order was an open invitation to would-be litigants seeking to mount a challenge. Along with Nebraska and Colorado, the state was on the radar of ASNN's post-election committee of legal advocates, committed to devising common strategies for litigation following state constitutional amendments.

48 Erin Davis, "Alabama Prison System Stops Publishing Monthly Death Reports," WFSA 12, January 5, 2023, https://www.wsfa.com/2023/01/05/alabama-prison-system-stops-publishing-monthly-death-reports/.

49 See Matt Kay's documentary about the case of Nathaniel Woods, *To Live and Die in Alabama* (2021).

50 Jeffrey Toobin, "The Legacy of Lynching, on Death Row," *The New Yorker*, August 15, 2016, https://www.newyorker.com/magazine/2016/08/22/bryan-stevenson-and-the-legacy-of-lynching. Also see Margaret A. Burnham, *By Hands Now Known: Jim Crow's Legal Executioners* (New York: Norton, 2022).

51 Nicholas Bogel-Burroughs, "Alabama Suspends Executions After Lethal Injection Problems," *The New York Times*, November 21, 2022, https://www.nytimes.com/2022/11/21/us/alabama-executions-lethal-injection.html.

52 Ivana Hrynkiw, "Airgas Refuses to Supply Nitrogen for Alabama Executions," *Alabama.com*, January 15, 2023, https://www.al.com/news/2023/01/airgas-refuses-to-supply-nitrogen-for-alabama-executions.html.

53 "'Astonishingly Cruel': Alabama Seeks to Test Execution Method on Death Row 'Guinea Pig,'" *The Guardian*, September 2, 2023, https://www.theguardian.com/world/2023/sep/02/alabama-execution-nitrogen-kenneth-smith.

54 Ed Pilkington, "Alabama Inmate Executed with Nitrogen Gas Was 'Shaking Violently', Witnesses Say," *The Guardian*, (March 26, 2024), https://www.theguardian.com/us-news/2024/jan/25/alabama-executes-kenneth-smith-nitrogen-gas.

55 No one had properly calculated the cost to Alabama of a sustained work stoppage, but, according to one estimate, the state of California had lost a whopping $636,068 of revenue, or $156,736 in profit, for each day of the 2016 strike "Prison Strike's Financial Impact in California," *Solidarity Research*, October 2016, http://solidarityresearch.org/wp-content/uploads/ 2016/10/Prison-Strike-in-California-10-07-16.pdf.

56 The lawsuit can be found at https://www.documentcloud.org/documents/
    24217214-1?responsive=1&title=1.

57 Michael Levenson, "Prisoners Sue Alabama, Calling Prison Labor System
    a 'Form of Slavery,'" *The New York Times*, December 12, 2023, https://
    www.nytimes.com/2023/12/12/us/alabama-prisons-lawsuit-labor.
    html#:~:text=According%20to%20the%20lawsuit%2C%20the,to%20
    state%20and%20county%20governments.

About the Authors

Andrew Ross is a social activist and Professor of Social and Cultural Analysis at NYU, where he also directs the Prison Education Program Research Lab. A contributor to the *Guardian*, *The New York Times*, *The Nation*, and *Al Jazeera*, he is the author or editor of more than twenty-five books, including, most recently, *Cars and Jails: Freedom Dreams, Debt*, and *Carcerality*.

Tommaso Bardelli is a Research Fellow at the NYU Prison Education Program Research Lab, where he conducts research on mass incarceration, financial debt, and their intersections. He holds a PhD in Political Science from Yale University.

Aiyuba Thomas is an MA graduate from NYU's Gallatin School of Individualized Study, and a justice impacted affiliate of the NYU Prison Education Program Research Lab. He is the project manager for "Movements Against Mass Incarceration," an archival oral history project at Columbia University.

Printed in the USA
CPSIA information can be obtained
at www.ICGtesting.com
JSHW020316260524
63609JS00001B/1

9 781682 193983